Socrates Digital™ for Learning and Problem Solving

Mark Salisbury
University of St. Thomas, USA

A volume in the Advances in
Computational Intelligence and
Robotics (ACIR) Book Series

Published in the United States of America by
    IGI Global
    Engineering Science Reference (an imprint of IGI Global)
    701 E. Chocolate Avenue
    Hershey PA, USA 17033
    Tel: 717-533-8845
    Fax: 717-533-8661
    E-mail: cust@igi-global.com
    Web site: http://www.igi-global.com

Library of Congress Cataloging-in-Publication Data

Names: Salisbury, Mark, 1955- author. | Socrates Digital (Firm)
Title: Socrates Digital for learning and problem solving / by Mark
    Salisbury.
Description: Hershey PA : Engineering Science Reference, [2021] | Includes
    bibliographical references and index. | Summary: "Readers of this book
    will learn how to build intelligent digital advisors that discern and
    provide the knowledge human users seek in fulfilling their
    responsibilities in the workplace through the aid of a new knowledge
    representation, called expert advice, that builds upon research in
    artificial intelligence, instructional design, cognitive psychology, and
    the learning sciences"-- Provided by publisher.
Identifiers: LCCN 2021030075 (print) | LCCN 2021030076 (ebook) | ISBN
    9781799879558 (hardcover) | ISBN 9781799879565 (paperback) | ISBN
    9781799879572 (ebook)
Subjects: LCSH: Expert systems (Computer science) | Problem solving--Data
    processing. | Knowledge, Theory of--Data processing. | Questioning--Data
    processing.
Classification: LCC QA76.76.E95 S25 2021 (print) | LCC QA76.76.E95
    (ebook) | DDC 006.3/3--dc23
LC record available at https://lccn.loc.gov/2021030075
LC ebook record available at https://lccn.loc.gov/2021030076

This book is published in the IGI Global book series Advances in Computational Intelligence and Robotics (ACIR) (ISSN: 2327-0411; eISSN: 2327-042X)

British Cataloguing in Publication Data
A Cataloguing in Publication record for this book is available from the British Library.

All work contributed to this book is new, previously-unpublished material.
The views expressed in this book are those of the authors, but not necessarily of the publisher.

For electronic access to this publication, please contact: eresources@igi-global.com.

Advances in Computational Intelligence and Robotics (ACIR) Book Series

ISSN:2327-0411
EISSN:2327-042X

Editor-in-Chief: Ivan Giannoccaro, University of Salento, Italy

MISSION

While intelligence is traditionally a term applied to humans and human cognition, technology has progressed in such a way to allow for the development of intelligent systems able to simulate many human traits. With this new era of simulated and artificial intelligence, much research is needed in order to continue to advance the field and also to evaluate the ethical and societal concerns of the existence of artificial life and machine learning.

The **Advances in Computational Intelligence and Robotics (ACIR) Book Series** encourages scholarly discourse on all topics pertaining to evolutionary computing, artificial life, computational intelligence, machine learning, and robotics. ACIR presents the latest research being conducted on diverse topics in intelligence technologies with the goal of advancing knowledge and applications in this rapidly evolving field.

COVERAGE

- Cognitive Informatics
- Heuristics
- Brain Simulation
- Automated Reasoning
- Algorithmic Learning
- Evolutionary Computing
- Pattern Recognition
- Neural Networks
- Computer Vision
- Cyborgs

IGI Global is currently accepting manuscripts for publication within this series. To submit a proposal for a volume in this series, please contact our Acquisition Editors at Acquisitions@igi-global.com or visit: http://www.igi-global.com/publish/.

Titles in this Series

For a list of additional titles in this series, please visit:
http://www.igi-global.com/book-series/advances-computational-intelligence-robotics/73674

Regulatory Aspects of Artificial Intelligence on Blockchain
Pardis Moslemzadeh Tehrani (University of Malaya, Malaysia)
Engineering Science Reference • © 2022 • 273pp • H/C (ISBN: 9781799879275) • US $245.00

Genetic Algorithms and Applications for Stock Trading Optimization
Vivek Kapoor (Devi Ahilya University, Indore, India) and Shubhamoy Dey (Indian Institute of Management, Indore, India)
Engineering Science Reference • © 2021 • 262pp • H/C (ISBN: 9781799841050) • US $225.00

Handbook of Research on Innovations and Applications of AI, IoT, and Cognitive Technologies
Jingyuan Zhao (University of Toronto, Canada) and V. Vinoth Kumar (MVJ College of Engineering, India)
Engineering Science Reference • © 2021 • 570pp • H/C (ISBN: 9781799868705) • US $325.00

Decision Support Systems and Industrial IoT in Smart Grid, Factories, and Cities
Ismail Butun (Chalmers University of Technology, Sweden & Konya Food and Agriculture University, Turkey & Royal University of Technology, Sweden)
Engineering Science Reference • © 2021 • 285pp • H/C (ISBN: 9781799874683) • US $245.00

Deep Natural Language Processing and AI Applications for Industry 5.0
Poonam Tanwar (Manav Rachna International Institute of Research and Studies, India) Arti Saxena (Manav Rachna International Institute of Research and Studies, India) and C. Priya (Vels Institute of Science, Technology, and Advanced Studies, India)
Engineering Science Reference • © 2021 • 240pp • H/C (ISBN: 9781799877288) • US $245.00

For an entire list of titles in this series, please visit:
http://www.igi-global.com/book-series/advances-computational-intelligence-robotics/73674

701 East Chocolate Avenue, Hershey, PA 17033, USA
Tel: 717-533-8845 x100 • Fax: 717-533-8661
E-Mail: cust@igi-global.com • www.igi-global.com

Table of Contents

Preface: A Data-Driven World – The Opportunity and Challenge for Human Learning and Problem Solving

THE OPPORTUNITY AND CHALLENGE

The Introduction Figure shows the history of our ability to learn and problem-solve with data and information. It illustrates that data and information processing has increased exponentially since the invention of the computer. For those history of technology buffs, we can place the beginning of this trend with the design and development of the ENIAC (Electronic Numerical Integrator and Computer) at the University of Pennsylvania in 1946 (Dyson, 2012). The U.S. Government funded the development of ENIAC for calculating ballistics tables for the military during World War II. While the end of World War II did not see the completion of ENIAC, it started the computer revolution in a post-war world.

As the top trend line, labeled "Data and Information Process" in Figure 1 shows, by the 1960s, businesses used computers for a variety of data and information processing. The amount of data that was processed had increased dramatically over the previous decade. With commercial database systems coming online and memory devices improving, the amount of data that could be processed was accelerating rapidly. When personal computers came along in the 1970s, the amount of data and information processed by computers began to increase at an even faster rate. By the time the spreadsheet applications came on the scene in the 1980s, computers' amount of data and information processed exponentially. This trend only has accelerated in the early 21st century with the advent of machine learning, business intelligence platforms, and the Internet of Things (IoT).

Figure 1. The History of Our Ability to Learn and Problem-Solve with Data and Information

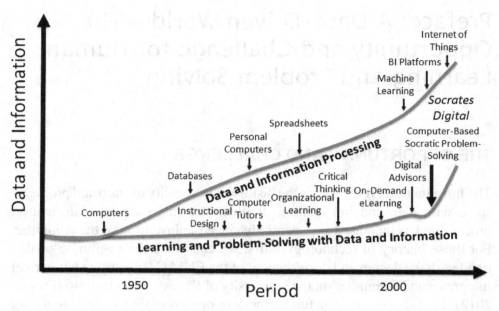

The lower trend line, labeled "Learning and Problem-Solving with Data and Information" in the Introduction Figure, shows that while the rate of data and information processing has been accelerating, our ability to learn and problem-solve with that data and information has not kept up. To effectively use this data and information for learning and problem-solving, we need to change how we reason with data and information. It seems as if our computers are using new and smarter methods to process more data, but we are using the same old ways for solving problems that we used before the invention of computers. If we can improve our ability to learn and problem-solve with data and information, we can more effectively address the complex problems that our world faces. Organizations will deliver better products and services, researchers will accelerate the advancement of science, and educational institutions can teach this new learning and problem solving to students entering a data-driven world.

DATA AND INFORMATION PROCESSING

As the Introduction Figure shows, the preponderance of big data is a relatively recent phenomenon that has emerged, starting in the mid-twentieth century -- powered by the expanding use of computer systems. As computer systems processed more information about the operations of government, companies, and non-profits, massive amounts of data became available for analysis. This big data provided the newfound ability to discover and predict trends in many aspects of our lives as citizens, employees, and customers.

However, the problem with big data is that it is not heterogeneous. Moreover, it is not uniform. For example, data about investment opportunities may reside in many different applications, such as spreadsheets, databases, business intelligence platforms, and internet sites. Furthermore, since this data comes from different applications, it will have been analyzed and processed with different methods. For example, data may be selected from a database with specific criteria to provide a subset of the larger dataset. Data in a spreadsheet may have undergone correlation analysis with other data in the spreadsheet. Furthermore, a machine-learning algorithm may have processed data in a business intelligence platform to identify what influences other data in a larger dataset.

In addition, since data is coming from different applications, the datasets will be of different sizes. Some datasets, perhaps, will be hundreds of items, while others are thousands of items, and some maybe millions of items. Not only are datasets of different sizes, but they are also of different quality. In other words, some datasets may have few errors in them while others have many errors – or have missing data.

All this means is that we have come to a point where we have lots of big data that provides the opportunity for analysis, discovery, and innovation, but much of it is disparate data. That is, the available data sources are vastly different in many ways. This new world of data brings the question, "how can we optimally reason with this big and disparate data?" The prevailing approach for analysts is to "pre-process" all the data into one giant heterogeneous dataset. This pre-process approach is the most common approach used by business intelligence platforms. These attempts, of course, have had limited success. That is because we cannot reduce all the ways we represent our shared experiences into a single dataset in real life. If we could do that, we could compile a "universal dataset" that captured all knowledge as we know it and solve any problem we encounter. This approach, of course, is not possible for many reasons. We need to develop a new approach for computers to help us learn and problem-solve with big and disparate data.

LEARNING AND PROBLEM-SOLVING WITH DATA AND INFORMATION

The Introduction Figure also shows our need for a new way to approach human learning and problem-solving. It illustrates that our ability to learn and problem-solve has increased very little since the invention of computers. That is because of the way we learn to problem-solve in school. We spend most of our time in school gaining factual knowledge about various phenomena and their problems. As for solving problems, we learn to solve them by recalling the problems and their associated solutions, matching the problem we are facing with one that we know, and applying the associated solution of that problem to the problem we are facing. From the field of logic, we call this deductive reasoning (LaFargue, 2016). We apply a general rule to a problem in order to solve it.

For most of us, problem-solving is recalling information and applying a known solution to the problem we are facing. With this perspective on learning, we then measure what students have learned by how much information they can recall about a topic. In the sciences, we may have them recall a solution then apply it to a given problem. An example of this is having students calculate the area of a circle after being given the diameter. In this view of education, learning is gaining information about problems. The problem-solving process is not essential since it is merely a simple deductive process to apply a known solution. "Real learning" for students is learning to recognize a problem and select the appropriate solution.

We carry this same perspective of learning and problem-solving into our workplaces. When we train our employees, we present information on topics and their associated problems hoping they will "absorb" it. When a problem presents itself in the workplace, they retrieve as much information about it as possible to match it to a known problem that has a known solution. When our employees were in school, problem-solving was the simple step of applying the solution they found. Since applying the solution is seen as so simple, we think there is no need to teach it to someone explicitly.

Surprisingly, many of our researchers also carry this same perspective of learning and problem-solving into their field of study. (I have seen this during my experience in chairing dozens of Ph.D. dissertations). They spend little time upfront with problem-solving to identify an appropriate topic to research. Instead, they will go on "hunches" or other anecdotal information to identify a question that needs an answer. Then, they will go to great lengths to create a well-designed study to test whether their insight was correct. Furthermore, they will go through lots and lots of detail about what study sample to use, measures to apply, analyzes to perform, and how to report the results. All good stuff -- but they begin with a hunch or anecdotal information. If they were to use better problem-solving upfront, they would identify more and better questions that need an answer provided by a study.

This perspective of learning and problem-solving is the main reason the trend line "Learning and Problem-Solving with Data and Information" in the Introduction Figure shows a relatively slight increase over time. However, there have been some improvements in human learning and problem-solving since the invention of computers. Some of the main contributing factors are the evolution of instructional design, the advent of organizational learning, and the development of e-learning. Computer-based, on-demand learning is probably one of the biggest reasons we have seen increased learning and problem-solving. The latest improvement is the development of computer-based Socratic problem solving – the topic of this book.

Despite these modest increases in our ability to solve problems, most of us believe that the prerequisite for problem-solving is learning about the problem and the possible solutions. Furthermore, we believe that if we have enough knowledge about a problem, we can stand back, and in our minds, "knit together" a solution for it. For example, if we are looking into the opportunity to invest in a motel chain, we might learn about common ways to measure the financial health of the motel chain. We might learn about the occupancy rate -- a measure of the percentage of total rooms rented -- and the average daily rate – a measure of average room price – and the revenue per available room – a measure of average room price that includes vacant rooms. After learning about these concepts, we might try to apply them to the motel chain to determine if the investment will boost total revenue enough to pay back the investors. We might even use a computer to help us calculate the values of these measures.

Moreover, if we live in the third decade of the 21st century, we might use a Business Intelligence platform to calculate these values. Then, we might paste the results on a dashboard of one of these platforms for others to see. Now, all the stakeholders in solving this problem can see the results in one place and "knit together" an answer to whether to invest in the motel chain. For many of us, we think that this is problem-solving. It is learning about the problem and then deciding what to do about it. The work is in learning about the problem and possible solutions. The problem-solving part is insignificant in comparison. In fact, we think little about it. Even though we do not understand how we knit together these solutions in our heads, we consider it relatively simple compared to learning about the problem.

This view of human problem-solving has tremendous implications for our work and the society in which we live. In the workplace, we focus on the many ways we can learn about a problem. Furthermore, we spend very little time on the problem-solving process itself. This view of human problem-solving also impacts our educational system. In fact, we reinforce this view in our educational systems, and our students take it to the workplace. As a result, we spend most of our energy and time teaching students about the nature of problems. Our practiced belief is to teach our students all about the problems they will face in their profession, equipping them to solve those problems when they encounter them. We spend very little time with them to learn a process to solve problems.

Meanwhile, problems have become too complex to solve in the workplace without a concerted effort to follow a problem-solving process. This problem-solving process must be able to deal with big and disparate data. Furthermore, it must solve problems that do not have a "rule" to apply in solving them. That means it needs to be inductive. Furthermore, it must deal with ambiguity and help humans use informed judgment to build on previous steps and create new understanding.

Computer-based Socratic problem-solving systems answer this need for a problem-solving process using big and disparate data. Furthermore, computer scientists, data scientists, and software developers need the knowledge to develop these systems.

This book presents the rationale for developing a Socratic problem-solving application. It describes how a computer-based Socratic problem-solving system called Socrates Digital™ can keep problem-solvers on track, document the outcome of a problem-solving session, and share those results with problem-solvers and larger audiences.

ORGANIZATION OF THIS BOOK

Chapter 1, "Problem-Solving With Data and Information," begins by looking at how humans learn and solve problems with data and information. However, we note that the actual steps for problem-solving remain a mystery to most problem-solvers. We also look at learning and problem-solving with technology in this chapter. This chapter also presents Digital advisors as a breakthrough technology for assisting humans in problem-solving. While promising, this approach relies on humans to ask the right questions. At the end of this chapter, we saw that computer-based Socratic problem-solving addresses this shortcoming by guiding the user through all the "right" questions needing answers to solve the problem at hand.

Chapter 2, "Critical Thinking and the Socratic Method," starts by answering the question, "What is Critical Thinking?" As it turns out, not everyone agrees on what critical thinking is. Nevertheless, researchers agree that critical thinking allows many people to reason together for solutions to complex problems. Also, in this chapter, we look at how computing capabilities enhance Socratic problem-solving. A computer-based Socratic problem-solving system can keep problem-solvers on track, document the outcome of a problem-solving session, and share those results with participants and a larger audience. In addition, Socrates Digital™ can also help problem-solvers combine evidence about their quality of reasoning for individual problem-solving steps and the overall confidence level for the solution.

In Chapter 3, "A Dialog With Socrates Digital™," the presented example dialog shows how Socrates Digital™ can guide users to learn and solve big and disparate data problems. In this example dialog, Socrates Digital™ takes the lead – as a human instructor or facilitator would – to guide the conversation with the user groups. It begins by guiding user groups in the examination of information, concepts, and assumptions. Next, Socrates Digital™ guides user groups to form conclusions and their implications. Finally, it guides user groups to summarize the conversation into a viewpoint about answering the question at hand.

Chapter 4, "System Design and Development," presents a Socrates Digital™ system's design and development process. It describes the four phases of design and development: Understand, Explore, Materialize, and Realize. The completion of these four phases results in a Socrates Digital™ system that leverages artificial intelligence services. The artificial intelligence services include a natural language processor provided by several artificial intelligence service providers, including Apple, Microsoft, Google, IBM, and Amazon.

Chapter 5 presents the Socrates Digital™ System Architecture – the inner workings of Socrates Digital™ module. It has most of the logic of a Socrates Digital™ system and describes how processes and subprocesses interact to create Socratic problem-solving. A Socrates Digital™ system allows the user to examine information, assumptions, and concepts in any order. Next,

Socrates Digital™ guides the user in developing a conclusion by applying concepts, using assumptions, and analyzing information. Afterward, Socrates Digital™ guides the user in predicting the implications of the conclusion and combining all the reasoning into a viewpoint that addresses the question at hand.

Chapter 6, "Problem Definition," begins with the Socrates Digital™ module calling the "Define Problem" process. This process identifies the problem area and gathers the problem-defining information from the user. In this chapter, we also see that this chapter provides pseudo-code for the subprocesses that make up the processes for Socrates Digital™. It has enough detail to implement the logic in any procedural and general-purpose computer programming language. This chapter shows that more questions follow after asking the user a question in many situations. The questions aimed at getting these answers are questions that target the quality of reasoning.

Chapter 7, "Information, Assumptions, and Concepts," shows the interrelationships between the processes to analyze information, identify assumptions, or apply concepts. This chapter uses an example to show how Socrates Digital™ examines the assumptions and the information they rest on simultaneously. If the user begins with analyzing information, then Socrates Digital™ asks the user to provide a data item that is relevant to the analysis. Next, it asks the user to identify the underlying assumptions used to analyze the data. After identifying the assumptions, Socrates Digital™ asks for the evidence that the assumption holds for a larger dataset.

Chapter 8, "Conclusions, Implications, and Viewpoints," shows how users can use Socrates Digital™ to analyze information, identify assumptions, and apply concepts to determine conclusions. After the user determines the conclusions, the next step for users is to predict the implications of those conclusions. Predicting the implications is followed by a step where the user summarizes the conclusions and implications into a viewpoint. Afterward, the user then evaluates this viewpoint, and Socrates Digital™ presents the opportunity to create another viewpoint. After the user decides there is no more evidence to gather, Socrates Digital™ then will calculate a score that provides a confidence level in the current viewpoint for the user.

Chapter 9, "Dialog Development Manager," shows how software development professionals use the provided flow charts and pseudo-code to create the Dialog Development Manager. Analysts then use the Dialog Development Manager to create the problem-specific knowledge needed by a natural language processor to support the conversation between Socrates Digital™ and end-users. The Dialog Development Manager guides the analysts through design and development of the Understand, Explore, Materialize, and Realize phases to create the conversational interface for Socrates Digital™.

Chapter 10, "Problem-Solving Manager," shows that Socrates Digital™ provides a submit, review, and approval process for a viewpoint to become a "best practice" for an organization to solve a particular problem. The Problem-Solving Manager makes these approved best practices available across the organization. This chapter presents the flow charts and pseudo-code for developing the Problem-Solving Manager. This chapter also shows that this additional role for the Problem-Solving Manager enables an innovative learning (iLearning) organization. Innovative learning begins with all team members having access to the same knowledge for the current "best way" of solving a problem. This knowledge is where the lessons learned from the past meet the best thinking of the present to learn how to do things better -- innovative learning.

Chapter 11, "The Road Ahead," notes that most discussions around critical thinking and Socratic problem-solving before this book was published described interactions between humans. However, as shown in this chapter, computers can not only automate the Socratic problem-solving process but can enhance its advantages for individuals, teams, and organizations in ways that only a computer can do. This chapter looks at eight ways that Socrates Digital™ can be enhanced to create better solutions for problem-solvers in less time.

REFERENCES

Dyson, G. (2012). *Turing's cathedral: The origins of the digital universe.* Pantheon Books.

LaFargue, M. (2016). *Rational spirituality and divine virtue in Plato: A modern interpretation and philosophical defense of Platonism.* SUNY Press.

Acknowledgment

I have many people to thank for their help with this book. First, I want to thank David Olson for introducing me to the world of computing so long ago. It truly transformed my life.

Also, thanks to my dissertation co-chairs, Dr. David Moursund and Dr. Mark Gall, I tried to share the wisdom you taught me with my doctoral students.

Thanks to Scott Moody, who provided his insights for an article that became the genesis for this book. Thanks, too, to Jason Sawin for early feedback and encouragement on the concept for the book.

I also thank Kevin Brady, Bob Grassberger, and Bill Meador from the University of New Mexico for sharing their ideas, resources, and interest in the future of work. They have been my "community of practice" for this work.

Thanks to Cris Zimmerman, too, for sharing his experience of how this technology can enhance human performance in the workplace.

I wish to thank my literary agent, Jeff Herman, for his help in making this book a reality.

Finally, thanks to my wife, Joan, for all her love and support while writing this book. I would also like to thank my three children, Luke, Jake, and Anya, for their patience waiting for me to complete this book before taking on more of life's adventures.

Chapter 1
Problem–Solving With Data and Information:
Accelerating Learning With Technology

ABSTRACT

This chapter begins by looking at how humans learn and solve problems with data and information. However, the authors note that the actual steps for problem-solving remain a mystery to most problem solvers. They also look at learning and problem solving with technology in this chapter. This chapter also presents digital advisors as a breakthrough technology for assisting humans in problem solving. While promising, this approach relies on humans to ask the right questions. At the end of this chapter, the authors saw that computer-based Socratic problem solving addresses this shortcoming by guiding the user through all the "right" questions needing answers to solve the problem at hand.

INTRODUCTION

We have made some small strides in our ability to learn and problem-solve since World War II. Several factors have contributed to this modest increase in our ability to reason. One factor was the adaptation of instructional systems design. Another factor was the focus on sharing learning across organizations, commonly known as organizational learning. Computer-based learning, or eLearning, was another factor that increased our ability to learn and problem-

DOI: 10.4018/978-1-7998-7955-8.ch001

solve. An actual increase began with computer-based, on-demand learning. This factor made learning available during problem-solving and improved our ability to reason about data and information. However, we are on the cusp of an exponential increase in our ability to reason with computer-based Socratic problem-solving. This chapter describes the developments that have paved the way for this new type of computer application, called Socrates Digital™.

Just as World War II launched the computer revolution, it also launched an industry focused on learning and development that spawned a new level of professionalism for training and educational programs. Out of this effort came an instructional design process featuring learning objectives and evaluating the instructional program.

Instructional Systems Design

Instructional designers are familiar with the major phases of instructional systems design (ISD) identified as analysis, design, development, implementation, and evaluation. The design phase uses the information from the analysis phase to formulate a plan for presenting instruction to learners. Most approaches in the design phase are rooted in the work of Robert Gagne, as described in his book, *The Conditions of Learning* (Gagne,1985), first published in 1965. Gagne's early work (1940s and 1950s) applied assumptions from behavioral psychology, notably that instruction is the reinforcement of appropriate learner responses to stimuli set up by the instructor. If students have learned, then it is more likely that they will exhibit the desired behavior in a given situation. Gagne's work did not apply operant conditioning in the behaviorist tradition. In his first edition of *The Conditions of Learning*, he incorporated cognitive information-processing views of learning. For Gagne, the behavior is complex and controlled primarily by internal mental processes rather than external stimuli and reinforcements. Therefore, Gagne saw instruction as organizing and providing information and activities that guide, support, and augment students' internal mental processes. Learning occurs when students incorporate new information that enables them to master new knowledge and skills. Gagne further developed cognitive views of learning and instruction in later editions of *The Conditions of Learning* (Gagne, 1985). This view of learning as a change in internal mental processes that results in improved performance is a cornerstone for modern applications of ISD.

Using an ISD process to solve a performance problem in an organization begins by noting the difference in the current state of performance and desired state of performance (Dick, Carey, & Carey, 2005). For example, an investment firm determines that the current rate of return on investments in commercial real estate is far below the targeted rate of return the firm has made for investments. In other words, there is a big gap between the desired rate of return and the actual rate of return on commercial real estate investments for the firm.

The next step in the ISD process is to determine the set of criteria, or performance objectives, that need to be met by its investors for the successful completion of an investment. These performance objectives sometimes called learning objectives, may be implicit or in the eye of the beholder. Recognizing the existence of these performance objectives without being able to articulate them easily is found in such phrases as "I know a good commercial real estate investment when I see one." These performance objectives spell out what is done and how well it is done for identifying successful commercial real estate investments. We can think of these as learning objectives since it is the performance we want to see in the learner after an instructional experience.

Using ISD, one way to identify performance objectives to determine a commercial real estate investment is to conduct a content analysis. It always starts with the same question. In this case, it is, "What knowledge does a person need to know to identify a successful commercial real estate investment?" (Davis, Alexander, & Yelon, 1974). This question focuses on identifying the cognitive skills needed for determining a successful commercial real estate investment. Cognitive skills underlie learning how to learn, that is, getting at the heart of the problem (Gagne, Briggs, & Wager, 1992). The next step is to rewrite these cognitive skills as performance objectives. For example, applying the cognitive skill occupancy rate is written as the performance objective, "To help determine if a motel chain is a good investment, the analyst will provide an accurate occupancy rate for each motel in the chain." (For a complete description of the steps for conducting a content analysis, see Rothwell & Kazanas, 2004).

Performance objectives make a precise statement of what a learner should "do" to accomplish the stated performance (Mager, 1997). They contain a performance component, a criterion component, and a condition component. The performance component describes how proficiency is demonstrated. The criterion component describes how well the proficiency is performed. The condition component describes what conditions must exist when proficiency is demonstrated.

Performance objectives also form the basis for evaluating the effectiveness of instruction. In the above occupancy rate performance objective example, effective instruction results in an accurate occupancy rate for each motel in the chain.

Bloom's Taxonomy

One of the advancements in ISD is the use of Bloom's Taxonomy for classifying learning objectives. In 1956, Benjamin Bloom, with collaborators Max Englehart, Edward Furst, Walter Hill, and David Krathwohl, published a framework for categorizing educational goals: *Taxonomy of Educational Objectives* (Bloom, 1956). Familiarly known as Bloom's Taxonomy, generations of K-12 teachers and college instructors have applied this framework to their teaching.

As shown in Figure 1, the taxonomy by Bloom and his collaborators consisted of six major categories: knowledge, comprehension, application, analysis, synthesis, and evaluation. The categories after knowledge were presented as "skills and abilities," with the understanding that knowledge was necessary for putting these skills and abilities into practice.

Figure 1. Bloom's Taxonomy of Educational Objectives

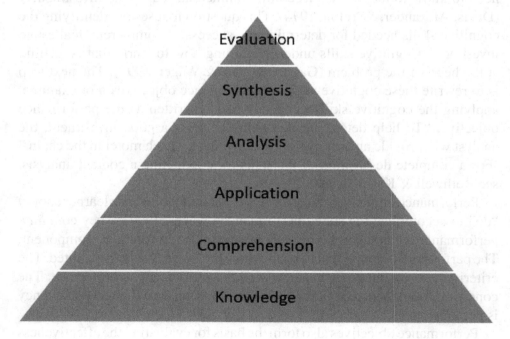

While each category contained subcategories, all lying along a continuum from simple to complex and concrete to abstract, the taxonomy is typically summarized by the six main categories.

Here are the authors' brief explanations of these main categories from the appendix of *Taxonomy of Educational Objectives* (Bloom, 1956):

- Knowledge "involves the recall of specifics and universals, the recall of methods and processes, or the recall of a pattern, structure, or setting."
- Comprehension "refers to a type of understanding or apprehension such that the individual knows what is being communicated and can make use of the material or idea being communicated without necessarily relating it to other material or seeing its fullest implications."
- Application refers to the "use of abstractions in particular and concrete situations."
- Analysis represents the "breakdown of a communication into its constituent elements or parts such that the relative hierarchy of ideas is made clear and/or the relations between ideas expressed are made explicit."
- Synthesis involves the "putting together of elements and parts so as to form a whole."
- Evaluation engenders "judgments about the value of material and methods for given purposes."

The use of Bloom's Taxonomy for classifying performance objectives has provided insight into how we perceive human problem-solving. For example, consider if we apply Bloom's Taxonomy to the performance objective discussed earlier, "To help determine if a motel chain is a good investment, the analyst will provide an accurate occupancy rate for each motel in the chain." We find that it belongs to the knowledge category since the analyst simply has to recall and use the process for determining an accurate occupancy rate for a motel to achieve the performance objective. Educators have used Bloom's Taxonomy to evaluate curriculum materials. They have been able to point out when instruction is based simply on recall.

While Bloom's Taxonomy has had tremendous influence in educational circles for over 75 years, it has had its distractors. For the most part, critics have pointed out that it breaks thinking up into these simple, hierarchical, and compartmentalized categories. Richard Paul, a proponent of critical thinking, argued that the categories are not a hierarchy. For Paul, this thinking has led educators to conclude that knowledge is always a simpler thinking process than comprehension. In turn, comprehension is simpler than application, and application is more simple than analysis. This thinking concludes with analysis as simpler than synthesis and synthesis as simpler than evaluation (Paul, 1993). Paul asserts that achieving knowledge always presupposes minimal comprehension, application, analysis, synthesis, and evaluation. Paul concludes that this creates obstacles for the development of what he calls "rational learning." For Paul, this perception that Bloom's six categories form a hierarchy leads to students being told -- and expecting to be told -- what to believe (belief inculcation) and being told what to do (the over-proceduralization of thought).

Making instruction development a professional process featuring learning objectives with methods for evaluating the instructional experience gave us a false sense of advancement in our ability to learn and problem-solve. We became focused on learning about the problem rather than on the process of solving the problem. We still believe that problem-solving is relatively simple once the problem is known. However, we cannot string together a chain of reasoning to solve our most complex problems for the most part.

Online Learning

Online learning is an extension of ISD. Developers still use the process of creating instructional materials for creating learning experiences online. However, three characteristics define online learning (Moore, 2013). The first characteristic is that geographic separation is inherent in online learning, and time may also separate students and teachers. Accessibility and convenience are essential advantages of this mode of education. Well-designed programs can also bridge intellectual, cultural, and social differences between students.

The second characteristic is that interactive telecommunications connect individuals within a learning group and with the instructor. Electronic communications, such as email, are often used, but traditional forms of communication, such as the postal system, may also be used. Whatever the medium, interaction is essential to online learning, as it is to any learning experience. The connections of learners, instructors, and instructional resources become less dependent on physical proximity as communications systems become more sophisticated and widely available. That means the Internet, mobile phones, and email have contributed to the rapid growth in online learning.

The third characteristic is that online learning, in many instances, creates a learning group, sometimes called a learning community, which is composed of students, a teacher, and instructional resources. The books, audio, video, and graphic displays allow the student to access the learning materials. Also, in the online learning environment, students can connect to reduce their sense of isolation.

Online learning has undoubtedly found a place in the education of our youth and for training and development in our organizations. However, it still has many of the advantages and disadvantages of traditional learning in face-to-face settings. Moreover, for the most part, the learning objectives can be judged with the help of Bloom's Taxonomy. As of yet, it has not 'reconceptualized" learning as we have known it. Like the ones in face-to-face settings, most online learning objectives fall into the last rungs of Bloom's Taxonomy – the knowledge and comprehension categories.

Critical Thinking

The critical thinking movement came into being as an answer to the perceived problem of American students having low problem-solving skills. Most educators familiar with the critical thinking movement begin with the book, *An Experiment in the Development of Critical Thinking*, written by Edward Glaser and published in 1941 (Glaser, 1941). As discussed in the following chapter, there are different interpretations of critical thinking. However, they all have four things in common: hunting assumptions, checking assumptions, seeing things from different viewpoints, and taking informed action (Brookfield, 2012).

During critical thinking, we try to find out the underlying assumptions that influence how we think or act (Flew, 2001). Identifying the assumptions that we have accepted, sometimes unknowingly, is the first step. It is a deliberate process that is sometimes difficult in that we are often unaware of the assumptions we take for granted in our thinking and actions.

Checking these assumptions that we have identified is the next step. We look at these assumptions guiding our thinking and begin to check to see if they are accurate. It begins by assessing if our assumptions are valid and reliable guides for our actions. In this assessment process, we look for times when our assumptions make sense and when they do not. We may find that our assumptions are too general in many situations and do not work for specific exceptions. We may end up checking our assumptions in many different ways, including conducting our investigations and relying on a source of authority.

The next step is to look at the situation from another viewpoint. We may do this from a different role than we may play – or from another person's point of view. An excellent way to determine if an assumption makes sense is to look at it from another point of view.

The last thing that all forms of critical thinking have in common is taking informed action. That means it is an action based on thought and analysis of evidence. Typically, we have analyzed the concepts we are using and have thought about the conclusions that result in the implications of doing that action.

Critical thinking forms the basis of Socratic questioning even though Socrates lived his life thousands of years before the critical thinking movement as we know it began. Critical thinking provides the conceptual tools for understanding the mind's reasons, and Socratic questioning employs those tools in framing questions essential to problem-solving. The goal, then of critical thinking, is to establish an additional level of thinking to our thinking – an inner voice of reason that monitors, assesses and reconstitutes our thinking and actions. Socratic discussion cultivates that inner voice by focussing on self-directed, disciplined questioning (Paul & Elder, 2019).

Organizational Learning

Although ISD is quite effective for solving acute organizational problems with instructional applications, it is not very effective for identifying the systemic relationships between organizational performance problems. This lack of a systems view (Senge, 1990) keeps instructional designers on a never-ending treadmill of responding to one performance crisis after another. They can keep the enterprise afloat but do not have the time, energy, and, most importantly, the big-picture perspective to make the necessary systemic improvements to improve organizational performance. What is needed is a "life cycle of knowledge" viewpoint from which to analyze, design, and implement systemic improvements for organizational performance problems.

The life cycle of knowledge is the ongoing cycle of creating, preserving, and disseminating knowledge in organizations. However, it is not just any knowledge but the knowledge that defines an organization's core competency— what the organization does best. To successfully manage the life cycle of knowledge in an organization requires recognition that organizational knowledge is complex. Lack of this recognition is why many traditional approaches to managing the life cycle of knowledge in organizations have failed. These failed approaches have assumed that this knowledge is relatively simple (only factual) and have used techniques to manage it (for example, document management). What is needed is a comprehensive framework that addresses the complexity of managing knowledge in an organizational setting.

The first phase of the ongoing life cycle of knowledge in successful organizations is creating new knowledge. This phase occurs when members of the organization solve a new unique problem or solve more minor parts of a more significant problem, such as those generated by an ongoing project. The next phase is preserving this newly created knowledge, which includes recording the description of the problem and its new solution. The dissemination and application phase involves sharing this new knowledge with the other members of the organization. It also includes sharing the solutions with the stakeholders affected by the problems that were solved. Disseminated knowledge then becomes an input for solving new problems in the following knowledge creation phase. An organization's ability to solve problems increases with the use of this disseminated knowledge. In this way, each knowledge life cycle phase constitutes input for the next phase, creating an ongoing cycle. Because this cycle continues to build on itself, it becomes a knowledge spiral in the organization, as described by Nonaka and Takeuchi (1995).

The growth and sharing of knowledge are essential elements in becoming a learning organization (Easterby-Smith, 1997; Marsick & Watkins, 1994; Senge, 1990). However, according to many researchers and practitioners in the field, what has been missing is the development of a cohesive theory for describing how people learn and perform in an organization (Raybould, 1995; Salisbury, 2000). Today's organizations need this coherent theory to avoid developing technological solutions that do not support their entire life cycle of knowledge (Plass & Salisbury, 2002). One coherent theory to meet this need describes how learning can occur with one individual, preserved by that individual, and transferred to other individuals in an organizational setting (Salisbury & Plass, 2001; Salisbury, 2003).

LEARNING AND PROBLEM-SOLVING WITH TECHNOLOGY

Since the invention of computers, we have sought to use them to help us solve problems. One of the first efforts was the General Problem Solver (GPS), a computer program first reported in 1959 by Herbert Simon, J. C. Shaw, and Allen Newell (Newell, Shaw, & Simon, 1959). The intention was to create a universal problem-solver machine. The developers employed an information processing model, and it attempted to explain all behavior as a function of memory operations, control processes, and rules. The intent for GPS was to be a general problem-solver, but it could only solve "well-defined" problems such as proving theorems in logic or geometry, word puzzles, and chess. The methodology for testing the theory involved developing a computer simulation and then comparing the simulation results with human behavior in a given task. This approach led to a synergy in their research between modeling human problem-solving to understand human cognitive processes better and creating computer programs with problem-solving capabilities (Newell & Simon, 1972).

Computer Tutors

Another line of research that started in the 1960s involved developing intelligent computer tutors to assist in human problem-solving. There was considerable research for creating intelligent tutors to assess learning difficulties in various areas, such as language, reading, spelling, and mathematics. The development goal for these tutors was to capture the "instructional strategy" of teaching. For example, consider the assessment of a child's arithmetic skills. Having determined that a student has difficulty in math with subtraction, the teacher must determine what aspects of subtraction are the problem for the student. In this process, the teacher may consider the question, "Is it poor knowledge of number facts that is the problem?" Alternatively, the teacher may consider the question, "Does the student not borrow correctly?" To determine the root cause of subtraction difficulties, a human diagnostician would generally undertake some informal evaluation of the student's performance. Programs with this type of expertise functioned as human teachers for diagnosing the student's root cause of misconceptions. Brown and Burton's BUGGY system demonstrated an excellent example of these intelligent tutors diagnosing student misconceptions about subtraction problems and "guiding" the student to correct those misconceptions (Brown & Burton, 1982). BUGGY, and the many others like it, was more focused on directing the students in their thought processes than working with them to solve a problem. These systems never reached their potential as the educational focus shifted from teacher-directed learning to student-centered learning (Papert, 1982). Intelligent tutors did not fit this new focus since they played the teacher's role and were essentially responsible for completing the planned learning for the student.

However, some early efforts did focus on student problem-solving. SOPHIE (SOPHisticated Instructional Environment) was an intelligent tutoring system for electronic troubleshooting that focused on student-centered learning than before (Brown, Burton, & de Kleer, 1982). Rather than instructing the student on electronics, SOPHIE provided the student with a learning environment to acquire problem-solving skills by trying different approaches. SOPHIE was a computer-based expert that helped the student to develop, test, and debug hypotheses. Nevertheless, like BUGGY and the others that came before, SOPHIE was still based on the assumption that students could not solve a problem because they were using a "faulty" cognitive strategy in pursuing a solution. The goal, then, was not to assist in solving the problem but, instead, in teaching the "correct" strategy to solve the problem.

In the 1980s, one of the most promising technologies for modeling human cognition in problem-solving was named an *expert system*, derived from the *knowledge-based expert system* (Luger, 2004). An expert system utilizes human knowledge captured in a computer program to solve a problem that ordinarily requires human expertise (Tyler, 2007). The idea behind these systems is to imitate the reasoning process that human experts use to solve specific problems. Nonexperts can improve their problem-solving capabilities using these systems, and human experts can use them as knowledgeable assistants.

At the time, it was an easy and natural conclusion that expert systems technology would be well suited for capturing and enhancing human problem-solving. However, while expert systems were proven to solve problems that had typically been considered solvable only by human experts, they were not very good at explaining why something needed doing. Several early expert systems bolted on "explanation systems" with deep domain knowledge to provide an explanation capability. MYCIN is a noteworthy example of this approach (Buchanan & Shortliffe, 1985). MYCIN, developed at Stanford, played the role of a physician and focused on choosing an antibiotic medicine (or combination of medicines) for treating a patient with a bacterial infection. MYCIN could walk its human users through the steps of how it came to its conclusions. However, the role of these new intelligent machines in relation to the humans who used them was not clearly established. It was not clear how much they were supposed to do without human intervention. As a result, they were never fully embraced.

Machine Learning

Since the turn of the 21st century, there has been a shift away from rule-based expert systems to machine learning systems to build intelligent applications. The central concept is to let the system learn its own "rules" by training on example problems. These new deep learning systems have reported performance as good or better than human performance in problem-solving. However, the new problem for these deep learning systems is explaining how they came to their decisions to a human being. The problem is not a new one. As noted previously, MYCIN could walk its human users through the steps of how it came to its conclusions (Buchanan & Shortliffe, 1985). While this is a similar requirement for users of the new deep learning systems, it is much more challenging to explain how decisions are made inside a "fuzzy" network. Inside deep learning systems are decision nodes with weighted values calculated by training specific instances of similar examples. So, the explanation for these new deep learning systems becomes a description of the weighted values used for making decisions, but not the reasons behind them. This lack of explanation makes the knowledge used to make decisions opaque to the users of these new deep learning systems.

Digital Advisors

Since the human users who use these intelligent applications are responsible for their operation and outcomes, they need expert advice about learning and solving problems. Instead of seeing the weights for decision-making on nodes that represent the problem space, these human users need to answer their questions: What do I do? Why do I do it? How do I do it? Moreover, When and Where do I do it? In other words, these users of intelligent systems need advice in human language about what their job is with the intelligent system. While users need to know what the intelligent machine does, they need to know, more importantly, what they need to learn and how they will go about solving the problem at hand. The development of intelligent digital advisors started to meet this need. These intelligent advisors can understand human language and find the right learning resource from a rich content library that includes descriptions, instruction, examples, and expert knowledge about a topic (Salisbury, 2019).

A revision of Bloom's Taxonomy (Bloom, 1956) developed by Anderson, Krathwohl, Airasian, Cruikshank, Mayer, Pintrich, Raths & Wittrock

(Anderson, L. W., et al., 1998) provided the path to create advice that provides access to the knowledge that users seek through their questions. As Figure 2 shows, one of the significant differences in Anderson and his colleagues' revised taxonomy is identifying knowledge as a separate dimension that describes it as factual, conceptual, procedural, and metacognitive. Another significant difference is that Anderson and his colleagues recast Bloom's other categories into a "process dimension," which describes the user's cognitive processes when processing knowledge of that category. These process dimension categories were also renamed from Bloom's original "knowledge, comprehension, application, analysis, synthesis, and evaluation" to "remember, understand, apply, analyze, evaluate, and create." Anderson and colleagues place "create" as the highest level of cognition; it describes individuals putting elements together to form a novel coherent whole or make an original product.

Figure 2. Revision of Bloom's Taxonomy by Anderson and Colleagues

Cognitive Dimension	Knowledge Dimension			
	Factual	Conceptual	Procedural	Metacognitive
Create	✓	✓	✓	✓
Evaluate	✓	✓	✓	✓
Analyze	✓	✓	✓	✓
Apply	✓	✓	✓	✓
Understand	✓	✓	✓	✓
Remember	✓	✓	✓	✓

While these categories of knowledge come from cognitive psychology, they are strikingly similar to the different types of knowledge identified in artificial intelligence research. Anderson and his colleagues described factual knowledge as similar to "declarative knowledge" described in expert systems. Anderson and his colleagues described conceptual knowledge as similar to "procedural knowledge" described in expert systems. In addition, procedural knowledge for Anderson and his colleagues is quite similar to "episodic knowledge," as described in case-based reasoning. Furthermore, Anderson and his colleagues' metacognitive knowledge corresponds to "metaknowledge" used to guide reasoning in knowledge-based systems. It is interesting to note that researchers in different fields have seen the advantages of distinguishing between different types of knowledge when attempting to model human reasoning and learning.

These four types of knowledge map very well to the types of questions users ask when solving a problem (Salisbury, 2009). When users ask what the definition of a task or procedure is, they are seeking factual knowledge (i.e., terminology, specific details, and elements). When users ask why it is essential, they seek conceptual knowledge – information about general principles and concepts. When users ask how to do a task or procedure, they seek procedural knowledge – the steps for completing it. When users ask when or where to do the task or procedure, they are seeking metacognitive knowledge – that knowledge about knowledge.

As shown in Figure 2, the revision of Bloom's Taxonomy realized in digital advisors addresses Paul's criticism about Bloom's original taxonomy. As discussed earlier, Paul argued that Bloom presented cognitive processing as hierarchical (Paul, 1993). Paul argues that cognitive processing is not hierarchical, and the different categories of processing coincide. For example, in Bloom's Application category, learners apply the knowledge they know about and already comprehend to a problem. That means they only do one cognitive process at a time – in this case, the application of knowledge. Paul would argue that learners must involve the other cognitive processing categories of Knowledge and Comprehension to apply that knowledge. For Paul, learners jump between Bloom's categories to learn what they need to know to accomplish the learning objective at hand.

Digital advisors created the flexibility needed to address this criticism by Paul of Bloom's Taxonomy. They can understand and deliver the type of knowledge learners are seeking to fulfill their cognitive processing requirements of the moment. For example, a learner interacting with a digital advisor could get access to factual knowledge to help the learner create a new way to measure the financial health of a motel chain. The checkmarks convey that a digital advisor can understand and answer a user for any cognitive processing category and knowledge type combination.

Digital advisors represent a breakthrough in assisting humans in problem-solving. However, while promising, this approach relies on humans to ask the right questions. What is needed is computer-based guidance to assist users in asking those right questions.

Computer-Based Socratic Problem-Solving

Figure 3 shows that computer-based Socratic problem-solving continues the flexibility shown by digital advisors for addressing the criticism by Paul of Bloom's Taxonomy. Note that it is also based on the revision of Bloom's Taxonomy by Anderson and his colleagues. In this adaptation of the revision of Bloom's Taxonomy, metacognitive knowledge breaks out into conclusions, implications, and viewpoints. Forming conclusions, predicting implications, and creating viewpoints are based upon information, concepts, and assumptions is "knowledge about knowledge" – the very definition of metacognitive knowledge as defined by Anderson and his colleagues (Anderson. et al., 1998). Anderson and his colleagues' revision of Bloom's Taxonomy adds information, concepts, and assumptions to factual, conceptual, and procedural knowledge in the computer-based Socratic problem-solving map.

Also, note that similarly to digital advisors, the checkmarks convey that Socrates Digital™ can understand and deliver an answer to a user for any combination of cognitive processing category and knowledge type. That means Socrates Digital™ can guide a user to create new information, concepts, assumptions, conclusions, implications, and viewpoints. It also means that Socrates Digital™ can guide users to evaluate information, concepts, assumptions, conclusions, implications, and viewpoints.

Figure 3. Revision of the Taxonomy of Anderson and Colleagues for Socratic Problem-Solving

Cognitive Dimension	Knowledge Dimension					
	Factual	Conceptual	Procedural	Metacognitive		
	Information	Concepts	Assumptions	Conclusions	Implications	Viewpoint
Create	✓	✓	✓	✓	✓	✓
Evaluate	✓	✓	✓	✓	✓	✓
Analyze	✓	✓	✓	✓	✓	✓
Apply	✓	✓	✓	✓	✓	✓
Understand	✓	✓	✓	✓	✓	✓
Remember	✓	✓	✓	✓	✓	✓

Figure 4 shows how cognitive processing and the four types of knowledge described by Anderson and his colleagues (Anderson. et al., 1998) come together in computer-based Socratic problem-solving. At the beginning of this problem-solving process, a questioning dialog between Socrates Digital™ and the system user identifies a purpose. Figure 4 shows that the outcome of this conversation is identifying a question at issue that needs answering. In the example dialog with Socrates Digital™ presented in Chapter 3, this question decides if the user will invest in a motel chain.

Figure 4. Socratic Problem-Solving from the Inside Out

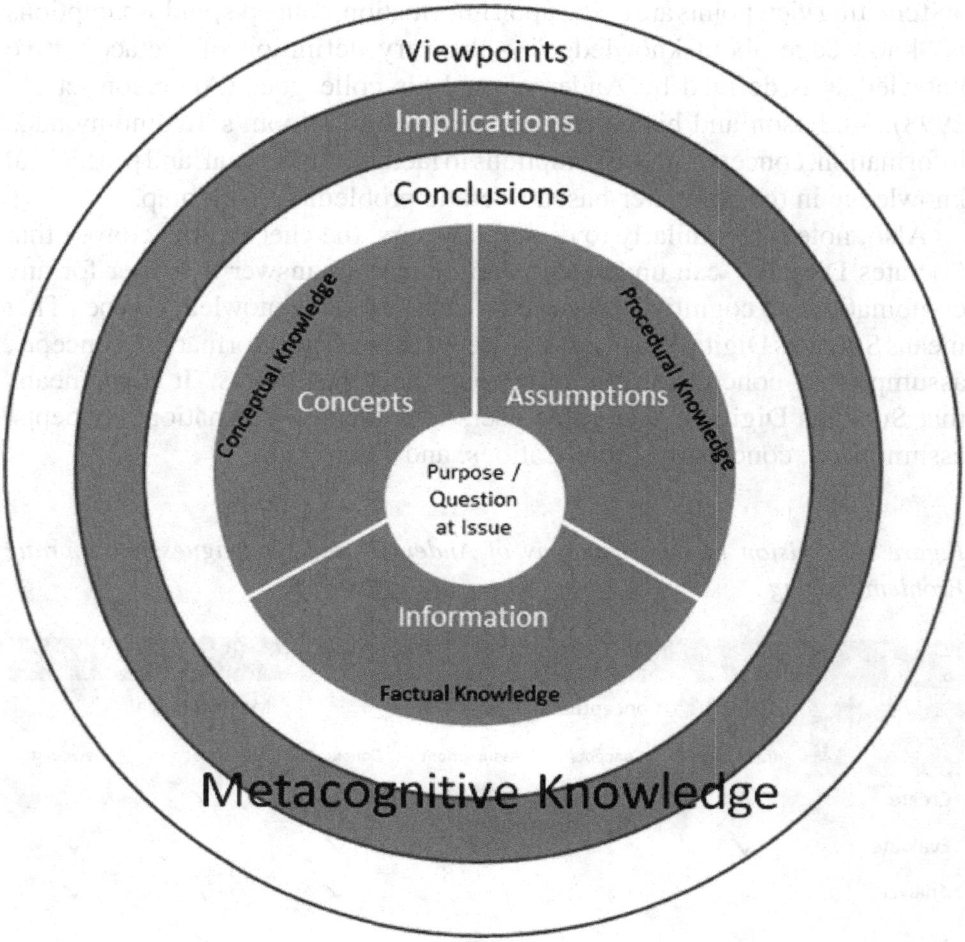

After identifying the question at issue, the next step depends on the human user of the system. The user can choose to analyze the concepts, assumptions, or information as the next step. As seen in Figure 4, these options are at the same level in the conversation between Socrates Digital™ and the user. In the example dialog coming up in Chapter 3, the user initially chooses "concepts" as the area to analyze first. After identifying "occupancy rate" as a concept used to judge the financial health of the motel chain for investment, the user is asked, "How well does this concept explain how to answer the question at hand." The user's answer informs Socrates Digital™ of the strength of the concept as judged by the user.

In the example dialog of Chapter 3, the human user chose "information" as the next step. Socrates Digital™ follows up with a question about what evidence the user has that shows that occupancy rate is a good measure of the financial health of the motel chain. The user responds with data on an individual motel that has low occupancy rates and low total revenue. Next, Socrates Digital™ asks the user to identify the assumption that underlies this observation. The user responds with the assumption that occupancy rate is positively correlated with total revenue. To which Socrates Digital™ asks if the user would like to apply this concept. The user replies with "probably apply it."

Socrates Digital™ follows up by asking if this assumption holds for the larger dataset. The user responds that yes, it does and provides information that shows occupancy rate is positively correlated with total revenue for all motels in the Rosebud Motel chain. Socrates Digital™ now asks the user to rate the accuracy of this data. To which the user replies, "I think that it is probably accurate."

As shown in Figure 4, Socrates Digital™ moves control to focus on making a conclusion and asks, "Given these concepts, assumptions, and information, what is the most reasonable conclusion?" The user replies, "Raising the occupancy rate for all the motels in the Rosebud Motel chain would raise total revenue for the chain." Socrates Digital™ now asks the user how they would rate the logic of that conclusion. The user responds with, "I would say that it is probably logical."

Next, Socrates Digital™ moves control to focus on identifying implications and asks the user to identify the implications of this conclusion. To which the user replies, "Increased marketing can raise the occupancy rate and total revenue for motels in the Rosebud Motel chain." When asked how you would rate your confidence in the implications of this conclusion, the user replies, "Insufficient evidence to judge."

The conversation takes a turn, and Socrates Digital™ and the user examine more information, concepts, and assumptions to form more conclusions and implications. Afterward, when prompted by Socrates Digital™, the user states this viewpoint, "The viewpoint is focused on increasing marketing to raise occupancy rates, average daily rates, and revenue per available room to increase total revenue for motels in the Rosebud Motel chain."

In this way, Socrates Digital™ begins with a dialog to identify the question at hand for solving the problem. Socrates Digital™ then works with the user to analyze information, apply concepts, and identify assumptions. Next, Socrates Digital™ works with the user to develop a conclusion and predict the implications. Finally, Socrates Digital™ guides the user to create a viewpoint that "tells a story" about how these factors answer the question at hand.

For the design and implementation of Socrates Digital™ in this book, Socrates Digital™ guides the user to examine information, concepts, and assumptions -- in any order. However, some of the design and implementation details were simplified for presentation purposes. For example, Socrates Digital™ guides the user to form conclusions, predict implications, and use all this analysis to create a viewpoint for answering the question at hand – in that order. This simplified design and implementation of Socrates Digital™ extends easily to guide the user to examine information, concepts, and assumptions, form conclusions, predict implications, and create a viewpoint – in any order.

SUMMARY

This chapter began by looking at how humans learn and solve problems with data and information. We noted that there had been some small increases in our ability to problem-solve due to instructional systems design (ISD), Bloom's Taxonomy, online learning, the critical thinking movement, and organizational learning. In general, these learning advancements have improved our ability to design and deliver instruction – and share that learning with others in our organizations. However, none of these advancements – except critical thinking -- have focused on increasing our ability to problem-solve. For the most part, they have focused on better methods for teaching the details of a problem and how to select the appropriate solution to solve it. The actual steps for problem-solving remain a mystery to most learners.

We also looked at learning and problem-solving with technology in this chapter. We noted that research in intelligent computer tutors has been – for the most part – focused on the teaching side of the details of a problem and the way to select the appropriate solution to solve it. We also noted that machine learning solved problems with outstanding success. However, since such systems cannot explain how they solved the problem to the humans who have to take responsibility for machine learning solutions, such systems are limited in their ability to increase human problem-solving. Digital advisors are a breakthrough in assisting humans in problem-solving. While promising, this approach relies on humans to ask the right questions. At the end of this chapter, we saw that computer-based Socratic problem-solving addresses this shortcoming by guiding the user through all the "right" questions needing answering to solve the problem at hand. In the next chapter, we will look closer at critical thinking and Socratic problem-solving to see how this perspective on human problem-solving informs the design of Socrates Digital™.

REFERENCES

Anderson, L., Krathwohl, D., Airasian, P., Cruikshank, K., Mayer, R., Pintrich, P., Raths, J., & Wittrock, M. (1998). *Taxonomy for learning, teaching and assessing: A revision of Bloom's taxonomy of educational objectives.* Longman.

Bloom, B. (1956). *Taxonomy of behavioral objectives. Handbook I: Cognitive Domain.* David McKay.

Brookfield, S. (2012). *Teaching for critical thinking: tools and techniques to help students question their assumptions.* Jossey-Bass.

Brown, J., & Burton, R. (1982). Diagnosing bugs in a simple procedural skill. In D. Sleeman & J. S. Brown (Eds.), *Intelligent Tutoring Systems* (pp. 157–183). Academic Press.

Brown, J., Burton, R., & de Kleer, J. (1982). Pedagogical, natural language and knowledge engineering techniques in SOPHIE I, II and III. In D. Sleeman & J. S. Brown (Eds.), *Intelligent Tutoring Systems* (pp. 227–282). Academic Press.

Buchanan, B., & Shortliffe, E. (1985). *Rule-Based Expert Systems: the MYCIN Experiments of the Stanford Heuristic Programming Project.* Addison-Wesley.

Davis, R., Alexander, L., & Yelon, S. (1974). *Learning systems design.* McGraw-Hill.

Dick, W., Carey, L., & Carey, J. (2005). *The systematic design of instruction* (6th ed.). Allyn & Bacon.

Easterby-Smith, M. (1997). Disciplines of organizational learning: Contributions and critiques. *Human Relations*, *50*(9), 1085–1113. doi:10.1177/001872679705000903

Flew, A. (2001). *How to think straight: An introduction*. Oxford University Press.

Gagne, R. (1985). *The conditions of learning* (4th ed.). Holt, Rinehart and Winston.

Gagne, R., Briggs, L., & Wager, W. (1992). *Principles of instructional design* (4th ed.). Harcourt Brace.

Glaser, E. (1941). *An experiment in the development of critical thinking*. AMS Press.

Luger, G. (2004). *Artificial intelligence: Structures and strategies for complex problem solving* (5th ed.). Addison-Wesley.

Mager, R. (1997). *Preparing instructional objectives: A critical tool in the development of effective instruction* (3rd ed.). Center for Effective Performance.

Marsick, V., & Watkins, K. (1994). The learning organization: An integrative vision for HRD. *Human Resource Development Quarterly*, *5*(4), 353–360. doi:10.1002/hrdq.3920050406

Moore, M. (2013). The theory of transactional distance. In M. G. Moore (Ed.), *Handbook of distance education*. Routledge. doi:10.4324/9780203803738.ch5

Newell, A., Shaw, J., & Simon, H. (1959). Report on a general problem-solving program. *Proceedings of the International Conference on Information Processing*, 256–264.

Newell, A., & Simon, H. (1972). *Human problem solving*. Prentice-Hall.

Nonaka, I., & Takeuchi, H. (1995). *The knowledge-creating company*. Oxford University Press.

Papert, S. (1982). *Mindstorms: Children, computers, and powerful ideas*. Basic Books. doi:10.1007/978-3-0348-5357-6

Paul, R. (1993). *Critical thinking: How to prepare students for a rapidly changing world*. Foundation for Critical Thinking.

Paul, R., & Elder, L. (2019). *The thinker's guide to Socratic questioning: Based on critical thinking concepts and tools*. Rowan & Littlefield.

Plass, J., & Salisbury, M. (2002). A living system approach to the development of knowledge management systems. *Educational Technology Research and Development*, *50*(1), 35–57. doi:10.1007/BF02504960

Raybould, B. (1995). Performance support engineering: An emerging development methodology for enabling organizational learning. *Performance Improvement Quarterly*, *8*(1), 7–22. doi:10.1111/j.1937-8327.1995.tb00658.x

Salisbury, M. (2000). Creating a process for capturing and leveraging intellectual capital. *Performance Improvement Quarterly*, *13*(3), 202–219. doi:10.1111/j.1937-8327.2000.tb00182.x

Salisbury, M. (2003). Putting theory into practice to build knowledge management systems. *Journal of Knowledge Management*, *7*(2), 128–141. doi:10.1108/13673270310477333

Salisbury, M. (2009). iLearning: How to Create an Innovative Learning Organization. New York: Wiley.

Salisbury, M. (2019). When Computers Advise Us: How to Represent the Different Types of Knowledge that Human Users Seek for Expert Advice. *IEEE Computer*, *52*(9), 44–51. doi:10.1109/MC.2019.2902137

Salisbury, M., & Plass, J. (2001). A conceptual framework for a knowledge management system. *Human Resource Development International*, *4*(4), 451–464. doi:10.1080/13678860010016913

Senge, P. (1990). *The fifth discipline: The art and practice of the learning organization*. Doubleday.

Tyler, A. (2007). *Expert systems research trends*. Nova Science Publishers.

ADDITIONAL READING

Rothwell, W., & Kazanas, H. (2004). *Mastering the instructional design process*. Pfeiffer.

Chapter 2
Critical Thinking and the Socratic Method:
Automating Socratic Questioning for Problem Solving

ABSTRACT

This chapter starts by answering the question, "What is critical thinking?" As it turns out, not everyone agrees on what critical thinking is. Nevertheless, researchers agree that critical thinking allows many people to reason together for solutions to complex problems. Also, in this chapter, the authors look at how computing capabilities enhance Socratic problem solving. A computer-based Socratic problem-solving system can keep problem solvers on track, document the outcome of a problem-solving session, and share those results with participants and a larger audience. In addition, Socrates Digital™ can also help problem solvers combine evidence about their quality of reasoning for individual problem-solving steps and the overall confidence level for the solution.

INTRODUCTION

Socrates set the foundation for critical thinking. He taught his students to question common beliefs and explanations reflectively and carefully

DOI: 10.4018/978-1-7998-7955-8.ch002

distinguish reasonable and logical beliefs from that lacking evidence or rational foundation (Paul, 1993).

Critical thinking, as described by Richard Paul, is clear, rational thinking involving critique. However, precisely what it varies between those who define it. The U.S. National Council for Excellence in Critical Thinking defines critical thinking as the "intellectually disciplined process of actively and skillfully conceptualizing, applying, analyzing, synthesizing, or evaluating information gathered from, or generated by, observation, experience, reflection, reasoning, or communication, as a guide to belief and action" (Glaser, 2017). However, this is not the only accepted definition of critical thinking.

WHAT IS CRITICAL THINKING?

As can be anticipated, not everyone agrees on what critical thinking is. Stephen Brookfield provides a good overview of the five most influential ways to conceptualize critical thinking (Brookfield, 2012). He categorizes the major camps for critical thinking as 1) analytic philosophy and logic, 2) natural science, 3) pragmatism, 4) psychoanalysis, and 5) critical theory.

The Analytic Philosophy and Logic Tradition

According to Brookfield, this is the most influential tradition informing how critical thinking is understood and taught in North America. This tradition focuses on the skills for constructing and deconstructing arguments. They focus on recognizing logical fallacies, distinguishing between bias and fact, opinion and evidence, judgment, and valid reference, and becoming skilled at using different forms of reasoning – inductive, deductive, formal, informal, and analogical. The analytic philosophy and logic tradition explain that if one can understand how bias and prejudice masquerade as an empirical fact or objective interpretation, one can better know what to believe or do. In this tradition, Paul and Elder (2019) wrote a guide for Socratic questioning heavily referenced throughout this chapter.

The Natural Science Tradition

As Brookfield notes, this critical thinking tradition is deeply rooted in the hypothetico-deductive method (Brookfield, 2012). Francis Bacon introduced this method in 1620 in his book, *Novum Organum*, where he presented a single way to investigate all the different fields of study (Bacon, 1620). The beginning of what we have come to call "the scientific method," Bacon's method was to seek the cause-and-effect relationship between two variables. Bacon argued that careful observation and experimentation were the basis of sound thinking.

Using the hypothetico-deductive method, a researcher posits a hypothesis – a cause-and-effect prediction of how one variable may impact one or more variables. The researcher then conducts an experiment to test whether or not the expected relationship between the variables is observable. Based on the outcome of the experiment, the hypothesis is either upheld or rejected. In this tradition, a critical thinker is always open to reformulating hypotheses to be tested. Said in another way, critical thinkers are constantly questioning the assumptions they use to understand the world.

This tradition of hypothesis formulation and testing has had a tremendous influence on society. It is what most people consider is the highest level of human reasoning. It has informed the other traditions of critical thinking to focus on observation and evidence gathering. In this tradition, the only truth revealed is by the careful collection and testing of evidence.

The Pragmatism Tradition

According to Brookfield, a third tradition that has influenced critical thinking is American pragmatism (Brookfield, 2012). It emphasizes the necessity of continuous experimentation to improve our society. American pragmatism is the idea that if we experiment, change, and constantly make adjustments, our democracy and society will continue to get better. Part of this ongoing process is the belief that we are all fallible. As a result, pragmatists believe in three strategies we should employ: 1) experimentation, 2) learning from our mistakes, and 3) deliberately seeking new information and understanding.

While scientists are at the forefront of using the hypothetico-deductive method, "ordinary people" are the ones at the forefront of pragmatism. The way a pragmatist would solve a problem is to consult those affected by the problem, those who have dealt with the problem in the past, and those who are specialists in the field of the problem – then, have them all reflect on their experiences to identify the possible causes and resolutions of the problem. For pragmatists, the essence of critical thinking is understanding one's assumptions more thoroughly by seeing them from multiple points of view.

The Psychoanalysis Tradition

Brookfield describes the fourth tradition as coming from the field of psychoanalysis and psychotherapy (Brookfield, 2012). The center of this tradition lies in the belief that each of us has a core, authentic personality waiting for realization. The connection between psychoanalysis and critical thinking is the notion that through critical analysis of our experiences, we can identify assumptions we hold that prevent us from realizing our full human potential. The process of psychoanalysis is then one of discovering the assumptions that govern our lives, frame our actions, and form our most personal choices. Once discovered, we can then challenge these assumptions from a radically different perspective. While the psychoanalysis tradition is less influential than the analytic philosophy, the natural sciences, or pragmatism traditions on critical thinking, its focus on uncovering our own deeply embedded assumptions does influence the field of critical thinking.

The Critical Theory Tradition

Finally, Brookfield identifies *critical theory* as a term traced to the Frankfurt School of Critical Social Theory (Brookfield, 2012). As Brookfield has noted, "Of all the traditions influencing how critical theory is understood, the fifth one I examine, critical theory, is the most overtly political." Brookfield argues that critical theory's debt is to Marxism and that this connection to social-democratic socialism promotes a conception of social justice and uncovering and redressing power inequities. As a result, one of the main criticisms of the critical theory view of critical thinking is that it has a preconceived goal – the creation of a society with democratic socialism (Bonner, 2011). This goal differs from the other critical thinking traditions where participants are always open to new possibilities and do not have a predetermined goal. However, the critical theory paradigm is also critical as it attempts to reconceptualize Marxist theory for conditions that Marx had not foreseen. This result is moving away from the idea of having a predetermined goal in mind for all its applications.

WHY CRITICAL THINKING IS NEEDED

Solving problems in a data-driven world is difficult because we have not been explicitly taught problem-solving in our education. What passes as problem-solving can at best be described as "shallow reasoning." According to Richard Paul, the dominant mode of teaching at all levels is didactic teaching (Paul, 1993). It is teaching by telling and learning by memorizing. Paul argues that didactic teaching encourages monological thinking from the beginning to the end of most so-called learning experiences. He describes monological thinking as approaching a problem from one point of view or perspective. Paul contends that this reduces teaching to simply telling students what to believe and think about a subject matter – and for students to reproduce it upon demand. Paul argues that this teaching mode falsely assumes that one can directly give knowledge without thinking about it. For Paul, in the end, didactic teaching confuses the ability to state a principle with the ability actually to understand that principle. Paul sums this situation up with the following conclusion (Paul, 1993):

"Unfortunately, students then come away with the impression that knowledge can be obtained without struggle, without having to hear from more than one point of view, without having to identify or assess evidence, without having to question assumptions, without having to trace implications, without having to analyze concepts, without having to consider objections."

We tend to solve problems in a data-driven world like we learned to solve them in school. We analyze the data using a known and accepted method – then use a visualization tool to display the results. Next, we will take these visualizations and place them on a computer display called a dashboard. Then we use the didactic teaching method to tell others what the data analysis means. We expect that our audience will be able to gain the knowledge that we have given them effortlessly. We then think if they can recall all of the results of the analyses we gave them, then our audience "knows" the results of the data analysis.

One might argue that when analyzing big and disparate data, that critical thinking is afoot when we try to divide our statements into "facts" and "opinions." For example, the results of our information analysis placed on a dashboard represent the analysis's facts. Our conclusions about these facts become opinions. While this seems like critical thinking, it is a shallow analysis of our data and situation. Paul says that this simplification of analysis into facts and opinions leaves out the most crucial part: reasoned judgment (1993). Paul argues that most important issues are not simply matters of opinion, nor are they matters of faith, taste, or preference. They are matters only fully understood from different points of view, having different assumptions, ideas and concepts, conclusions, and implications.

Establishing the facts is simply the beginning of a chain of reasoning for solving problems which Paul calls "multilogical." These problems, only understood from different points of view, lead to multiple competing solutions. An example of these problems is answering the question, "Should we invest in a motel chain?" These "real-life" problems are markedly different from monological problems, which have an established step-by-step procedure for solving them. Examples of monological problems include finding the square root of a number, determining the distance between two points, and calculating the force of a gust of wind. Sometimes, we try to simplify our real-life problems by treating them as monological problems having a step-by-step solution. For example, we might use a step-by-step approach to determine if we should invest in a motel chain. We apply one point of view, say maximizing rate of return, and decide by stepping through a process for that end. However, we have probably oversimplified our problem-solving analysis in this situation since we have not considered other points of view. For example, another point is that investors may want to diversify their portfolios by not taking on more motel investments.

Solving complex problems requires considering multiple points of view. Those differing points of view usually come from different people. Critical thinking provides a way for many people to reason together for solutions to complex problems.

Critical Thinking Is a Social Process

Vygotsky makes an excellent case that all vital learning happens in a social context (Vygotsky, 1978). Stephen Brookfield (Brookfield, 2012) argues that critical thinking only works well as a social process. He points out that this is hardly surprising if we consider how difficult it is to learn about our motives, assumptions, and worldviews through our self-examination. He continues by saying that our most influential assumptions are too close to us to be seen clearly without the help of others.

Richard Paul also sees critical thinking as a social process (Paul, 1993). According to Paul, we are reasoning *dialectically* when we reason from different points of view, comprised of different assumptions, ideas and concepts, conclusions, and implications. It is the process of arriving at truth through a process of comparing and contrasting various solutions. However, when discussing these different points of view with different assumptions, ideas and concepts, conclusions, and their implications -- with others -- we are reasoning *dialogically*. For Paul, dialogical and dialectical thinking involves dialogue about different points of view. Both are multilogical in that there is more than one line of reasoning to consider. Dialogue becomes dialectical when different lines of reasoning come into conflict, and we need to assess their various strengths and weaknesses.

Socratic Questioning

Most historians place the beginning of critical thinking with the teachings of Socrates. Socrates stressed that one should seek evidence, closely examine reasoning and assumptions, analyze basic concepts, and recognize implications of that said and done. His method of questioning is now known as "Socratic questioning" and is the most widely used critical thinking teaching strategy. He questioned beliefs, closely inspected assumptions, and built conclusions on evidence and sound rationale with his questions. What we know about Socrates we learned from Plato's writings (LaFargue, 2016). Aristotle and others refined Socrates' teachings by using systematic thinking and asking questions to ascertain the true nature of reality beyond how others may present it (West, 1979).

In the Thinker's Guide to Socratic Questioning (Paul & Elder, 2019), Richard Paul and Linda Elder layout a conceptual framework for Socratic questioning. This framework focuses on analyzing thought (focusing on the parts of thinking) and assessing reasoning (focusing on the standards for thinking). Their work is in the analytic philosophy and logic tradition (Brookfield, 2012).

QUESTIONS THAT TARGET THE PARTS OF THINKING

Figure 1 shows the questions that target the parts of thinking in Paul and Elder's conceptual framework (Paul & Elder, 2019). They call these questions "elements of thought" since they focus on reasoning or thinking parts. Figure 1 also shows that questions that target the parts of thinking fall into eight categories in Paul and Elder's conceptual framework (Paul & Elder, 2019). We examine these categories with their example questions on the following pages.

Figure 1. Questions that Target the Parts of Thinking

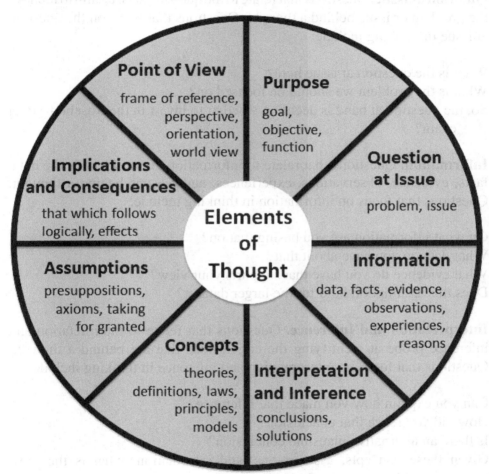

Purpose. Questions that relate to the purpose aim to identify the purpose, goal, or function behind a thought. Questions that focus on purpose in thinking include:

What is the purpose behind this?

What is the goal in doing this?
What function will this serve?
What are we trying to accomplish here?
What can I help you with today?

Question at Issue. Questions that relate to the question at issue aim to identify the problem or issue behind a thought. Questions that focus on the question at issue in thinking include:

What is the question at issue here?
What is the problem we should be focused on?
So, the question at hand is deciding whether to invest in the Rosebud Motel chain?

Information. Questions that relate to information aim to identify the data, facts, evidence, observations, experiences, and reasons behind a thought. Questions that focus on information in thinking include:

On what information are you basing that on?
What data do you have about that?
What evidence do you have that supports your view?
Does this assumption hold for the larger dataset?

Interpretation and Inference. Questions that relate to interpretation and inference probe at identifying the conclusions that are behind a thought. Questions that focus on interpretation and inference in thinking include:

Can you explain how you made that inference?
How did you reach that conclusion?
Is there an alternative plausible conclusion?
Given these concepts, assumptions, and information, what is the most reasonable conclusion?

Concepts. Questions that relate to concepts aim to identify the theories, definitions, laws, principles, and models behind a thought. Questions that focus on concepts in thinking include:

What is the main idea that you are using in your reasoning?
Are we using the most appropriate concept?

What is the main concept that you will use to make for your decision?

Assumptions. Questions related to concepts examine the presuppositions, axioms, and those things taken for granted behind a thought. Questions that focus on assumptions in thinking include:

What exactly are you taking for granted here?
Why are you assuming that?
What alternative assumptions might we make?
Do any of the following assumptions underlie this observation?

Implications and Consequences. Questions that relate to implications and consequences aim to identify that which logically follows the effects behind a thought. Questions that focus on implications and consequences in thinking include:

If we do this, what is likely to happened as a result?
What are you implying when you say that?
What are the implications of this conclusion?

Point of View. Questions related to the point of view aimed to define the frame of reference, perspective, orientation, and world view behind a thought. Questions that focus on the point of view in thinking include:

From what point of view are you looking at this?
Which of these points of view make the most sense given the situation?
Is there another viewpoint that should be considered?
Can you restate the implications of the current conclusions listed below as
    a viewpoint for answering the question at hand?

QUESTIONS THAT TARGET THE QUALITY OF REASONING

Figure 2 shows the questions that target the quality of reasoning in Paul and Elder's conceptual framework (Paul & Elder, 2019). They call these questions "standards for thinking" since the questions focus on the assessment of reasoning. They can be used to access the thinking behind any of the answers given to questions in the elements of thought category. For example, a question about clarity could follow a question about the purpose of the thought, the question at issue, or a question from any other category of questions in the elements of thought. Figure 2 also shows that questions that target the quality of reasoning make up nine categories in Paul and Elder's conceptual framework (Paul & Elder, 2019). We examine these categories with their example questions on the following pages.

Figure 2. Questions that Target the Quality of Reasoning

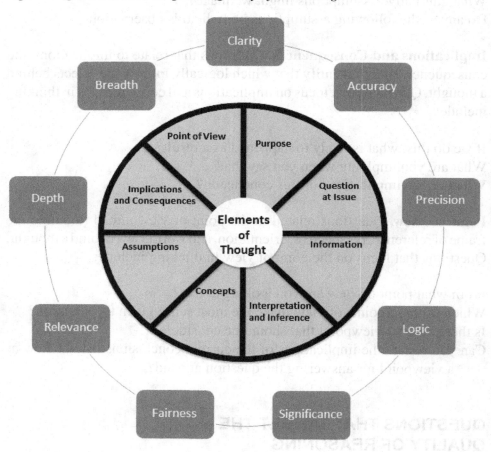

Clarity. Questions that relate to clarity are aimed at clarifying a thought. Questions that focus on clarity in thinking include:

Can you elaborate on this?

Can you give me an example or illustration of your point?
Can you give me an example data point about this?

Accuracy. Questions that relate to accuracy are aimed at checking to see if thinking represents things as they are. Questions that focus on accuracy in thinking include:

How could we check that to see if it's true?
How could we verify these alleged facts?
How would you rate the accuracy of this information? Which following statement more closely represents your confidence in its accuracy?
- ○ Accurate
- ○ Probably Accurate
- ○ Unknown Accuracy
- ○ Probably Not Accurate
- ○ Inaccurate

Precision. Questions that relate to precision are aimed at providing more precision to a thought. Questions that focus on precision in thinking include:

Could you give me more details about that?
Could you be more specific?
What will the investment be used for?

Logic. Questions that relate to logic check to see if thinking follows a line of reasoning and is logically consistent. Questions that focus on logic in thinking include:

Does all this make sense together?
Does what you say follow from the evidence?
Given this is all the evidence that you currently have, how would you rate the logic of this conclusion?
- ○ Very Logical
- ○ Probably Logical
- ○ Unknown How Logical
- ○ Probably Not Logical
- ○ Illogical

Significance. Questions that relate to breadth aim to decern if thinking focuses on more than one point of view or frame of reference. Questions that focus on breadth in thinking include:

Is this the central concept to focus on?
Is this the most important idea to consider?
How well does this concept explain how to answer the question at hand?
- ○ Always Explains
- ○ Mostly Explains
- ○ Sometimes Explains
- ○ Rarely Explains
- ○ Never Explains

Fairness. Questions that relate to fairness aim to check if a vested interest compromises or creates a bias for certain viewpoints. Questions that focus on fairness in thinking include:

Do I have any vested interest in this issue?
Am I sympathetically representing the viewpoints of others?
Before we get started, do you have vested interest in the question at hand?

Relevance. Questions related to relevance check to see if thinking focuses on the task, question, problem, or issue under consideration. Questions that focus on relevance in thinking include:

How does it relate to the question at hand?
I don't see what you said bears on the question. Could you show me how it is relevant?
Could you explain how what you just said relates to the problem?

Depth. Questions that relate to depth check to see if thinking needs to get beneath the surface to explore deeper matters or issues. Questions that focus on depth in thinking include:

Have we identified all the factors that make this a difficult problem?
How are we dealing with the complexities inherit in the question?
Have we described all the difficulties we need to deal with?
How would you rate your confidence in the implications of this conclusion?
- ○ Highly Justified

- ○ Probably Justified
- ○ Insufficient Evidence to Judge
- ○ Not Justified by the Evidence
- ○ Refuted by the Evidence

Breadth. Questions that relate to breadth check to see if thinking focuses on more than one point of view or frame of reference. Questions that focus on breadth in thinking include:

Do we need to look at this from another perspective?
Do we need to look at this in other ways?
Is there another viewpoint that should be considered?

ENHANCING SOCRATIC PROBLEM-SOLVING WITH COMPUTING

Up until this point, we have discussed critical thinking and Socratic problem-solving in its "original form" – interactions between humans (Vaughn, 2009). However, computers can automate the Socratic problem-solving process and enhance its advantages for individuals, teams, and organizations. As any teacher committed to Socratic problem-solving knows, learning how to do it effectively is challenging (Willingham, 2007). It also takes planning for its successful application and considerable guidance to keep it on track with a group of learners and problem-solvers (Overholser, 1992). In addition, it is labor-intensive to document the outcome of a Socratic problem-solving session and make those results available to the participants and any larger audience.

Computer systems can help with all these challenges (Howard, 2006). As an expert teacher in Socratic problem-solving, a computer program can help guide the conversation to answer all the important questions to solve the problem. Problem-solvers can immediately use a computer-based system without having the expertise to conduct a Socratic problem-solving session by themselves. This computer-based system dramatically reduces the time needed to get up to speed on how to conduct sessions, plan for sessions, and guide those sessions. An added benefit is that a computer-based system can use knowledge management techniques to capture results during problem-solving sessions and make those results immediately available to participants and any larger audience (Osterlund & Carlile, 2005). This added benefit is knowledge management at its potential since it can provide the most essential knowledge any organization will ever manage – how it solves problems -- to its members instantly. Managing this knowledge moves an organization from a learning organization to a "teaching-learning organization" (French & Bazalgette, 1996).

A computer-based Socratic problem-solving system can also enhance problem-solving in ways that only a computer can do. For example, Socrates Digital™ can guide human problem-solvers in assessing the quality of their reasoning. It can assist human problem-solvers in determining a numerical value for their level of confidence in a single step in a session – such as how much confidence they have in the information analysis step. A computer-based Socratic problem-solving system can also combine the confidence levels from several steps into an overall confidence level for the solution produced in the session. This capability to assist human problem-solving harks back to the MYCIN program (Buchanan & Shortliffe, 1985). MYCIN used "confidence factors" to combine evidence in a chain of reasoning to detect the type of bacteria that caused the illness observed in a human patient. The difference – an important one – is that Socrates Digital™ helps human problem-solvers set these confidence factors as they problem-solve. Another important difference is that MYCIN reasoned deductively – it sought the one and only right answer – the bacteria responsible for the infection. On the other hand, Socrates Digital™ guides human problem-solvers to find a "good solution" to a complex problem.

Problem-Solving with Inductive Reasoning

Michael LaFargue describes Socratic reasoning as what philosophers call "inductive" reasoning (LaFargue, 2016). Inductive reasoning is generalizing from observations in specific concrete cases. LaFargue argues that Isaac Newton was using inductive reasoning when he derived the general law of gravity from many specific concrete observations about falling apples and the movement of the planets.

When we contrast inductive reasoning with deductive reasoning, we note that deductive reasoning deduces conclusions from a general principle. Deductive reasoning assumes that we can be sure about general abstract principles. Euclidean geometry is built on deductive reasoning since it starts from general abstract axioms assumed to be self-evident, such as "The shortest distance between two points is a straight line."

LaFargue points out that inductive Socratic reasoning assumes that we can be more certain about our perceptions in clear concrete cases than we can ever be about general principles (LaFargue, 2016). As in all inductive reasoning, when some general principle conflicts with a specific concrete observation (a "counterexample"), this is assumed to show a weakness in the general principle, which will need revising in the light of the concrete observation.

This "improvement by approximation" makes inductive Socratic reasoning a better approach than deductive reasoning for solving complex problems that do not have a single "right answer." In solving many problems, we are not sure what general principles we should start with. For example, if we are trying to determine if investing in a motel chain is a good investment, we might start with the question, "Which concept do you want to use to explain how to answer the question at hand?" We might answer that we wish to start with the concept of occupancy rate to determine if the investment will boost total revenue in the motel chain enough to produce the rate of return offered.

The next question we could ask is, "What information, data, or experience do you have that supports or informs this analysis?" To answer this question, we might find that the Dundalk Inn & Suites motel has low occupancy rates and low total revenue. This answer should prompt the question, "Do any assumptions underlie this observation?" After some examination, we find that we assume occupancy rate positively correlates with total revenue. This discovery brings us to the next question, "Given these concepts, assumptions, and information, what is the most reasonable conclusion?" We conclude that raising the occupancy rate for the motels would raise the total revenue for the chain – possibly enough to pay the offered rate of return.

Note that we have decided that the concept, information, and assumptions naturally imply the conclusion. This chain of reasoning is the basis for inductive thinking. We are moving from specific statements to a general conclusion. We can take this a step further by seeking the implications of the conclusion by answering this question, "What are the implications of this conclusion?" We may decide that this conclusion implies that occupancy rate, say, through increased marketing, will increase, and total revenue will rise to meet the projected rate of return for the investment in the motel chain.

After determining the implications, the question at hand demands an answer. That question is whether to invest in the Rosebud Motel chain. Each step is evaluated in this inductive thinking process to see if it implies the following step. These steps called the "elements of thought" by Paul and Elder, form a chain of inductive reasoning representing a point of view. That is, the concepts, information, assumptions, conclusions, and implications form a line of reasoning that answers the question at hand -- whether to invest in the Rosebud Motel chain. Note that a different set of concepts, information, assumptions, conclusions, and implications will describe a different point of view that may form the basis for a different answer for the question at hand.

Assessing the Quality of Reasoning

This evaluation of each step to see how well it implies the next step is what Paul and Elder call the "standard of reasoning" or the quality of reasoning. For example, identifying the concept to be used to determine if investing in a motel chain is a good investment gives rise to its own questions such as, "How well does this concept explain how to answer the question at hand?" In this example dialog, we might respond with "sometimes explains." This answer shows some – but not a high level – confidence in this concept to determine if investing in the motel chain is a good investment. In examining the quality of our reasoning about this concept, we might determine that it is relatively "weak" for its part in implying the conclusion. Similarly, when asked this question after identifying the assumption that occupancy rate positively correlates with total revenue, "Do you want to apply this assumption in your reasoning," our response might have been, "Probably keep it." This favorable response would mean we had a high confidence level for using the assumption to form a conclusion. We should have also been asked the question, "How would you rate the accuracy of this information?" Our response might have been, "I think that it is probably accurate" – meaning a high level of confidence in using the information analysis to form a conclusion.

When Socratic questioning occurs between humans, the evidence for implying the next step is a "reasoned judgment" arrived at after much consideration. As seen in later chapters, Socrates Digital™ can help problem-solvers in arriving at this reasoned judgment. Socrates Digital™ can also help problem-solvers combine evidence about their reasoning quality for these individual steps into an overall confidence level for the solution. Adding this computing ability to the Socratic problem-solving process can significantly enhance the advantages of Socratic problem-solving.

SUMMARY

We began this chapter by answering the question, "What is Critical Thinking?" As it turns out, not everyone agrees on what critical thinking is. We looked at the five most influential ways to conceptualize critical thinking: 1) analytic philosophy and logic, 2) natural science, 3) pragmatism, 4) psychoanalysis, and 5) critical theory. After getting a handle on what critical thinking is, we next discussed why critical thinking is needed. One reason it is needed is that the dominant mode of teaching at all levels is didactic teaching. It is teaching by telling and learning by memorizing. Another reason is that solving complex problems requires considering multiple points of view. Those differing points of view usually come from different people. Critical thinking provides a way for many people to reason together for solutions to complex problems.

We next looked at Paul & Elder's conceptual framework for Socratic questioning. We noted that their work is in the analytic philosophy and logic tradition of critical thinking. Two parts make up their conceptual framework. The first part focuses on analyzing thought (the parts of thinking) with its eight categories of questions. We followed this with an overview of the second part of their framework, assessing reasoning (focusing on the standards for thinking) – which has nine categories of questions.

Finally, we looked at how computing capabilities enhance Socratic problem-solving. A computer-based Socratic problem-solving system can keep problem-solvers on track, document the outcome of a problem-solving session, and share those results with participants and a larger audience. In addition, Socrates Digital™ can also help problem-solvers combine evidence about their quality of reasoning for individual problem-solving steps and the overall confidence level for the solution. In the next chapter, we will see this at work by stepping through a problem-solving session with Socrates Digital™.

REFERENCES

Bacon, F. (1620). *Novum Organum*. American University of Beirut.

Bonner, S. (2011). *Critical theory: A very short introduction*. Oxford University Press. doi:10.1093/actrade/9780199730070.001.0001

Brookfield, S. (2012). *Teaching for critical thinking: Tools and techniques to help students question their assumptions*. Jossey-Bass.

Buchanan, B., & Shortliffe, E. (1985). *Rule-Based Expert Systems: the MYCIN Experiments of the Stanford Heuristic Programming Project*. Addison-Wesley.

French, R., & Bazalgette, J. (1996). From learning organization to teaching-learning organization. *Management Learning, 27*(1), 113–128. doi:10.1177/1350507696271007

Glaser, E. (2017). *Defining critical thinking*. The International Center for the Assessment of Higher Order Thinking (ICAT, US)/Critical Thinking Community.

Howard, G. (2006). Socrates and technology a new millennium. *International Journal of Instructional Media, 1*(33).

LaFargue, M. (2016). *Rational spirituality and divine virtue in Plato: A modern interpretation and philosophical defense of Platonism*. SUNY Press.

Osterlund, C., & Carlile, P. (2005). Relations in practice: Sorting through practice theories on knowledge sharing in complex organizations. *The Information Society, 21*(2), 91–107. doi:10.1080/01972240590925294

Overholser, J. (1992). Socrates in the classroom. *College Teaching, 1*(40), 14–18. doi:10.1080/87567555.1992.10532256

Paul, R. (1993). *Critical thinking: How to prepare students for a rapidly changing world*. Foundation for Critical Thinking.

Paul, R., & Elder, L. (2019). *The thinker's guide to Socratic questioning: Based on critical thinking concepts and tools*. Rowan & Littlefield.

Vaughn, L. (2009). *The power of critical thinking: Effective reasoning about ordinary and extraordinary claims* (3rd ed.). Oxford University Press.

Vygotsky, L. (1978). *Mind and society: The development of higher psychological processes*. Harvard University Press.

West, T. (1979). *Plato's "Apology of Socrates": An interpretation, with a new translation*. Cornell University Press.

Willingham, D. (2007). Critical thinking: Why is it so hard to teach? *American Educator, 31*(2), 8–19.

Chapter 3
A Dialog With Socrates Digital™:
Socratic Problem Solving for Investment Opportunities

ABSTRACT

*In this chapter, the presented example dialog shows how Socrates Digital™
can guide users to learn and solve big and disparate data problems. In this
example dialog, Socrates Digital™ takes the lead—as a human instructor or
facilitator would—to guide the conversation with the user groups. It begins
by guiding user groups in the examination of information, concepts, and
assumptions. Next, Socrates Digital™ guides user groups to form conclusions
and their implications. Finally, it guides user groups to summarize the
conversation into a viewpoint about answering the question at hand.*

INTRODUCTION

Socratic problem-solving is of interest in the business world (Peterson,
2009). The following dialog shows how Socrates Digital™ can guide users
to learn and solve big and disparate data problems in a business setting. In
the following scenario, Socrates Digital™ helps guide users to combine data
and reasoning from multiple sources such as spreadsheets, databases, survey
data, and firsthand reports to determine if an investment opportunity is a good

DOI: 10.4018/978-1-7998-7955-8.ch003

one. This data is not only from multiple sources but processed with different methods. For some data, processing resulted in totals and subtotals. Other data resulted from selection with criteria through search queries. Furthermore, other data resulted from applying statistical methods to measure central tendencies and correlations between values. Recently, new data results from analysis with techniques from artificial intelligence, including textual analysis and the application of machine learning algorithms.

In the following example dialog, the story is that investment analysts configure Socrates Digital™ for a conversation with end-users – who are also analysts – about how to analyze a commercial real estate investment opportunity. This initial configuration includes investment concepts and assumptions that investment analysts routinely use to evaluate investment opportunities in the motel real estate industry. In this example dialog, Socrates Digital™ begins with these concepts and assumptions and guides two groups of users to learn about a particular investment opportunity and decide whether to invest in that opportunity. "UP1" is the first user group and "UP2" is the second user group. During the dialog, Socrates Digital™ uses questions from Socratic Questioning categories based on critical thinking concepts and tools taken from Paul and Elder's *The Thinker's Guide to Socratic Questioning* (2019). The example dialog notes the Socratic Questioning category for each question. Chapter 2 describes Paul and Elder's Socratic Questioning categories.

AN EXAMPLE DIALOG WITH SOCRATES DIGITAL™

SOCRATES DIGITAL™: What can I help you with today? (Questions that Target the Parts of Thinking -- Questioning Goals and Purposes)

UP1: Deciding whether to invest in the Rosebud Motel[1] chain.

SOCRATES DIGITAL™: So, the question at hand is deciding whether to invest in the Rosebud Motel chain? (Questions that Target the Parts of Thinking – Question at Issue)

UP1: Yes.

SOCRATES DIGITAL™: What is the main concept that you will use to make your decision? (Questions that Target the Parts of Thinking -- Questioning Concepts and Ideas)

UP1: We need to know if the investment will boost total revenue enough to pay back the investors.

SOCRATES DIGITAL™: How does it relate to the question at hand? (Questions that Target the Quality of Reasoning -- Questioning Relevance)

UP1: We need to know if the investment will increase the total revenue for the Rosebud Motel chain so that it can repay the investment at the projected rate of return.

SOCRATES DIGITAL™: OK – are you ready to answer some questions about the terms of the investment? (Questions that Target the Parts of Thinking -- Questioning Questions)

UP1: Sure.

SOCRATES DIGITAL™: What is the projected rate of return? (Questions that Target the Parts of Thinking -- Questioning Precision)

UP1: They are offering a 10% rate of return.

SOCRATES DIGITAL™: What is the investment amount? (Questions that Target the Parts of Thinking -- Questioning Precision)

UP1: $3,500,000.

SOCRATES DIGITAL™: What is the repayment period? (Questions that Target the Parts of Thinking -- Questioning Precision)

UP1: Five years.

SOCRATES DIGITAL™: What will the investment be used for? (Questions that Target the Parts of Thinking -- Questioning Precision)

UP1: It will be used for motel renovations and promotional services.

SOCRATES DIGITAL™: Could you elaborate further about what the investment will be used for? (Questions that Target the Quality of Reasoning -- Questioning Clarity)

UP1: Yes. It will be used for a marketing campaign and for making repairs, painting the interior and exterior, staff training on customer service, and creating a program with local restaurants and stores which will provide gift cards for their services to motel guests.

SOCRATES DIGITAL™: Before we get started, do you have a vested interest in the question at hand? For example, you would have a vested interest in this business opportunity if the Rosebud Motel was owned by one of your relatives. (Questions that Target the Quality of Reasoning -- Questioning Fairness)

UP1: No, I do not have a vested interest.

SOCRATES DIGITAL™: OK, of the following, what would you like to work on? (Questions that Target the Parts of Thinking -- Questioning Questions)

- *Information*
- *Assumptions*
- *Concepts*

UP1: Concepts, I believe.

SOCRATES DIGITAL™: Which concept do you want to use to explain how to answer the question at hand? "We need to know if the investment will boost total revenue enough to pay back the investors." (Questions that Target the Parts of Thinking -- Questioning Concepts and Ideas)

The investment analysts, who initially configured Socrates Digital™, provided these concepts widely used to evaluate investment opportunities in the motel real estate industry.

- *Occupancy Rate – a measure of the percentage of total rooms rented*
- *Average Daily Rate – a measure of average room price*
- *Revenue per Available Room – a measure of average room price, including vacant rooms*
- *Another Concept*

UP1: Occupancy rate.

SOCRATES DIGITAL™: How well does this concept explain how to answer the question at hand? (Questions that Target the Quality of Reasoning -- Questioning Significance)

The values for each option that Socrates Digital™ will use to calculate the strength of the concept have been displayed for this example dialog. These values are not typically displayed to users.

- *Always Explains (0.75)*
- *Mostly Explains (0.5)*
- *Sometimes Explains (0)*
- *Rarely Explains (-0.5)*
- *Never Explains (-0.75)*

UP1: Sometimes explains.

SOCRATES DIGITAL™: OK, of the following, what would you like to work on? (Questions that Target the Parts of Thinking -- Questioning Questions)

- *Information*
- *Assumptions*

UP1: Information.

SOCRATES DIGITAL™: What information, data, or experience do you have that supports or informs this analysis? (Questions that Target the Parts of Thinking – Information, Data, and Experience)

UP1: I have spreadsheet data on occupancy rates and revenue for the Rosebud Motel chain.

Figure 1. The Dundalk Inn & Suites Motel has Low Occupancy Rates and Low Total Revenue

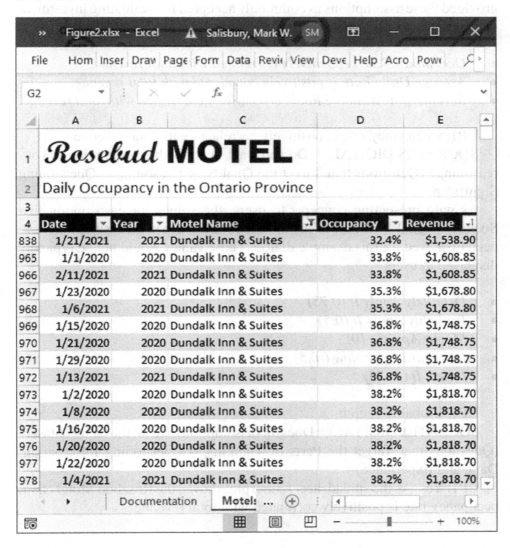

SOCRATES DIGITAL™: Can you give me an example data point about this? (Questions that Target the Quality of Reasoning -- Questioning Clarity)

UP1: As the spreadsheet shows, the Dundalk Inn & Suites motel has low occupancy rates and low total revenue.

SOCRATES DIGITAL™: Do any of the following assumptions underlie this observation? (Questions that Target the Parts of Thinking -- Questioning Assumptions)

The investment analysts, who initially configured Socrates Digital™, provided these assumptions as commonly accepted for evaluating investment opportunities in the motel real estate industry.

- *Occupancy Rate is positively correlated with total revenue.*
- *Average Daily Rate is positively correlated with total revenue.*
- *Revenue per Available Room is positively correlated with total revenue.*

UP1: Occupancy rate is positively correlated with total revenue.

SOCRATES DIGITAL™: Do you want to apply this assumption in your reasoning? (Questions that Target the Quality of Reasoning -- Questioning Significance)

As with presenting concepts to users, the values for each option that Socrates Digital™ will use to calculate the confidence in the assumption have been displayed for this example dialog. These values would not be typically displayed to users.

- *Definitely Apply It (0.75)*
- *Probably Apply It (0.5)*
- *Maybe Apply it (0)*
- *Disregard It for Now (-0.5)*
- *Delete It (-0.75)*

UP1: Probably keep it.

SOCRATES DIGITAL™: Does this assumption hold for the larger dataset? (Questions that Target the Parts of Thinking -- Questioning Information, Data, and Experience)

UP1: Yes. As the spreadsheet scatterplot shows, the Rosebud Motel chain occupancy rate is positively correlated with total revenue.

Figure 2. The Rosebud Motel Chain Occupancy Rate is Positively Correlated with Total Revenue

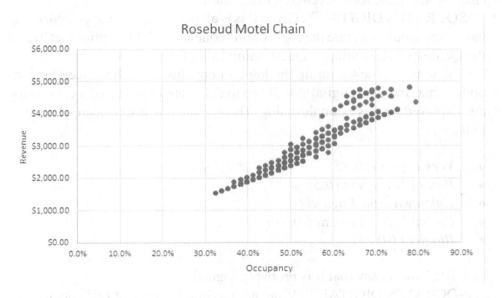

Only about half the year shows in Figure 3.2 since the spreadsheet program cannot graph the entire year. The result is a truncated data set.

SOCRATES DIGITAL™: How would you rate the accuracy of this information? Which following statement more closely represents your confidence in its accuracy? (Questions that Target the Quality of Reasoning -- Questioning Accuracy)

As with presenting concepts and assumptions to users, Socrates Digital™ displays the values for each option to calculate the accuracy of the information for this example dialog. These values are not typically displayed to users.

- *Accurate (0.75)*
- *Probably Accurate (0.5)*
- *Unknown Accuracy (0)*
- *Probably Not Accurate (-0.5)*
- *Inaccurate (-0.75)*

UP1: I think that it is probably accurate.

SOCRATES DIGITAL™: Given these concepts, assumptions, and information, what is the most reasonable conclusion? (Questions that Target the Parts of Thinking -- Questioning Inferences and Conclusions)

UP1: Raising the occupancy rate for all the motels in the Rosebud Motel chain would raise total revenue for the chain.

SOCRATES DIGITAL™: Given this is all the evidence that you currently have, how would you rate the logic of this conclusion? (Questions that Target the Quality of Reasoning -- Questioning Logic)

The same is true for rating the logic of conclusions. The values for each option that Socrates Digital™ will use to calculate the logic of a conclusion are displayed for this example dialog. These values are not typically displayed to users.

- *Very Logical (0.75)*
- *Probably Logical (0.5)*
- *Unknown How Logical (0)*
- *Probably Not Logical (-0.5)*
- *Illogical (-0.75)*

UP1: I would say that it is probably logical.

SOCRATES DIGITAL™: What are the implications of this conclusion? (Questions that Target the Parts of Thinking -- Questioning Implications and Consequences)

UP1: Increased marketing can raise the occupancy rate and total revenue for motels in the Rosebud Motel chain.

SOCRATES DIGITAL™: How would you rate your confidence in the implications of this conclusion? (Questions that Target the Quality of Reasoning -- Questioning Depth)

Again, the values for each option that Socrates Digital™ will use to calculate the confidence in the implications of a conclusion are displayed for this example dialog. These values are not typically displayed to users.

- *Highly Justified (0.75)*
- *Probably Justified (0.5)*
- *Insufficient Evidence to Judge (0)*
- *Not Justified by the Evidence (-0.5)*
- *Refuted by the Evidence (-0.75)*

UP1: Insufficient evidence to judge.

SOCRATES DIGITAL™: Can we get more confirming evidence about this? (Questions that Target the Parts of Thinking -- Questioning Information, Data, and Experience)

UP1: Yes, I believe we can.

SOCRATES DIGITAL™: OK, of the following, what would you like to work on? (Questions that Target the Parts of Thinking -- Questioning Questions)

Figure 3. The Shelburne Lodge Has a Low Average Daily Rate Indicating a Low Average Room Price

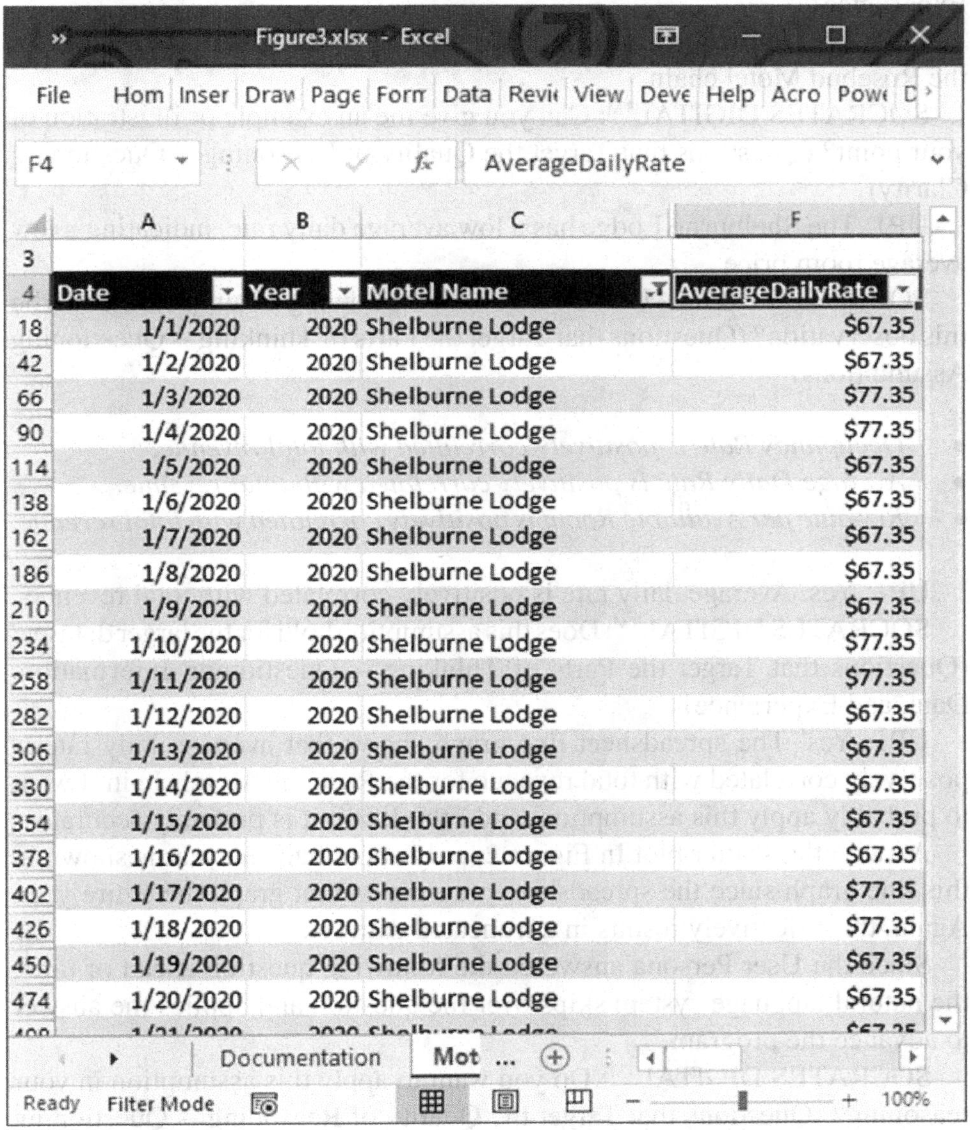

Date	Year	Motel Name	AverageDailyRate
1/1/2020	2020	Shelburne Lodge	$67.35
1/2/2020	2020	Shelburne Lodge	$67.35
1/3/2020	2020	Shelburne Lodge	$77.35
1/4/2020	2020	Shelburne Lodge	$77.35
1/5/2020	2020	Shelburne Lodge	$67.35
1/6/2020	2020	Shelburne Lodge	$67.35
1/7/2020	2020	Shelburne Lodge	$67.35
1/8/2020	2020	Shelburne Lodge	$67.35
1/9/2020	2020	Shelburne Lodge	$67.35
1/10/2020	2020	Shelburne Lodge	$77.35
1/11/2020	2020	Shelburne Lodge	$77.35
1/12/2020	2020	Shelburne Lodge	$67.35
1/13/2020	2020	Shelburne Lodge	$67.35
1/14/2020	2020	Shelburne Lodge	$67.35
1/15/2020	2020	Shelburne Lodge	$67.35
1/16/2020	2020	Shelburne Lodge	$67.35
1/17/2020	2020	Shelburne Lodge	$77.35
1/18/2020	2020	Shelburne Lodge	$77.35
1/19/2020	2020	Shelburne Lodge	$67.35
1/20/2020	2020	Shelburne Lodge	$67.35
1/21/2020	2020	Shelburne Lodge	$67.35

- *Information*
- *Assumptions*
- *Concepts*

UP1: Let's go with information again.

SOCRATES DIGITAL™: What information, data, or experience do you have? (Questions that Target the Parts of Thinking – Information, Data, and Experience)

UP1: I have spreadsheet data on average daily rate and total revenue for the Rosebud Motel chain.

SOCRATES DIGITAL™: Can you give me an example or illustration of your point? (Questions that Target the Quality of Reasoning -- Questioning Clarity)

UP1: The Shelburne Lodge has a low average daily rate, indicating a low average room price.

SOCRATES DIGITAL™: Do any of the following assumptions underlie this observation? (Questions that Target the Parts of Thinking -- Questioning Assumptions)

- *Occupancy Rate is positively correlated with total revenue.*
- *Average Daily Rate is positively correlated with total revenue.*
- *Revenue per Available Room is positively correlated with total revenue.*

UP1: Yes. Average daily rate is positively correlated with total revenue.

SOCRATES DIGITAL™: Does this assumption hold for the larger dataset? (Questions that Target the Parts of Thinking -- Questioning Information, Data, and Experience)

UP1: Yes. The spreadsheet line graph shows that average daily rate is positively correlated with total revenue for the Rosebud Motel chain. I want to probably apply this assumption, and I think that it is probably accurate.

As with the scatter plot In Figure 2, only about half the year is shown in this line graph since the spreadsheet program cannot graph the entire year. Again, this effectively results in a truncated data set.

Since the User Persona answered the following question ahead of time, the natural language system skips over the question and applies the answer to advance the program.

SOCRATES DIGITAL™: Do you want to apply this assumption in your reasoning? (Questions that Target the Quality of Reasoning -- Questioning Significance)

Figure 4. Average Daily Rate is Positively Correlated with Total Revenue for the Rosebud Motel Chain

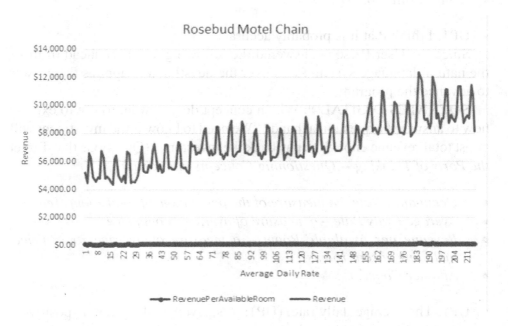

- *Definitely Apply It (0.75)*
- *Probably Apply It (0.5)*
- *Maybe Apply it (0)*
- *Disregard It for Now (-0.5)*
- *Delete It (-0.75)*

UP1: I want to probably apply this assumption.

Since the User Persona answered the following question ahead of time, the natural language system skips over the question and applies the answer to advance the program.

SOCRATES DIGITAL™: How would you rate the accuracy of this information? Which following statement more closely represents your confidence in its accuracy? (Questions that Target the Quality of Reasoning -- Questioning Accuracy)

- *Accurate (0.75)*
- *Probably Accurate (0.5)*
- *Unknown Accuracy (0)*

- *Probably Not Accurate (-0.5)*
- *Inaccurate (-0.75)*

UP1: I think that it is probably accurate.

Since the User Persona answered the following question ahead of time, the natural language system skips over the question and applies the answer to advance the program.

SOCRATES DIGITAL™: Which concept do you want to use to explain how to answer the question at hand? "We need to know if the investment will boost total revenue enough to pay back the investors." (Questions that Target *the Parts of Thinking -- Questioning Concepts and Ideas*)

- *Occupancy Rate – a measure of the percentage of total rooms rented*
- *Average Daily Rate – a measure of average room price*
- *Revenue per Available Room – a measure of average room price, including vacant rooms*
- *Another Concept*

UP1: The average daily rate. (UP1: Yes. Average daily rate is positively correlated with total revenue.)

SOCRATES DIGITAL™: For the question at hand, how well does this concept explain how to answer it? (Questions that Target the Quality of Reasoning -- Questioning Significance)

- *Always Explains (0.75)*
- *Mostly Explains (0.5)*
- *Sometimes Explains (0)*
- *Rarely Explains (-0.5)*
- *Never Explains (-0.75)*

UP1: Sometimes explains.

SOCRATES DIGITAL™: With these concepts, assumptions, and information, what is the best conclusion? (Questions that Target the Parts of Thinking -- Questioning Inferences and Conclusions)

UP1: Raising the average room price would raise total revenue for the Rosebud Motel chain.

SOCRATES DIGITAL™: Given all this evidence, how would you rate this logic? (Questions that Target the Quality of Reasoning -- Questioning Logic)

- *Very Logical (0.75)*
- *Probably Logical (0.5)*
- *Unknown How Logical (0)*
- *Probably Not Logical (-0.5)*
- *Illogical (-0.75)*

UP1: I would say that it is probably logical.

SOCRATES DIGITAL™: For this conclusion, what do you think are the implications? (Questions that Target the Parts of Thinking -- Questioning Implications and Consequences)

UP1: Increased marketing is needed to raise the total revenue for motels in the Rosebud Motel chain. It's probably justified.

Since the User Persona answered the following question ahead of time, the natural language system skips over the question and applies the answer to advance the program.

SOCRATES DIGITAL™: How would you rate your confidence in the implications of this conclusion? (Questions that Target the Quality of Reasoning -- Questioning Depth)

- *Highly Justified (0.75)*
- *Probably Justified (0.5)*
- *Insufficient Evidence to Judge (0)*
- *Not Justified by the Evidence (-0.5)*
- *Refuted by the Evidence (-0.75)*

UP1: It's probably justified.

SOCRATES DIGITAL™: Is there more information that supports this? (Questions that Target the Parts of Thinking -- Questioning Information, Data, and Experience)

UP1: Yes, I think so.

SOCRATES DIGITAL™: OK, of the following, what would you like to work on? (Questions that Target the Parts of Thinking -- Questioning Questions)

- *Information*
- *Assumptions*
- *Concepts*

UP1: Let's do assumptions.

SOCRATES DIGITAL™: Any of these assumptions underlie this observation? (Questions that Target the Parts of Thinking -- Questioning Assumptions)

- *Occupancy Rate is positively correlated with total revenue.*
- *Average Daily Rate is positively correlated with total revenue.*
- *Revenue per Available Room is positively correlated with total revenue.*

UP1: Revenue per available room is positively correlated with total revenue.

SOCRATES DIGITAL™: Do you want to apply this assumption in your reasoning? (Questions that Target the Quality of Reasoning -- Questioning Significance)

- *Definitely Apply It (0.75)*
- *Probably Apply It (0.5)*
- *Maybe Apply it (0)*
- *Disregard It for Now (-0.5)*
- *Delete It (-0.75)*

UP1: Definitely keep it.

The Natural Language Processing Unit recognizes this response as "Definitely Apply It."

SOCRATES DIGITAL™: OK, of the following, what would you like to work on? (Questions that Target the Parts of Thinking -- Questioning Questions)

- *Information*
- *Concepts*

UP1: Let's do Concepts.

SOCRATES DIGITAL™: Which concept do you want to use for this question at hand? "We need to know if the investment will boost total revenue enough to pay back the investors." (Questions that Target the Parts of Thinking -- Questioning Concepts and Ideas)

- *Occupancy Rate – a measure of the percentage of total rooms rented*
- *Average Daily Rate – a measure of average room price*
- *Revenue per Available Room – a measure of average room price, including vacant rooms*
- *Another Concept*

UP1: Revenue per available room.

SOCRATES DIGITAL™: For the question at hand, how well does this concept explain how to answer it? (Questions that Target the Quality of Reasoning -- Questioning Significance)

- *Always Explains (0.75)*
- *Mostly Explains (0.5)*
- *Sometimes Explains (0)*
- *Rarely Explains (-0.5)*
- *Never Explains (-0.75)*

Figure 5. The Little Britain Motel has Low Revenue per Available Room Indicating Many Vacant Rooms

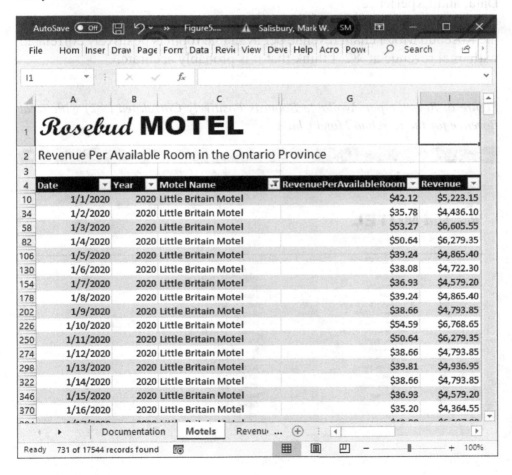

UP1: Mostly explains.

SOCRATES DIGITAL™: What information, data, or experience do you have? (Questions that Target the Parts of Thinking – Information, Data, and Experience)

UP1: I have information on revenue per available room for the Rosebud Motel chain.

SOCRATES DIGITAL™: Can you provide an example data point that shows this? (Questions that Target the Quality of Reasoning -- Questioning Clarity)

UP1: The Little Britain Motel has a low revenue per available room score which means that it has many vacant rooms.

SOCRATES DIGITAL™: For the larger dataset, does this assumption hold? (Questions that Target the Parts of Thinking -- Questioning Information, Data, and Experience)

UP1: Yes. As the Pearson Correlation shows in the spreadsheet program, the Rosebud Motel chain revenue per available room is positively correlated with total revenue at .82. I think that it is probably accurate.

Figure 6. Revenue per Available Room is Positively Correlated (.82) with Total Revenue for the Rosebud Motel Chain

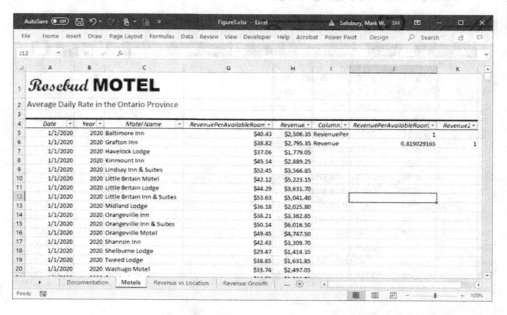

Since the User Persona answered the following question ahead of time, the natural language system skips over the question and applies the answer to advance the program.

SOCRATES DIGITAL™: How would you rate the accuracy of this information? Which following statement more closely represents your confidence in its accuracy? (Questions that Target the Quality of Reasoning -- Questioning Accuracy)

- *Accurate (0.75)*
- *Probably Accurate (0.5)*
- *Unknown Accuracy (0)*
- *Probably Not Accurate (-0.5)*
- *Inaccurate (-0.75)*

UP1: I think that it is probably accurate.

SOCRATES DIGITAL™: What is the most reasonable conclusion with these concepts, assumptions, and information? (Questions that Target the Parts of Thinking -- Questioning Inferences and Conclusions)

UP1: The Rosebud Motel chain can increase revenue by filling more of its vacant rooms. I would say that it is very logical.

Since the User Persona answered the following question ahead of time, the natural language system skips over the question and applies the answer to advance the program.

SOCRATES DIGITAL™: Given this is all the evidence that you currently have, how would you rate the logic of this conclusion? (Questions that Target the Quality of Reasoning -- Questioning Logic)

- *Very Logical (0.75)*
- *Probably Logical (0.5)*
- *Unknown How Logical (0)*
- *Probably Not Logical (-0.5)*
- *Illogical (-0.75)*

UP1: I would say that it is very logical.

SOCRATES DIGITAL™: Can you explain the implications of this conclusion? (Questions that Target the Parts of Thinking -- Questioning Implications and Consequences)

UP1: A viewpoint such as increasing marketing is needed to increase revenue per available room for motels in the Rosebud Motel chain.

SOCRATES DIGITAL™: Is this the same as the implication that increased marketing is needed to raise the total revenue for motels in the Rosebud Motel chain? (Questions that Target the Quality of Reasoning -- Questioning Precision)

UP1: Yes.

SOCRATES DIGITAL™: For this implication of the conclusion, how would you rate your confidence? (Questions that Target the Quality of Reasoning -- Questioning Depth)

- *Highly Justified (0.75)*
- *Probably Justified (0.5)*
- *Insufficient Evidence to Judge (0)*
- *Not Justified by the Evidence (-0.5)*
- *Refuted by the Evidence (-0.75)*

UP1: Highly justified. There is no more information at this time.

Since the User Persona answered the following question ahead of time, the natural language system skips over the question and applies the answer to advance the program.

SOCRATES DIGITAL™: Can we get more confirming evidence about this? (Questions that Target the Parts of Thinking -- Questioning Information, Data, and Experience)

UP1: There is no more information at this time.

SOCRATES DIGITAL™: Can you restate the implications of the current conclusions listed below as a viewpoint for answering the question at hand? (Questions that Target the Parts of Thinking -- Questioning Viewpoints and Perspectives)

- *Increased marketing can raise the occupancy rate and total revenue for motels in the Rosebud Motel chain.*
- *Increased marketing is needed to raise the total revenue for motels in the Rosebud Motel chain.*
- *A viewpoint such as increasing marketing is needed to increase revenue per available room for motels in the Rosebud Motel chain.*

UP1: The viewpoint is focused on increasing marketing to raise occupancy rates, average daily rates, and revenue per available room to increase total revenue for motels in the Rosebud Motel chain.

SOCRATES DIGITAL™: You have expressed an overall confidence of .54 (some confidence) for this viewpoint:

The viewpoint is focused on increasing marketing to raise occupancy rates, average daily rates, and revenue per available room to increase total revenue for motels in the Rosebud Motel chain.

Is there another viewpoint that should be considered? (Questions that Target the Parts of Thinking -- Questioning Breadth)

UP1: Not that I can think of at this time.

Meanwhile, on the other side of the world, but within the same organization, another user group has just seen the summary and results of this conversation. However, they know about another viewpoint that should be considered.

SOCRATES DIGITAL™: Is there another viewpoint that should be considered? (Questions that Target the Parts of Thinking -- Questioning Breadth)

UP2: Yes! We know that price is only one of the influencing factors for customers of motel rooms. For example, customers are influenced by clean rooms in good repair, friendly staff, and complimentary gifts.

SOCRATES DIGITAL™: OK, of the following, what would you like to work on? (Questions that Target the Parts of Thinking -- Questioning Questions)

- *Information*
- *Assumptions*
- *Concepts*

UP2: Let's do information like they did.

SOCRATES DIGITAL™: What information, data, or experience do you have supporting or informing this analysis? (Questions that Target the Parts of Thinking – Information, Data, and Experience)

UP2: I have sentiment scores from customer comments for several motels in the Rosebud Motel chain.

SOCRATES DIGITAL™: Do you have an example data item that illustrates this? (Questions that Target the Quality of Reasoning -- Questioning Clarity)

UP2: As these records in the database show, Saint Ola Inn has high sentiment scores for customer comments (0.5 is neutral) and also high total revenue numbers. Sentiment scores of customer comments are a measure of customer experience. One customer comment was, "Great stay. Nice fresh paint and complimentary gift cards to local stores. Friendly staff. Clean rooms."

Figure 7. Saint Ola Inn has High Customer Comments Scores and High Total Revenue

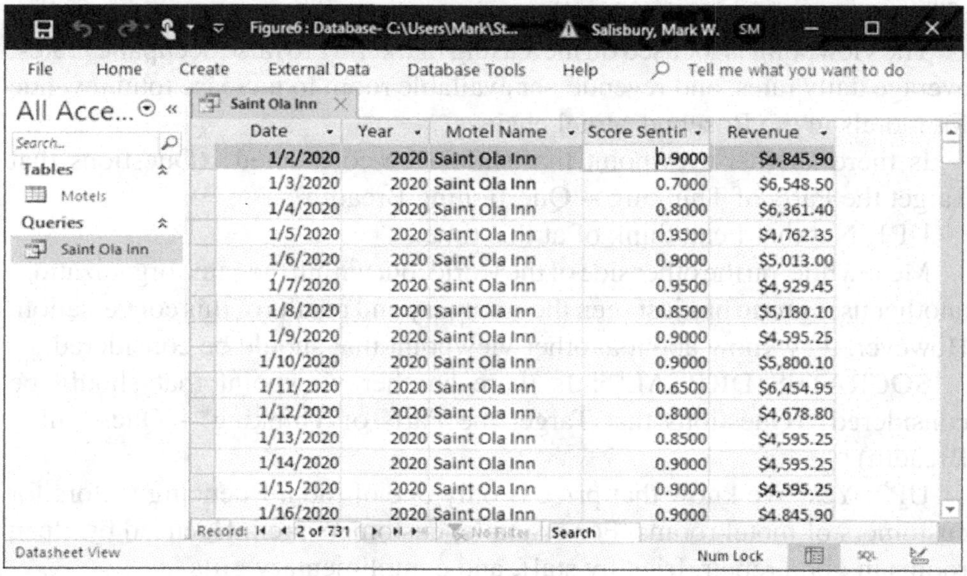

Date	Year	Motel Name	Score Sentir	Revenue
1/2/2020	2020	Saint Ola Inn	0.9000	$4,845.90
1/3/2020	2020	Saint Ola Inn	0.7000	$6,548.50
1/4/2020	2020	Saint Ola Inn	0.8000	$6,361.40
1/5/2020	2020	Saint Ola Inn	0.9500	$4,762.35
1/6/2020	2020	Saint Ola Inn	0.9000	$5,013.00
1/7/2020	2020	Saint Ola Inn	0.9500	$4,929.45
1/8/2020	2020	Saint Ola Inn	0.8500	$5,180.10
1/9/2020	2020	Saint Ola Inn	0.9000	$4,595.25
1/10/2020	2020	Saint Ola Inn	0.9000	$5,800.10
1/11/2020	2020	Saint Ola Inn	0.6500	$6,454.95
1/12/2020	2020	Saint Ola Inn	0.8000	$4,678.80
1/13/2020	2020	Saint Ola Inn	0.8500	$4,595.25
1/14/2020	2020	Saint Ola Inn	0.9000	$4,595.25
1/15/2020	2020	Saint Ola Inn	0.9000	$4,595.25
1/16/2020	2020	Saint Ola Inn	0.9000	$4,845.90

SOCRATES DIGITAL™: Of the following assumptions, do any underly this observation? (Questions that Target the Parts of Thinking -- Questioning Assumptions)

- *Occupancy Rate is positively correlated with total revenue.*
- *Average Daily Rate is positively correlated with total revenue.*
- *Revenue per Available Room is positively correlated with total revenue.*

UP2: No.

SOCRATES DIGITAL™: What assumption underlies this example?

UP2: Customer experience is positively correlated with total revenue.

SOCRATES DIGITAL™: Is this the assumption you want to use right now? (Questions that Target the Quality of Reasoning -- Questioning Significance)

- Definitely Apply It (0.75)
- Probably Apply It (0.5)
- Maybe Apply it (0)
- Disregard It for Now (-0.5)
- Delete It (-0.75)

UP2: Definitely apply it.

SOCRATES DIGITAL™: For the larger dataset, does this assumption hold? (Questions that Target the Parts of Thinking -- Questioning Information, Data, and Experience)

UP2: Yes. These records from a crosstab query in the database show that customer experience is positively correlated with total revenue in the Rosebud Motel chain. I think that it is probably accurate.

Figure 8. Customer Experience is Positively Correlated with Total Revenue in the Rosebud Motel Chain

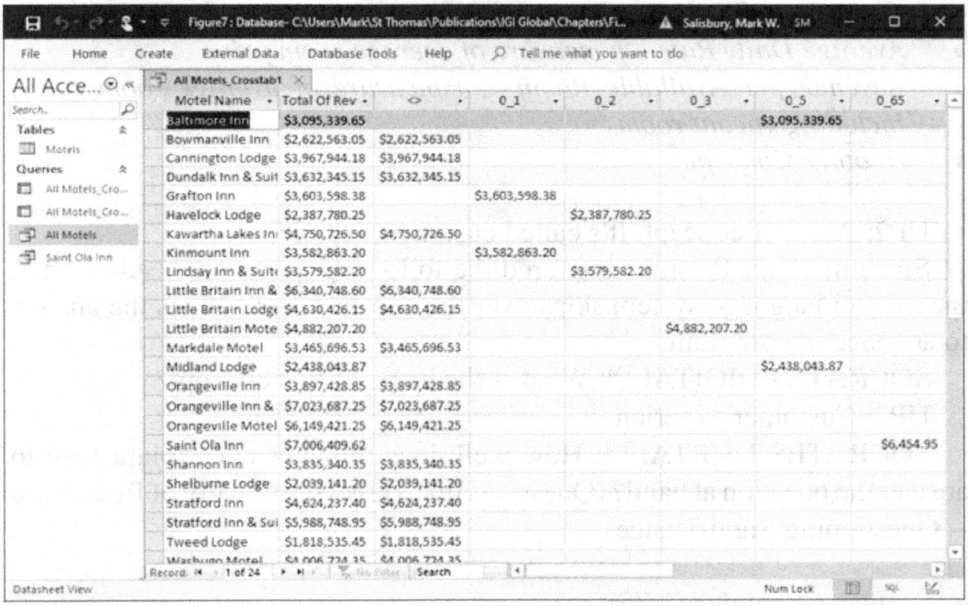

Motel Name	Total Of Rev	<>	0_1	0_2	0_3	0_5	0_65
Baltimore Inn	$3,095,339.65					$3,095,339.65	
Bowmanville Inn	$2,622,563.05	$2,622,563.05					
Cannington Lodge	$3,967,944.18	$3,967,944.18					
Dundalk Inn & Suit	$3,632,345.15	$3,632,345.15					
Grafton Inn	$3,603,598.38		$3,603,598.38				
Havelock Lodge	$2,387,780.25			$2,387,780.25			
Kawartha Lakes Inn	$4,750,726.50	$4,750,726.50					
Kinmount Inn	$3,582,863.20		$3,582,863.20				
Lindsay Inn & Suite	$3,579,582.20			$3,579,582.20			
Little Britain Inn &	$6,340,748.60	$6,340,748.60					
Little Britain Lodge	$4,630,426.15	$4,630,426.15					
Little Britain Mote	$4,882,207.20				$4,882,207.20		
Markdale Motel	$3,465,696.53	$3,465,696.53					
Midland Lodge	$2,438,043.87					$2,438,043.87	
Orangeville Inn	$3,897,428.85	$3,897,428.85					
Orangeville Inn &	$7,023,687.25	$7,023,687.25					
Orangeville Motel	$6,149,421.25	$6,149,421.25					
Saint Ola Inn	$7,006,409.62						$6,454.95
Shannon Inn	$3,835,340.35	$3,835,340.35					
Shelburne Lodge	$2,039,141.20	$2,039,141.20					
Stratford Inn	$4,624,237.40	$4,624,237.40					
Stratford Inn & Sui	$5,988,748.95	$5,988,748.95					
Tweed Lodge	$1,818,535.45	$1,818,535.45					
Washago Motel	$4,006,724.35	$4,006,724.35					

Since the User Persona answered the following question ahead of time, the natural language system skips over the question and applies the answer to advance the program.

SOCRATES DIGITAL™: How would you rate the accuracy of this information? Which following statement more closely represents your confidence in its accuracy? (Questions that Target the Quality of Reasoning -- Questioning Precision)

- *Accurate (0.75)*

- *Probably Accurate (0.5)*
- *Unknown Accuracy (0)*
- *Probably Not Accurate (-0.5)*
- *Inaccurate (-0.75)*

UP2: I think that it is probably accurate.

SOCRATES DIGITAL™: Of the following, which do you want to use to answer the question at hand? "We need to know if the investment will boost total revenue enough to pay back the investors." (Questions that Target the Parts of Thinking -- Questioning Concepts and Ideas)

- *Occupancy Rate – a measure of the percentage of total rooms rented*
- *Average Daily Rate – a measure of average room price*
- *Revenue per Available Room – a measure of average room price, including vacant rooms*
- *Another Concept*

UP2: Another concept. It's called customer experience.

Since the User Persona answered the following question ahead of time, the natural language system skips over the question and applies the answer to advance the program.

SOCRATES DIGITAL™: What is the name of this concept?

UP2: Customer experience

SOCRATES DIGITAL™: How well does this concept explain how to answer the question at hand? (Questions that Target the Quality of Reasoning -- Questioning Significance)

- *Always Explains (0.75)*
- *Mostly Explains (0.5)*
- *Sometimes Explains (0)*
- *Rarely Explains (-0.5)*
- *Never Explains (-0.75)*

UP2: Always explains.

SOCRATES DIGITAL™: What is the most reasonable conclusion with these concepts, assumptions, and information? (Questions that Target the Parts of Thinking -- Questioning Inferences and Conclusions)

UP2: The Rosebud Motel chain can increase revenue by improving customer experience, as measured by sentiment analysis scores of comments about staying at their motels. I would say that it is very logical.

Since the User Persona answered the following question ahead of time, the natural language system skips over the question and applies the answer to advance the program.

SOCRATES DIGITAL™: Given this is all the evidence that you currently have, how would you rate the logic of this conclusion? (Questions that Target the Quality of Reasoning -- Questioning Logic)

- *Very Logical (0.75)*
- *Probably Logical (0.5)*
- *Unknown How Logical (0)*
- *Probably Not Logical (-0.5)*
- *Illogical (-0.75)*

UP2: I would say that it is very logical.

SOCRATES DIGITAL™: For this conclusion, what do you think are the implications? (Questions that Target the Parts of Thinking -- Questioning Implications and Consequences)

UP2: A viewpoint is needed for making repairs, painting the interior and exterior, staff training on customer service, and creating promotional programs with local restaurants and stores that improves customer experience and increases total revenue in the Rosebud Motel chain.

SOCRATES DIGITAL™: For this implication of the conclusion, how would you rate your confidence? (Questions that Target the Quality of Reasoning -- Questioning Depth)

- *Highly Justified (0.75)*
- *Probably Justified (0.5)*
- *Insufficient Evidence to Judge (0)*
- *Not Justified by the Evidence (-0.5)*
- *Refuted by the Evidence (-0.75)*

UP2: Highly Justified.

SOCRATES DIGITAL™: Is there more information that supports this? (Questions that Target the Parts of Thinking -- Questioning Information, Data, and Experience)

UP2: Yes, the background about the St. Ola Inn provides more evidence for this viewpoint. Let's start with Concepts. It's customer experience, again.

Since the User Persona answered the following questions ahead of time, the natural language system skips over the questions and applies the answers to advance the program.

SOCRATES DIGITAL™: Which concept do you want to use to explain how to answer the question at hand? "We need to know if the investment will boost total revenue enough to pay back the investors." (Questions that Target the Parts of Thinking -- Questioning Concepts and Ideas)

- *Occupancy Rate – a measure of the percentage of total rooms rented*
- *Average Daily Rate – a measure of average room price*
- *Revenue per Available Room – a measure of average room price, including vacant rooms*
- *Another Concept*

UP2: Another concept. It's called customer experience.
SOCRATES DIGITAL™: What is the name of this concept?
UP2: It's customer experience, again.
SOCRATES DIGITAL™: How well does this concept explain how to increase the total revenue for the Rosebud Motel chain? (Questions that Target the Quality of Reasoning -- Questioning Significance)

- *Always Explains (0.75)*
- *Mostly Explains (0.5)*
- *Sometimes Explains (0)*
- *Rarely Explains (-0.5)*
- *Never Explains (-0.75)*

UP2: Always explains. Let's look at information.

Since the User Persona answered the following question ahead of time, the natural language system skips over the question and applies the answer to advance the program.

SOCRATES DIGITAL™: OK, of the following, what would you like to work on? (Questions that Target the Parts of Thinking -- Questioning Questions)

- *Information*
- *Assumptions*

UP2: Let's look at information.

SOCRATES DIGITAL™: Do you have an example data item that illustrates this? (Questions that Target the Quality of Reasoning -- Questioning Clarity)

UP2: Rosebud Motels put $145,000 into Saint Ola Inn and raised the sentiment analysis score for comments from 0.3 (average for Rosebud Motels) to 0.9 by making repairs, painting the interior and exterior, staff training on customer service, and creating promotional programs with local restaurants and stores to improve customer experience and raise total revenue in the Rosebud Motel chain. Saint Ola raised its total revenue by 4.6%.

SOCRATES DIGITAL™: Any of these assumptions underlie this observation? (Questions that Target the Parts of Thinking -- Questioning Assumptions)

- *Occupancy Rate is positively correlated with total revenue.*
- *Average Daily Rate is positively correlated with total revenue.*
- *Revenue per Available Room is positively correlated with total revenue.*
- *Customer Experience is positively correlated with total revenue.*

UP2: Customer experience is positively correlated with total revenue. Let's definitely apply it.

Since the User Persona answered the following question ahead of time, the natural language system skips over the question and applies the answer to advance the program.

SOCRATES DIGITAL™: Do you want to apply this assumption in your reasoning? (Questions that Target the Quality of Reasoning -- Questioning Significance)

- *Definitely Apply It (0.75)*
- *Probably Apply It (0.5)*
- *Maybe Apply it (0)*
- *Disregard It for Now (-0.5)*
- *Delete It (-0.75)*

UP2: Let's definitely apply it.

SOCRATES DIGITAL™: Is this assumption true for the larger dataset? (Questions that Target the Parts of Thinking -- Questioning Information, Data, and Experience)

UP2: Yes. In the Rosebud Motel chain, an analysis of key influencers shows that customer experience influences total revenue. A more detailed analysis of key influencers shows that total revenue is more likely to increase when the sentiment score is higher than 0.5 (neutral). I think that it is probably accurate.

Figure 9. Key Influencers Show that Customer Experience Influences Total Revenue

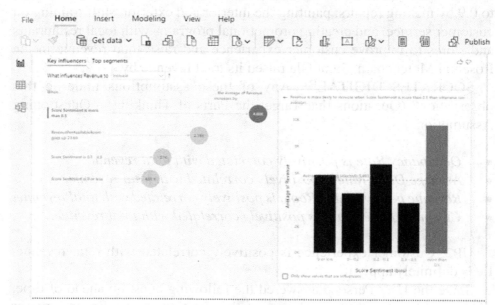

Since the User Persona answered the following question ahead of time, the natural language system skips over the question and applies the answer to advance the program.

SOCRATES DIGITAL™: How would you rate the accuracy of this information? Which following statement more closely represents your confidence in its accuracy? (Questions that Target the Quality of Reasoning -- Questioning Accuracy)

- *Accurate (0.75)*
- *Probably Accurate (0.5)*
- *Unknown Accuracy (0)*
- *Probably Not Accurate (-0.5)*
- *Inaccurate (-0.75)*

UP2: I think that it is probably accurate.

SOCRATES DIGITAL™: With these concepts, assumptions, and information, what is the best conclusion? (Questions that Target the Parts of Thinking -- Questioning Inferences and Conclusions)

UP2: This is more evidence that the Rosebud Motel chain can increase revenue by improving customer experience, as measured by sentiment analysis scores of comments about staying at their motels. I would say that it is very logical.

Since the User Persona answered the following question ahead of time, the natural language system skips over the question and applies the answer to advance the program.

SOCRATES DIGITAL™: Given this is all the evidence that you currently have, how would you rate the logic of this conclusion? (Questions that Target the Quality of Reasoning -- Questioning Logic)

- *Very Logical (0.75)*
- *Probably Logical (0.5)*
- *Unknown How Logical (0)*
- *Probably Not Logical (-0.5)*
- *Illogical (-0.75)*

UP2: I would say that it is very logical.

SOCRATES DIGITAL™: Can you explain the implications of this conclusion? (Questions that Target the Parts of Thinking -- Questioning Implications and Consequences)

UP2: This is more evidence that the viewpoint for making repairs, painting the interior and exterior, staff training on customer service, and creating promotional programs with local restaurants and stores that improves customer experience and increases total revenue in the Rosebud Motel chain. I think it is highly justified.

Since the User Persona answered the following question ahead of time, the natural language system skips over the question and applies the answer to advance the program.

SOCRATES DIGITAL™: How would you rate your confidence in the implications of this conclusion? (Questions that Target the Quality of Reasoning -- Questioning Depth)

- *Highly Justified (0.75)*
- *Probably Justified (0.5)*
- *Insufficient Evidence to Judge (0)*

- *Not Justified by the Evidence (-0.5)*
- *Refuted by the Evidence (-0.75)*

UP2: I think it is highly justified.

SOCRATES DIGITAL™: Can you rephrase these current implications, listed below, into a viewpoint? (Questions that Target the Parts of Thinking -- Questioning Viewpoints)

- *A viewpoint is needed for making repairs, painting the interior and exterior, staff training on customer service, and creating promotional programs with local restaurants and stores that improves customer experience and increases total revenue in the Rosebud Motel chain.*
- *This is more evidence that the viewpoint for making repairs, painting the interior and exterior, staff training on customer service, and creating promotional programs with local restaurants and stores that improves customer experience and increases total revenue in the Rosebud Motel chain.*

UP2: The viewpoint is focused on making repairs, painting the interior and exterior, staff training on customer service, and creating promotional programs with local restaurants and stores that improves customer experience to increase total revenue in the Rosebud Motel chain.

SOCRATES DIGITAL™: Can you provide more data that backs this up? (Questions that Target the Parts of Thinking -- Questioning Information, Data, and Experience)

UP2: Not at this time.

SOCRATES DIGITAL™: You have expressed an overall confidence of .81 (good confidence) for this viewpoint:

The viewpoint is focused on making repairs, painting the interior and exterior, staff training on customer service, and creating promotional programs with local restaurants and stores that improves customer experience to increase total revenue in the Rosebud Motel chain.

At this time, is there another viewpoint we should look at? (Questions that Target the Parts of Thinking -- Questioning Breadth)

UP2: Not at this time

SOCRATES DIGITAL™: Would you like to see all the viewpoints and their confidence levels for answering the question at hand? (Questions that Target the Parts of Thinking -- Questioning Viewpoints and Perspectives)

UP2: Yes.

SOCRATES DIGITAL™: UP1 has expressed an overall confidence of .54 (some confidence) for the following viewpoint:

The viewpoint is focused on increasing marketing to raise occupancy rates, average daily rates, and revenue per available room to increase total revenue for motels in the Rosebud Motel chain.

UP2 has expressed an overall confidence of .81 (good confidence) for the following viewpoint:

The viewpoint is focused on making repairs, painting the interior and exterior, staff training on customer service, and creating promotional programs with local restaurants and stores that improves customer experience to increase total revenue in the Rosebud Motel chain.

SOCRATES DIGITAL™: Can you combine these viewpoints based upon their information, concepts, assumptions, conclusions, and implications into a single composite viewpoint? (Questions that Target the Parts of Thinking -- Questioning Viewpoints)

UP2: Yes, we can.

SOCRATES DIGITAL™: What is this composite viewpoint for answering the question at hand?

UP2: Rosebud Motels uses its investment funds for marketing and make the motel renovations it did with Saint Ola for all its motels.

Does this help answer the question at hand about deciding whether to invest in the Rosebud Motel chain? (Questions that Target the Parts of Thinking – Question at Issue)

UP2: Yes

SOCRATES DIGITAL™: What is that answer? (Questions that Target the Parts of Thinking -- Questioning Goals and Purposes)

UP2: We decided to recommend investing in the Rosebud Motel chain.

SOCRATES DIGITAL™: What are the implications of this decision? (Questions that Target the Parts of Thinking -- Questioning Implications and Consequences)

UP2: If Rosebud Motels uses its investment funds for marketing and make the motel renovations it did with Saint Ola for all its motels, it would increase the Rosebud Motel chain revenue by $2,000,000 in the first year. This would make it easily possible to repay the $4,800,000 for the loan over five years. It would provide a good return for investors at 10% and increase revenues for the Rosebud Motel chain in the future.

SOCRATES DIGITAL™: OK, that completes this session.

SUMMARY

The presented example dialog shows how Socrates Digital™ can guide users to learn and solve big and disparate data problems. In the example scenario, Socrates Digital™ helped guide users to combine data from multiple sources such as spreadsheets, databases, survey data, and firsthand reports. The data was from multiple sources and analyzed with different methods. Data were analyzed with statistical methods to measure central tendencies and correlations between values. Also, data were analyzed with techniques from artificial intelligence, including textual analysis and the application of machine learning algorithms.

In this example dialog, Socrates Digital™ takes the lead – as a human instructor or facilitator would – to guide the conversation with the user groups. It begins by guiding user groups in the examination of information, concepts, and assumptions. Next, Socrates Digital™ guides user groups to form conclusions and their implications. Finally, it guides user groups to summarize all the conversation into a viewpoint about how to answer the question at hand. Note that Socrates Digital™ works with the humans to arrive at this answer. It does not dictate the criteria for judging the factors that make up the answer. Good human facilitators do it this way. However, Socrates Digital™ can work with multiple user groups with the same data at the same time. Humans cannot manage the complexity of this task. The result is that Socrates Digital™ can make the reasoning made by one user group available to another user group in real-time. This speeds communication of findings across organizations in a way that was not possible before Socrates Digital™. As a result, the ability for organizations to learn and solve problems – organizational learning – is greatly accelerated. Later, Chapter 10 presents the technology and process for supporting organizational learning. The next chapter shows how to design and develop a Socrates Digital™ system.

REFERENCES

Paul, R., & Elder, L. (2019). *The thinker's guide to Socratic questioning: Based on critical thinking concepts and tools*. Rowan & Littlefield.

Peterson, E. (2009). Socratic problem-solving in the business world. *American Journal of Business Education*, 2(5), 101–104. doi:10.19030/ajbe.v2i5.4074

ENDNOTE

[1]   Any similarity to the Rosebud Motel in the situation comedy "Schitt's Creek (TV Series 2015–2020) is merely coincidental.

Chapter 4

System Design and Development:
Understand, Explore, Materialize, and Realize

ABSTRACT

This chapter presents the Socrates Digital™ system's design and development process. It describes the four phases of design and development: understand, explore, materialize, and realize. The completion of these four phases results in a Socrates Digital™ system that leverages artificial intelligence services. The artificial intelligence services include a natural language processor provided by several artificial intelligence service providers, including Apple, Microsoft, Google, IBM, and Amazon.

INTRODUCTION

A Socrates Digital™ system, as presented in this book, is a hybrid, modular system. It is designed and developed over four phases: Understand, Explore, Materialize, and Realize.

The completion of these four phases results in a Socrates Digital™ system that leverages artificial intelligence services. Figure 1 shows the Socrates Digital™ system architecture. The artificial intelligence services include a natural language processor, an optional speech recognition processor, and

DOI: 10.4018/978-1-7998-7955-8.ch004

a text-to-speech generator. Several artificial intelligence service providers, including Apple, Microsoft, Google, IBM, and Amazon, offer these services. This book will not cover the ways to configure these services since they are well documented. Instead, this book focuses on designing and developing a Socrates Digital™ architecture's other processes and components.

Figure 1. Socrates Digital™ System Architecture

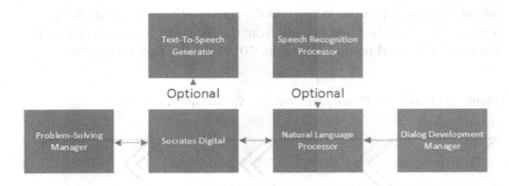

Figure 1 shows that the Socrates Digital™ module has the main logic that controls the behavior of Socrates Digital™. It asks the user persona questions and passes the answers to the natural language processor for processing. The natural language processer utilizes a domain-specific knowledge-base created by the system developer with the Dialog Development Manager. The natural language processor parses the user responses and matches them against a list of predicted answers, and returns the answer with the highest confidence. The Socrates Digital™ module then processes the answers and advances users to the following questions.

The Socrates Digital™ module reads and writes summaries about information, assumptions, concepts, and conclusions of viewpoints for solving problems to and from the process "Problem-Solving Manager." Chapter 10 presents the details.

DESIGN AND DEVELOPMENT PHASES

Figure 2 shows the design and development phases for Socrates Digital™ – Understand, Explore, Materialize, and Realize. Inspired by Design Thinking (Brooks, 2010; Lewrick, Link, & Leifer, 2018), these phases have emerged to design the user experience for modern complex computer interfaces that utilize a conversational interface. Since Socrates Digital™ leverages artificial intelligence services to handle processing natural human language, the design and development process focuses on the conversational user experience. As a result, this book borrows heavily from the YouTube video created by Jeff Humble of CareerFoundry (Humble, 2019) for the first three phases. The

Figure 2. Design and Development Phases for Socrates Digital™

last phase, Realize, was added for the implementation portion of Socrates Digital™. For our investment dialog example presented in Chapter 3, as design and developers, investment analysts would have followed this phased process to create the Socrates Digital™ system presented.

Understand Phase

The Understand phase of design and development for Socrates Digital™ has three steps. The first step of this phase, the User Persona step, is to identify the system's potential users and construct a user persona for them. In the Understand phase, the second step, the system persona, determines how the persona will ask the user persona the questions that will lead to a viewpoint that will solve the problem. The third step of this phase, the User Journey Mapping, is to identify the most critical parts of the conversation that the system persona and user persona will have.

User Persona

In our investment dialog example, the potential users of the completed system are analysts in an investment firm who evaluate commercial real estate investment opportunities. These potential users of the system were used to create a profile of the user persona who will use the resulting Socrates Digital™ system for these investment evaluations.

An essential aspect of constructing the user persona is identifying the information, assumptions, and concepts the potential users apply. In our investment dialog example, the information provided to the potential investors was the business data related to revenue for daily operations of each motel in the Rosebud Motel chain. This information comes into perspective through the lens of the concepts and the underlying assumptions. Note that it is vital to provide some initial concepts and assumptions to start the learning and problem-solving process for the system's users.

In the investment dialog example, the concepts provided initially by the system included the following:

- Occupancy Rate
- Average Daily Rate
- Revenue per Available Room

These concepts provided initially by the system are standard ways to conceptualize financial performance in the motel industry. Applying these standard concepts provides critical first steps for the system's users to analyze the investment opportunity. These concepts relate to the following assumptions that were also initially provided:

- Occupancy Rate is positively correlated with total revenue.
- Average Daily Rate is positively correlated with total revenue.
- Revenue per Available Room is positively correlated with total revenue.

Applying these assumptions provides industry-standard ways to interpret the information for analyzing the opportunity for investing in the Rosebud Motel chain.

Another important aspect of constructing the user persona is identifying how the user persona interacts with the system. The investment dialog example assumes that the user persona will interact with the system through a laptop PC. Access by PC allows users to use a browser for applications such as spreadsheets, databases, and business intelligence platforms. However, other devices can run Socrates Digital™ systems. For example, a smartphone might be the preferred device if a spoken conversation without access to other applications suffices.

System Persona

In our investment dialog example, the Socrates Digital™ system walked potential users through various ways to examine the investment opportunity. The questions that Socrates Digital™ asked the user persona focused on analyzing an investment opportunity in the motel industry. In designing the system persona for Socrates Digital™ in the investment dialog example, the investment analysts who designed and developed the system decided what the behavior and the personality would be for the Socrates Digital™ system.

For the behavior aspect of the system persona, Socrates Digital™ guides the user persona in conversation to first address the information, concepts, and assumptions of decision making. After addressing these aspects of decision-making, Socrates Digital™ guides the user persona in conversation to discover the conclusions implied by the information, concepts, and assumptions. Next, Socrates Digital™ guides the user persona in conversation to identify the implications of those conclusions. Finally, Socrates Digital™ guides the user persona in summarizing how all these -- information, concepts, assumptions, conclusions, and implications, form a viewpoint about evaluating an investment opportunity in the commercial real estate industry.

As for the personality of the system persona, Socrates Digital™ asks its questions in different ways – as a human person would. Being able to ask each question in three different ways was judged to meet this requirement. To realize this flexibility meant that Socrates Digital™ required three forms of each question created by the investment analysts who designed and developed the system.

User Journey Mapping

User journey mapping starts by deciding the most important conversations between the system and user persona. These important conversations are then modeled with the system persona and user persona to ensure that the system persona provides what the user persona needs to solve the problem at hand. In our investment example, the most important part of the conversation for the system persona and user persona concerns examining the ability of the Rosebud Motel to raise total revenue as a result of the investment. Raising total revenue enough to pay the project rate of return for the motel chain would ensure that the investment meets the terms specified. Other parts of this conversation may also be deemed important such as the cost side of the motel chain operation. For example, lowering costs for motel operations may also be a way to ensure that the investment meets the terms specified. In this case, modeling the cost-side conversation ensures that the system persona provides the user persona what it needs to decide about investing in the chain. Other conversations between the system persona and user persona conversation may become important. For example, the system persona may have to answer general economic questions, such as the current interest rate and economic outlook.

Explore Phase

The Explore phase of design and development for Socrates Digital™ also has three steps. The first step of this phase, Sample Dialog, is creating a sample dialog between the system and user persona. In the Explore phase, the second step, Table Reading, is to practice the sample dialog with actors to determine if it accurately models the intended conversation between the system and user persona. The third step of this phase, Wizard of Oz Testing, is to test the Sample Dialog with the system and user personas, where an actor plays the part of the system persona from a remote location.

Sample Dialog

In this step, sample dialogs model those "most important" conversations identified in the User Journey Mapping of the Understand Phase. The "happy path" approach assumes there are no misunderstandings in the conversation in these sample dialogs. This approach keeps the conversations simple and allows the designers to focus on the information exchanged in the conversation. That means that the system or user persona will not respond to each other with replies such as "I did not understand" what you meant. It also means there will not be follow-up questions like those seen in the investment example where the system persona asks for more details or clarification from the user persona.

For all Socrates Digital™ systems, this sample dialog should guide the user persona through the steps to identify the information the user persona will examine, what concepts it will use to make sense of the information, and what assumptions underlie the analysis of the information.

As demonstrated in the investment dialog example, the sample dialog should conclude by guiding the user persona to make a conclusion and identify the implications. Finally, the sample dialog should guide the user into taking all the information, concepts, assumptions, conclusions, and implications into account to create a viewpoint for answering the question at hand. Our investment dialog example was a viewpoint that answered whether the investment would raise motel total revenue enough to pay off the investors.

Table Reading

This next step of the Explore Phase is to use actors to see if the sample dialog created in the previous step provides the answers for the user persona to solve the problem. No, you do not have to hire Brad Pit and Sandra Bullock for this step. All you need to do is get a couple of volunteers familiar with the problem area. Our example is to get people familiar with motel investing and have them read the sample dialog script. Have one volunteer read the system persona part and another volunteer read the user persona part.

Afterward, conduct a debrief where you ask both volunteers for their impressions of the system persona. Specifically, ask them if the system persona asked the right questions – and in the right way. Ask them if some questions were redundant. Then, ask them if some questions were missing. The most important aspect of the debrief is to have your volunteer actors look at the line of reasoning to see if it makes sense. Have them look for weak spots where the reasoning makes too big of a leap, such as a conclusion based on shaky concepts or assumptions. Early sample dialogs had a big leap from the information, concepts, and assumptions to our investment dialog example conclusions. Rewriting the questions and adding more questions enhanced the quality of reasoning (clarity and precision) about the information, concepts, and assumptions to reduce the distance for leaping to a conclusion.

The last thing to do in this step is to take all this feedback and update the sample dialog to represent a clear and logical progression from reasoning about information to constructing a viewpoint for solving the problem at hand.

Wizard of Oz Testing

After the updates to the sample dialog during the Table Reading step, the next step is Wizard of Oz Testing. It is Toto's actions in the movie that gives this step the fun name. The Wizard is unseen until Toto pulls the curtain to reveal him. So, the idea with this step is to have an actor play the role of the user persona and have that person communicate with the unseen system persona in another room. This distanced interaction provides a way to test the sample dialog in a setting more closely representing the planned communication between the system and user persona.

The first thing to do in this step is to have your volunteers go through the sample dialog. As before, you will be looking to see if the sample dialog represents a clear and logical progression from reasoning about information to constructing a viewpoint for solving the problem at hand. As before, look for weak spots where the reasoning makes too big of a leap. For example, a conclusion made on shaky concepts or unreliable assumptions.

The next thing to do is identify the places that the system persona will need to have a clear and precise answer. The need for these clear and precise answers shows in the following exchange in the motel investment example:

SP: What will the investment be used for? (Questions that Target the Parts of Thinking -- Questioning Clarity)

UP: It will be used for motel renovations and promotional services.

SP: Could you give me more details about that? (Questions that Target the Quality of Reasoning -- Questioning Precision)

UP: Yes. It will be used for making repairs, painting the interior and exterior, staff training on customer service, and creating a program with local restaurants and stores which will provide gift cards for their services to motel guests.

The request for more details is a question that gets at precision and focuses on the quality of reasoning. These questions by the system persona will aim at gaining clear and precise information from the user persona. Use your volunteer actors to help edit the questions, so the user persona will know what the system persona needs.

Materialize Phase

After a tested and revised sample dialog has been created, the next step for designing and developing a Socrates Digital™ system is the Materialize phase.

Like the other phases, it has three steps. The first step, User Flow Charts, is about creating the user flow charts for the questions that make up the parts of thinking and the questions that make up the parts of the quality of reasoning. Documentation of the Voice Scripts, with all questions and possible responses, is in the second step. The third step, Multimodal Interactions, addresses the multimodal interactions between the system and user personas.

User Flow Charts

In this first step of the Materialize Phase, mapping the entire experience between the system and user persona occurs. This mapping is an essential step since it outlines most of the design decisions needed to create the voice scripts in the next step of the Materialize Phase. These voice scripts become the vocabulary for the natural language processor in the Realize Phase.

This step documents the flow of control for all the modules processing questions that target the parts of thinking. The flow charts are updated using the sample dialog resulting from the Wizard of Oz testing and revision to address possible user persona responses.

Voice Scripts

In this second step of the Materialize Phase, developers document all questions and possible responses using a word processing or spreadsheet application. Most natural language processing services can process single question/answer pairs. The temptation for developers is to skip this step and just input the questions and answers one at a time. However, two good reasons for this step are documenting the question/answer pairs in a file and uploading them as a batch to a natural language processing service.

The first reason is that systematic changes in the system may affect many related question/answer pairs. With a documented "knowledge base" of question/answer pairs, developers can easily see what needs to be changed, make those changes, and upload the question/answer pairs as a batch to make those systematic changes. All the natural language processing services support this way of managing your knowledge base. These services will allow designers to delete all the question/answer pairs and upload a new knowledge base or simply overwrite the current knowledge base when a new one is uploaded.

The second reason to document the question/answer pairs is to create a way to divide up the work for designing and developing a Socrates Digital™

system. A designer can do the upfront design work described in these first three phases of design and development. Then, the designer hands off the file containing the knowledge base of questions and answer pairs to a programmer for the Realize Phase. The knowledge base file provides a clean hand-off and division of duties between a designer and programmer. These two reasons explain why Figure 1 shows the natural language processor getting its knowledge base from the Dialog Development Manager, which manages all the other artifacts for developing the knowledge base. Chapter 10 describes the Dialog Development Manager.

Multimodal Interactions

In this third step of the Materialize Phase, the developer identifies the multimodal interactions between the system and user personas. In the investment dialog example, the user persona interacts with data sources such as spreadsheets, databases, and business intelligence platforms while the user persona is interacting with Socrates Digital™. In these interactions, the user persona interacts with these data sources through a PC or smartphone browser. However, in the investment example dialog, Socrates Digital™ is not integrated with the data sources. Socrates Digital™ relies on the user persona to provide values from the data sources.

The conversation between Socrates Digital™ and the user persona changes dramatically when Socrates Digital™ interacts directly with the data sources. For example, this could change the interaction when the system persona asks the user persona if a relation between data items holds for the larger dataset. Socrates Digital™ could interact with the data source, run the correlation, and present the results to the user to evaluate. This level of interaction between the Socrates Digital™, user persona, and the data sources would require additional design, development, and system user testing to ensure the system works as envisioned. Note that this system interaction would be played out in the Wizard of Oz step of the Explore Phase to ensure that the resulting system would work as designed.

Realize Phase

After the developer has created the flow charts, voice scripts, multimodal interactions, the next step is the implementation of the system in the Realize Phase. Furthermore, like the other phases, it has three steps. In the first step,

Natural Language Vocabulary, the developer creates the vocabulary for the natural language processor. In the second step, Implementation Logic, the developer codes the logic for the system. Moreover, in the last step, Calculation Weights, the developer sets the calculation weights for how Socrates Digital™ combines logic and evidence.

Natural Language Vocabulary

In this first step of the Realize Phase, the developer builds the vocabulary for the natural language processing service. This process is typically a simple, straightforward, and well-documented process. This process to create the vocabulary for the natural language processing service is similar across artificial intelligence service providers such as Apple, Microsoft, Google, and Amazon.

Creating a vocabulary for a natural language processing service typically has the following steps:

1) Create an account with the artificial intelligence service provider.
2) Create an entity that will process the string of words that you send it. These are usually called a "bot," "agent," or a similar name.
3) Upload the knowledge base of question/answer pairs.
4) Train the bot on the knowledge base.
5) Test the bot to see if it answers the questions in the way you expect.
6) Revise the question/answer pairs.
7) Publish the bot.
8) Access the bot from the Socrates Digital™ system. Access is by calling the published endpoint (URL address) of the bot.

Implementation Logic

In this second step of the Realize Phase, the developer codes the implementation logic for the Socrates Digital™ system. There are several approaches for implementation. The chosen approach will depend on several factors. One factor is concerns which artificial intelligence service provider is selected. Some have no code application programming interfaces (APIs), while others have APIs that developers access with a general programming language such as Java, C, or Python. Another factor is how much the Socrates Digital™ system is integrated with the user persona's data sources. The more integration with the data sources, the more likely a developer will use a general programming language for the implementation logic. Nevertheless, another factor relates to how easily the user base (or developers) can modify the implementation logic of the Socrates Digital™ system. Developers can more easily modify the logic with no code APIs than the logic of a general programming language.

To sort through these options, consider using Microsoft's Power Virtual Agent as the natural language processor for Socrates Digital™. Developers can develop the implementation logic for this natural language processor in three ways.

The first and most straightforward way is to develop the logic in Power Virtual Agent itself. It has a no-code authoring system that allows designers to flowchart the responses by the user persona to questions posed by the system. The downside is that this no-code approach tends to make the entire system an all-Microsoft implementation. See Appendix C for an overview of using Demo of Microsoft's Power Virtual Agent to develop a Socrates Digital™ application.

The second way to develop the logic for Power Virtual Agent is to use Microsoft Power Automate (formally called flow) – which is part of the Microsoft Power Platform. Technically, Power Automate is also a no-code solution. Similar to the flowcharting authoring system in Power Virtual Agent, Power Automate can also flowchart the responses to questions posed by the system. However, Power Automate does have more operators and conditional statements to make it a powerful tool for creating the implementation logic. Furthermore, using the no-code Virtual Agent option makes the entire system an all-Microsoft implementation. However, the upside is that logic created in Power Automate can tap into the data sources if those data sources are in Microsoft's Power BI. Power Automate can then manipulate and display those data sources for the user.

The third way to develop the logic for Power Virtual Agent is to program the logic in a general programming language and connect to Power Virtual Agent via an API. This choice, of course, involves the most work but provides the most flexibility for customizing the implementation logic. Also, this option would allow manipulation and display of data in Power BI through its APIs. This book presents the pseudo-code for developing most of the logic in a general programming language. Developers can then use this pseudo-code for the parts they choose for implementation in a general programming language.

By the time this book is published, all of the above options and tradeoffs for the implementation logic will be available, more or less, across all of the artificial intelligence service providers, including Apple, Microsoft, Google, and Amazon.

Calculation Weights

The last step in the Realize Phase is setting the numerical weights for the calculations in the implementation logic. The upcoming chapters describe these calculation weights in the pseudo-code of the modules.

Below, all the calculations that are spread across the modules are listed in one place.

```
/* Factor weighting used for calculating overall confidence for
an approach after analysis
Dataset_Weight
Concept_Weight
Assumption_Weight
Conclusion_Weight
Implication_Weight
Approach_Weight

/* The default value for the additional multiplier of each
Dataset, Concepts, Assumption, Conclusion,
/* and Implication.  The idea is that each additional one of
these increases confidence in the results.
Additional_Dataset_Multiplier
Additional_ Concept_Multiplier
Additional_ Assumption_Multiplier
Additional_ Conclusion_Multiplier
Additional_ Implication_Multiplier

/* The default settings for the example investment dialog
/* Set the multiplier that increases the adjusted average of
multiple datasets
Additional_Dataset_Multiplier:= 0.1
/* Set the dataset weight for calculating overall confidence
for an approach
Dataset_Weight:= 0.3

/* Set the multiplier that increases the adjusted average of
multiple concepts
Additional_ Concept_Multiplier:= 0.1
/* Set the concept weight for calculating overall confidence
for an approach
Concept_Weight:= 0.1

/* Set the multiplier that increases the adjusted average of
```

```
multiple assumptions
Additional_ Assumption_Multiplier:= 0.1
/* Set the assumption weight for calculating overall confidence
for an approach
Assumption_Weight:= 0.1

/* Set the multiplier that increases the adjusted average of
multiple conclusions
Additional_ Conclusion_Multiplier:= 0.1
/* Set the conclusion weight for calculating overall confidence
for an approach
Conclusion_Weight:= 0.2

/* Set the multiplier that increases the adjusted average of
multiple implications
Additional_ Implication_Multiplier:= 0.1
/* Set the implication weight for calculating overall
confidence for an approach
Implication_Weight:= 0.3
```

SUMMARY

The design and development of a Socrates Digital™ system has four phases: Understand, Explore, Materialize, and Realize. The completion of these four phases results in a Socrates Digital™ system that leverages artificial intelligence services. The artificial intelligence services include a natural language processor provided by several artificial intelligence service providers, including Apple, Microsoft, Google, IBM, and Amazon.

In the design and development of a Socrates Digital™ system, the Understand phase has three steps. The first step of this phase, the User Persona step, is to construct a user persona. The second step of the Understand phase is to determine how the system persona will ask the user persona to solve the problem. User Journey Mapping, the third step, identifies the most important parts of the conversation that the system and user persona will have.

The Explore phase for designing and developing a Socrates Digital™ also has three steps. The first step of this phase, Sample Dialog, is creating a sample dialog between the system and user persona. In the Explore phase, the second step, Table Reading, is to practice the sample dialog with actors. In the third step of this phase, Wizard of Oz Testing, the Sample Dialog is tested with an actor playing the part of the system persona from a remote location.

The Materialize phase of the design and development of a Socrates Digital™ system also has three steps. The first step, User Flow Charts, is creating the user flow charts for all the user interactions with the system. In the second step, Voice Scripts, developers document all questions and possible responses. The third step, Multimodal Interactions, addresses the multimodal interactions between the system and user personas.

Finally, the Realize Phase, like the other phases, has three steps. In the first step, Natural Language Vocabulary, the developer creates the vocabulary for the natural language processor. In the second step, Implementation Logic, the developer codes the logic for the system. Moreover, in the last step, Calculation Weights, the developer sets the calculation weights for how Socrates Digital™ combines logic and evidence.

REFERENCES

Brooks, F. (2010). *The design of design*. Addison-Wesley.

Humble, J. (2019). *The Voice Design Process For Voice User Interfaces (VUIs)*. CareerFoundry [YouTube channel]. Retrieved November 22, 2019, from https://www.youtube.com/watch?v=8OXN0ZDpwrM&t=1s

Lewrick, M., Link, P., & Leifer, L. (2018). *The design thinking playbook*. Wiley.

Chapter 5
Socrates Digital™ System Architecture:
Overview of the Socrates Digital™ Module

ABSTRACT

This chapter presents the inner workings of the Socrates Digital™ module. It has most of the logic of a Socrates Digital™ system and describes how processes and subprocesses interact to create Socratic problem solving. A Socrates Digital™ system allows the user to examine information, assumptions, and concepts in any order. Next, Socrates Digital™ guides the user in developing a conclusion by applying concepts, using assumptions, and analyzing information. Afterward, Socrates Digital™ guides the user in predicting the implications of the conclusion and combining all the reasoning into a viewpoint that addresses the question at hand.

INTRODUCTION

As described in Chapter 4, the design and development of a Socrates Digital™ system presented in this book is a hybrid, modular system. This chapter describes how the Socrates Digital™ processes and subprocesses interact with each other. The upcoming chapters present details of each process with flow charts and pseudo-code.

DOI: 10.4018/978-1-7998-7955-8.ch005

Figure 5.1 provides an overview of Socrates Digital™ module. The example dialog from Chapter 3 illustrates how it guides user groups through a Socratic Questioning session to learn and solve a problem.

DEFINE PROBLEM PROCESS

As Figure 1 shows, Socrates Digital™ begins with the "Define Problem" process to define the problem that the user persona is trying to solve. Socrates Digital™ starts this process by asking the user persona, "What can I help you with today?"

In the investment example dialog presented in Chapter 3, the user persona asks for help deciding whether to invest in the Rosebud Motel chain. Socrates Digital™ verifies that this will be the main question that the user persona is aiming to answer.

Next, Socrates Digital™ questions the user persona to determine the main concept for making the decision. The user persona responds that it needs to know if the investment will boost total revenue enough to pay back the investors. Next, Socrates Digital™ verifies that this is the central idea to make the decision. After getting a "Yes" from the user persona, Socrates Digital™ next asks how it relates to the question at hand. The user persona explains that it needs to know if the investment will increase the total revenue for the Rosebud Motel chain so that it can repay the investment at the projected rate of return.

In this investment example dialog, Socrates Digital™ has identified that this is about determining if this is a good investment and begins to ask questions about the details of the investment. It begins by asking the user persona to identify the projected rate of return for the investment. After the user persona answers that they are offering a 10% rate of return, Socrates Digital™ goes to the next question and asks, "What is the investment amount?" The user persona responds that the investment amount is three and one-half million dollars. Socrates Digital™ follows up by asking what the repayment period will be and gets the answer of 5 years from the user persona.

After getting an answer to these questions, Socrates Digital™ asks the user persona what the investment will be used for. The user persona initially offers a high-level answer that the investment will fund motel renovations and promotional services. However, Socrates Digital™ asks for more details around the plans for the investment. The user persona then responds that the investment will fund repairs, paint the interior and exterior, staff training on

Figure 1. Define Problem Process of the Socrates Digital™ Module

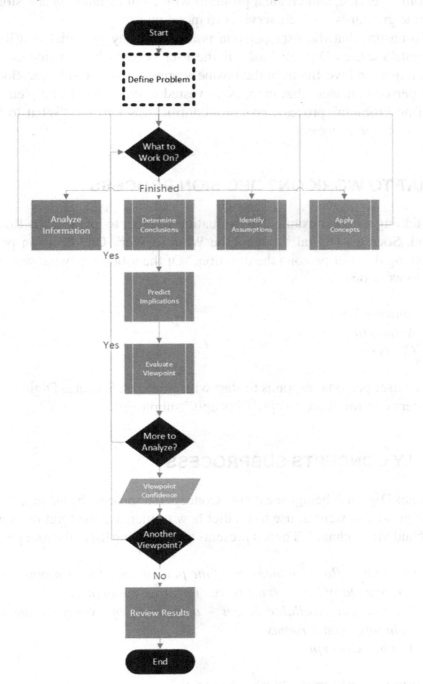

customer service, and create a program with local restaurants and stores to provide gift cards for their services to motel guests.

To ensure that the user persona is aware of any potential conflicts of interest, Socrates Digital™ asks if the user persona has an interest other than return on investment in the business opportunity. To this question, the user persona answers that there is no vested interest. After completing the "Define Problem" process, program control passes to the "What to Work On?" decision process.

WHAT TO WORK ON? DECISION PROCESS

Continuing with our example of evaluating whether to invest in the Rosebud Motel, Socrates Digital™ begins the What to Work On? decision process by asking the user persona the question, "Of the following, what would you like to work on?

- *Information*
- *Assumptions*
- *Concepts*

The user persona responds to start with concepts. Socrates Digital™ then transfers control to the "Apply Concepts" subprocess.

APPLY CONCEPTS SUBPROCESS

Socrates Digital™ beings the Apply Concepts subprocess by asking, "Which concept do you want to use to predict how to increase the total revenue for Rosebud Motel chain?" Then, it presents the following list to the user persona.

- *Occupancy Rate – a measure of the percentage of total rooms rented*
- *Average Daily Rate – a measure of average room price*
- *Revenue per Available Room – a measure of average room price, including vacant rooms*
- *Another Concept*

The user persona replies, "Occupancy rate."

Figure 2. Apply Concepts Process of the Socrates Digital™ Module

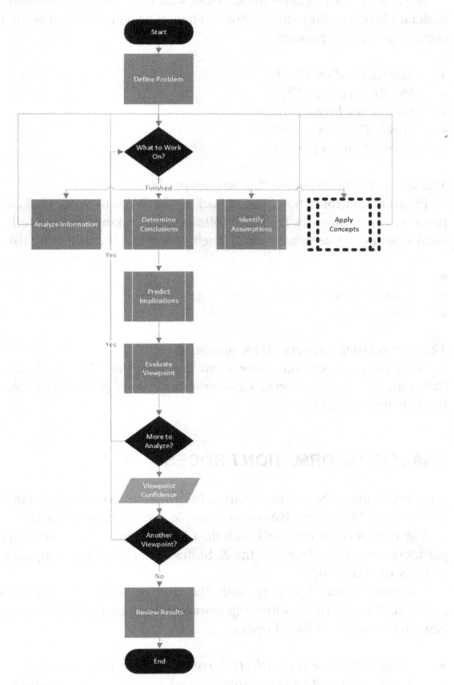

Next, Socrates Digital™ asks, "How well does this concept predict the Rosebud Motel chain total revenue?" Then, it provides the following list of options to the user persona.

- *Always Predicts (0.75)*
- *Mostly Predicts (0.5)*
- *Sometimes Predicts (0)*
- *Rarely Predicts (-0.5)*
- *Never Predicts (-0.75)*

The user persona responds, "Sometimes predicts."

Program control is now passed back to the What to Work On? decision process, where Socrates Digital™ follows up by asking, "Of the following, what would you like to work on?" Then, it presents the following list.

- *Information*
- *Assumptions*
- *Concepts*

The user persona answers "Information."

After the user persona answers this question, the "What to Work On?" that completes the decision process, program control passes to the "Analyze Information" process.

ANALYZE INFORMATION PROCESS

Socrates Digital™ begins the Analyze Information process, shown in Figure 3, by asking, "Can you give me an example data point about this?"

The user persona responds with data from a spreadsheet showing that a particular motel, the Dundalk Inn & Suites motel, has low occupancy rates and low total revenue.

Socrates Digital™ then presents the user persona with the following question, "Do any of the following assumptions underlie this observation?" Next, it provides this list of options.

- *Occupancy Rate is positively correlated with total revenue.*
- *Average Daily Rate is positively correlated with total revenue.*
- *Revenue per Available Room is positively correlated with total revenue.*

Figure 3. Analyze Information Process of the Socrates Digital™ Module

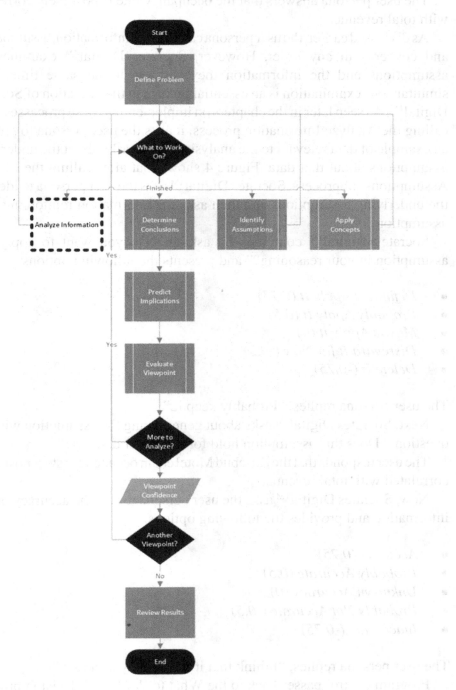

The user persona answers that the occupancy rate is positively correlated with total revenue.

As discussed earlier, the user persona can analyze information, assumptions, and concepts in any order. However, Socrates Digital™ examines the assumptions and the information they rest on at the same time. This simultaneous examination is an essential linkage in the operation of Socrates Digital™. As seen later in the chapters on implementing these processes, after calling the Analyze Information process, it asks the user persona to provide an example of data relevant to the analysis. Then it asks about the underlying assumptions about that data. Figure 4 shows that after calling the Identify Assumptions subprocess, Socrates Digital™ asks the user persona to identify the underlying assumptions and then asks for information reinforcing each assumption.

Socrates Digital™ continues by asking, "Do you want to apply this assumption in your reasoning?" and presents the following options.

- *Definitely Apply It (0.75)*
- *Probably Apply It (0.5)*
- *Maybe Apply it (0)*
- *Disregard It for Now (-0.5)*
- *Delete It (-0.75)*

The user persona replies, "Probably keep it."

Next, Socrates Digital™ asks about generalizing the assumption with the question, "Does this assumption hold for the larger data set?"

The user responds that the Rosebud Motel chain occupancy rate is positively correlated with total revenue.

Now, Socrates Digital™ asks the user persona to rate the accuracy of this information and provides the following options.

- *Accurate (0.75)*
- *Probably Accurate (0.5)*
- *Unknown Accuracy (0)*
- *Probably Not Accurate (-0.5)*
- *Inaccurate (-0.75)*

The user persona replies, "I think that it is probably accurate."

Program control passes back to the What to Work On? decision process, which determines that all three – information, assumptions, and concepts –

Figure 4. Identify Assumptions Subprocess of the Socrates Digital™ Module

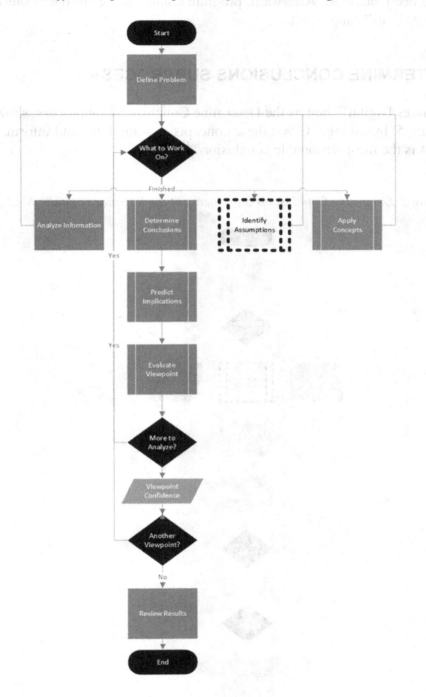

have been analyzed. Afterward, program control passes to the "Determine Conclusions" subprocess.

DETERMINE CONCLUSIONS SUBPROCESS

Socrates Digital™ begins the Determine Conclusions subprocess, shown in Figure 5, by asking, "Given these concepts, assumptions, and information, what is the most reasonable conclusion?"

Figure 5. Determine Conclusions Subprocess of the Socrates Digital™ Module

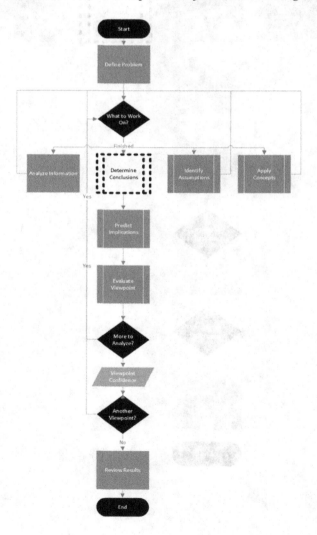

The user persona replies with the answer, "Raising the occupancy rate for all the motels in the Rosebud Motel chain would raise total revenue for the chain."

Socrates Digital™ follows up with this question, "Given this is all the evidence that you currently have, how would you rate the logic of this conclusion?" Then, Socrates Digital™ provides the following list of possible responses.

- *Very Logical (0.75)*
- *Probably Logical (0.5)*
- *Unknown How Logical (0)*
- *Probably Not Logical (-0.5)*
- *Illogical (-0.75)*

The user persona replies with, "I would say that it is probably logical."

With the Determine Conclusions subprocess completed, program control passes to the "Predict Implications" subprocess.

PREDICT IMPLICATIONS SUBPROCESS

Socrates Digital™ begins the Predict Implications subprocess, shown in Figure 5.6, by asking, "What are the implications of this conclusion?"

The user persona responds with, "Increased marketing can raise the occupancy rate and total revenue for motels in the Rosebud Motel chain."

After completing the Predict Implications process, control is advanced to the "Evaluate Viewpoint" subprocess.

Figure 6. Predict Implications Subprocess of the Socrates Digital™ Module

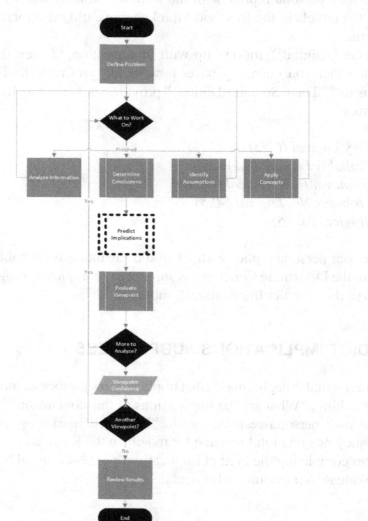

EVALUATE VIEWPOINT SUBPROCESS

Socrates Digital™ begins the Evaluate Approach subprocess by asking, "How would you rate your confidence in the viewpoint to increase marketing for increasing occupancy rate and total revenue for motels in the Rosebud Motel chain?"

- *Highly Justified (0.75)*
- *Probably Justified (0.5)*
- *Insufficient Evidence to Judge (0)*
- *Not Justified by the Evidence (-0.5)*
- *Refuted by the Evidence (-0.75)*

The user persona replies that there is insufficient evidence to judge. Control is now passed to the "More to Analyze?" decision process.

MORE TO ANALYZE? DECISION PROCESS

Socrates Digital™ begins the More to Analyze? Decision process by asking, "Can we get more confirming evidence about this?"

In the investment dialog example presented in Chapter 3, the user persona replies, "Yes, I believe we can." This answer takes the user persona back to the What to Work On? decision process to add more evidence to the current approach under analysis. Since the What to Work On? decision process has already been described, the investment dialog example is now changed to have the user persona say, "No, I don't think so." Program control is advanced to the "Viewpoint Confidence" output process.

VIEWPOINT CONFIDENCE OUTPUT PROCESS

In this output process, Socrates Digital™ lists the confidence level calculated for the current viewpoint. The first time it is called in our investment dialog example, Socrates Digital™ states, "You have expressed an overall confidence of .54 (some confidence) for the viewpoint to increase marketing is needed to raise the total revenue for motels in the Rosebud Motel chain."

After displaying this confidence level to the user persona, program control passes to the "Another Viewpoint?" decision process.

ANOTHER VIEWPOINT? DECISION PROCESS

At the beginning of this decision process, Socrates Digital™ asks the user persona, "Is there another approach that should be considered?"

After skipping over the investment example dialog where more evidence determined the need for increased marketing, the scene changes to another user group with the following statement.

Meanwhile, on the other side of the world, but within the same organization, another user group has just seen the summary and results of this conversation. However, they know about another viewpoint that should be considered.

To this new user group, labeled "UP2," Socrates Digital™ asks this question, "Is there another viewpoint that should be considered?"

UP2 answers, "Yes! We know that price is only one of the influencing factors for customers of motel rooms. For example, customers are influenced by clean rooms in good repair, friendly staff, and complimentary gifts."

This answer takes the user persona (UP2) back to the What to Work On? decision to create a new approach and add evidence to the analysis of this new approach. Since the What to Work On? decision process has already been described, the investment dialog example is now changed to have the user persona say "No, not at this time," and program control passes to the "Review Results" process.

REVIEW RESULTS PROCESS

Figure 5.7 shows that Socrates Digital™ begins this process by asking if the user persona would like to see all the viewpoints and their confidence levels for this question at hand.

In our investment example, the user persona answers "Yes."

Socrates Digital™ then displays the following results to the user persona (UP2):

"UP1 has expressed an overall confidence of .54 (some confidence) for the following viewpoint:

The viewpoint is focused on increasing marketing to raise occupancy rates, average daily rates, and revenue per available room to increase total revenue for motels in the Rosebud Motel chain.

UP2 has expressed an overall confidence of .81 (good confidence) for the following viewpoint:

The viewpoint is focused on making repairs, painting the interior and exterior, staff training on customer service, and creating promotional programs with local restaurants and stores that improve customer experience to increase total revenue in the Rosebud Motel chain."

Socrates Digital™ then asks, "Can you combine these viewpoints based upon their information, concepts, assumptions, conclusions, and implications into a composite single viewpoint?"

To which the user persona (UP2) replies, "Yes, we can."

Socrates Digital™ responds with, "What is this composite viewpoint for answering the question at hand?"

The user persona (UP2) replies, "Rosebud Motels uses its investment funds for marketing and make the motel renovations it did with Saint Ola for all its motels."

Socrates Digital™ then asks the user persona (UP2), "Does this help answer the question at hand question at hand about deciding whether to invest in the Rosebud Motel chain?"

In our investment dialog example, the user persona (UP2) answers "Yes."

In response to this, Socrates Digital™ asks, "What is that answer?"

The user persona replies, "We decided to recommend investing in the Rosebud Motel chain."

Socrates Digital™ follows up with this question "What are the implications of this decision?"

To which, the user persona (UP2) makes the following response.

"If Rosebud Motels uses its investment funds for marketing and make the motel renovations it did with Saint Ola for all its motels, it would increase the Rosebud Motel chain revenue by $2,000,000 in the first year. This would make it easily possible to repay the $4,800,000 for the loan over five years. It would provide a good return for investors at 10% and increase revenues for the Rosebud Motel chain in the future."

Socrates Digital™ ends the session by asking, "OK, that completes this session. Would you like to save your recommendation for investing?"

In response, the user persona says, "Yes – thanks."

Figure 8. shows that Socrates Digital™ provides additional functionality with the Dialog Development Manager module after exiting the session.

The Dialog Development Manager provides a submit, review, and approval process for all the steps – Understand, Explore, Materialize, and Realize – of the dialog development process described in Chapter 4. This dialog development process is a file of question/answer pairs uploaded to a natural language processor. The Dialog Development Manager guides users through this dialog development process and makes all the results available to the user group that created them and other organizational members. These other

Figure 7. Review Results Process of the Socrates Digital™ Module

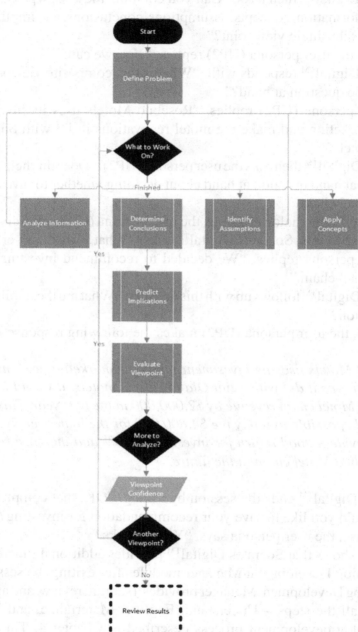

Figure 8. The Dialog Development Manager Process

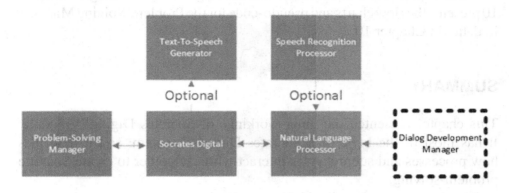

Figure 9. The Problem-Solving Manager Process

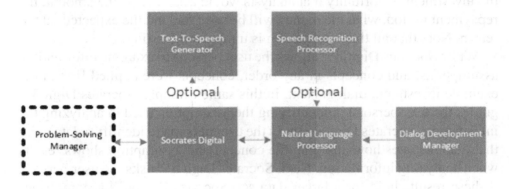

organizational members will apply lessons from previous efforts to develop their questions/answers file for other problem areas. Chapter 9 presents the Dialog Development Manager in detail – with flow charts and pseudo-code.

The other module where Socrates Digital™ provides additional functionality is with the Problem-Solving Manager. As discussed in this chapter, the Socrates Digital™ module reads and writes summaries about information, assumptions, concepts, and conclusions of viewpoints for solving problems with the process "Problem-Solving Manager." As shown in Figure 9, the Problem-Solving Manager also provides a submit, review, and approval process for viewpoints created during problem-solving sessions, which become "best practices" for the organization. These best practice viewpoints then become invaluable knowledge that the Problem-Solving Manager manages. Chapter 10 presents the flow charts and pseudo-code for the Problem-Solving Manager in detail in Chapter 10.

SUMMARY

This chapter presented the inner workings of Socrates Digital™ module. It has most of the logic of a Socrates Digital™ system, and it describes how processes and subprocesses interact with each other to create Socratic problem-solving.

The first process described is the "Define Problem" process to define the problem the user persona tries to solve. Socrates Digital™ asks questions upfront to describe the problem and determine the main question at hand. In the investment example dialog, Socrates Digital™ asked questions about the investment opportunity that analysts would ask, such as the amount, the repayment period, what the money will be used for, and the expected rate of return. Note that all this information is unique to investing.

While Socrates Digital™ allows the user persona to examine information, assumptions, and concepts in any order, concepts were applied first in the example investment dialog. Next, in this same example, Socrates Digital™ guides the user persona in identifying the assumption used in analyzing the information. Socrates Digital™ asks the user persona to identify a data point that demonstrates how applying the concept and assumption shows results when analyzing information. Next, Socrates Digital™ asks the user persona if these results hold for a larger data set. Socrates Digital™ accomplishes these interactions through the Analyze Information Process, Apply Concepts subprocess, and the Identify Assumptions subprocess. Note that processes contain subprocesses, and subprocesses are the smallest unit of logic. Later chapters show the pseudo-code of the subprocesses.

As this chapters presents, Socrates Digital™ uses the Determine Conclusions module to guide the user persona in developing a conclusion from applying concepts, using assumptions, and analyzing information. Socrates Digital™ then uses the Predict Implications module to guide the user persona in predicting the implications of the conclusion just developed. Finally, Socrates Digital™ uses the Evaluate Viewpoint module to guide the user persona into combining all this reasoning into a viewpoint that addresses the question at hand.

Also described in this chapter are the Dialog Development Manager and the Problem-Solving Manager. Both are part of Socrates Digital™ design goal to support knowledge management and organizational learning. The Dialog Development Manager guides the user persona through the development steps for creating the problem domain vocabulary used by an artificial intelligence service to interact with the user persona. The Dialog Development Manager makes the result of this process available to the developers and other organization members for use in developing the vocabulary for other problem domains.

Socrates Digital™ uses the Problem-Solving Manager to identify, review, and approve viewpoints – with their concepts, assumptions, information, conclusions, and implications – to solve problems. These viewpoints can become "best practices" for organizations as Socrates Digital™ enables knowledge management and organizational learning.

Chapter 6
Problem Definition:
Specifying the Problem and Solution Requirements

ABSTRACT

This chapter begins with the Socrates Digital™ module calling the "Define Problem" process. This process identifies the problem area and gathers the problem-defining information from the user. This chapter provides pseudo-code for the subprocesses that make up the processes for Socrates Digital™. It has enough detail to implement the logic in any procedural and general-purpose computer programming language. This chapter shows that more questions follow after asking the user a question in many situations. The questions aimed at getting these answers are questions that target the quality of reasoning.

INTRODUCTION

As Figure 6.1 shows, the first process that the Socrates Digital™ module calls is the "Define Problem" process. This first process identifies the problem area and collects the problem-defining information from the user persona. The investment example dialog is again revisited in this chapter to show how the Define Problem process gathers this information. Since this example is on reasoning about investments, this initial process defines what type of investment it is, the financial details of the investment, and whether the user group has any vested interest in the investment.

DOI: 10.4018/978-1-7998-7955-8.ch006

INSIDE THE DEFINE PROBLEM PROCESS

Figure 1. The Define Problem Process of the Socrates Digital™ Module

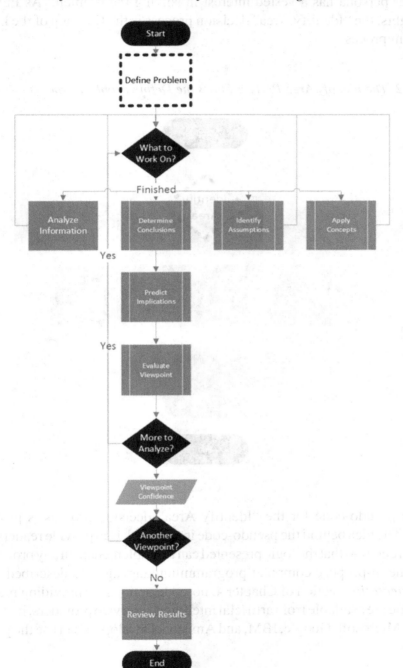

Figure 2 shows the inner workings of the Define Problem process. The first question is to identify the problem area, or type of problem, collect information from the user persona about the problem area, and identify if the user persona has a vested interest in solving the problem. As Figure 2 highlights, the "Identify Area" decision process is the first step of the Define Problem process.

Figure 2. The Identify Area Process Starts the Define Problem Process

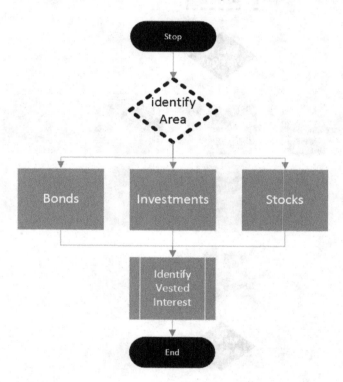

The pseudo-code for the "Identify Area" decision process is provided below. The idea behind the pseudo-code in this book is to provide readers with enough detail so that the logic presented can be implemented in any procedural and general-purpose computer programming language. As described in the *Implementation* section of Chapter 4, no-code options for providing much of this logic are available from artificial intelligence service providers, including Apple, Microsoft, Google, IBM, and Amazon. Developers can use the pseudo code provided in this book to implement the parts they choose in a general programming language.

The first line of this listing is a comment (denoted by the "/*" symbols at the beginning of the line). The comment states that the question asked by Socrates Digital™ of the user persona belongs to one of the two main categories of Socratic Questions called "Questions that Target the Parts of Thinking." The second part of this first comment, "Questioning Goals and Purposes," tells us that the question belongs to a subcategory of Socratic Questions aimed at determining the goals and purposes of the user persona for engaging Socrates Digital™.

```
/* Questions that Target the Parts of Thinking -- Questioning
Goals and Purposes

/* Ask user persona to identify the area that help is needed
BEGIN Process Decision_Process_Identify_Area

/* Generate a Random Number Between 1 and 3 - the Possible
Forms of the Question
RandomInteger:= GenerateRandomInteger[1,3]

/* Select a Form of the Question
    CASE RandomInteger OF
    1: Question:= "What can I help you with today?"
    2: Question:= "What can I do for you?"
    3: Question:= "Can I help you with something today?"
    END_CASE

OUTPUT Question
INPUT Answer

Problem_Description:= Answer

User_Response:= Answer

/* Understood_Response should come back as "Bonds,"
"Investments," or "Stocks"
Natural_Language_Processor (User_Response, Understood_Response)

IF Understood_Response <>  "Bonds" OR "Investments" OR "Stocks"
THEN OUTPUT "Sorry I didn't understand you. Do you want help
with bonds, investments, or stocks?"
INPUT Answer
User_Response:= Answer
END_IF
```

```
Problem_Area:= Understood_Response

/* Save Session_ID, Problem_Description, Problem_Area in
database
INSERT INTO Define_Problem_Table (Session_ID, Problem_
Description, Problem_Area) VALUES (Current_Session_ID, Problem_
Description, Problem_Area)

END Process Decision_Process_Identify_Area
```

Pseudo Code for the Decision_Process_Identify_Area

The second line in the listing is also a comment. It describes what the process, Decision_Process_Identify_Area, does. The comment describes that the code asks the user persona to identify the problem area for learning and problem-solving guidance.

When Decision_Process_Identify_Area runs, the first action is to call a function, GenerateRandomInteger, to generate a random integer between 1 and 3. As seen in the pseudo-code, this provides the logic to randomly select a form of the question to present to the user persona. This presentation of different forms of a question is an essential feature for Socrates Digital™.

Natural language processing will identify the "intent" behind a question even if worded differently. However, when Socrates Digital™ asks questions of user personas, they typically do it the same way every time. That is our history of conversations with computers, and it reinforces for users that they are talking with a computer. Providing multiple ways to ask the same question makes a Socrates Digital™ system seem more "natural" and "human-like." This behavior improves the conversational interaction for the user persona.

Socrates Digital™ asks the user persona in the investment example dialog, "What can I help you with today?" The user persona replies with, "Deciding whether to invest in the Rosebud Motel chain." This answer is assigned to the Problem_Description variable after it was input by the user persona. The answer is also assigned to the User_Response variable and used to call the natural language processor. It will process the user persona's answer and return "Bonds," "Investments," or "Stocks." In our investment example dialog, the natural language processor identified the user persona's answer as "Investments." If an unknown value is returned, it means that the natural language processor did not recognize the user persona's answer to Socrates Digital™'s question, "What can I help you with today?" In this case, Socrates Digital™ replies with the options, "Bonds," "Investments," or "Stocks." The answer stated by the user persona is then assigned to the variable User_Response.

The next step is to assign the User_Response to the variable Problem_Area.

Figure 3. The Investments Process is a Second Step Option in the Define Problem Process

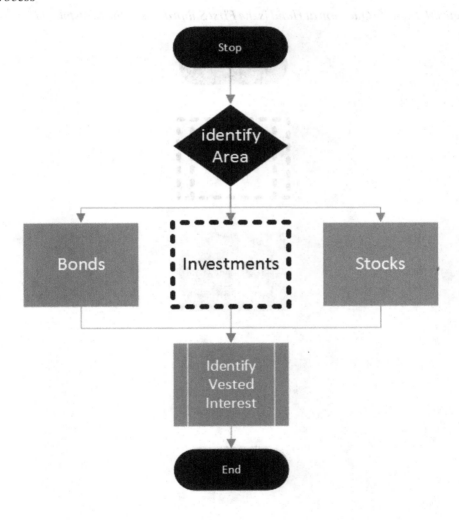

The following step saves the Problem_Description and Problem_Area in the database using the INSERT command. Note that the variable names in the subprocess are the same as the field names in the database. Problem_ Description and Problem_Area are local variables in the subprocess, and they are also the field names of the database table. This name sharing is a standard convention used to make the code more readable. This book follows this convention except when the names get too long, and it becomes difficult to keep the proper indentation in the code.

Figure 4. Identify Question at Hand is the First Subprocess in the Investment Process

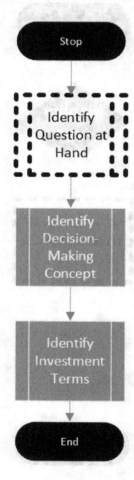

Selecting a database as the external storage for session data with the investment example dialog simplified things. However, Socrates Digital™ can use other external storage choices. For example, it can use Microsoft's

Sharepoint, a spreadsheet, external files, or a business intelligence platform for external storage.

After completing the Decision_Process_Identify_Area process, the identified problem area is the next to be processed. In our investment example dialog, program control passes to the Investments problem area. As Figure 3 highlights, the "Investments" process is the second step option in the Define Problem process.

As highlighted in Figure 4, the first subprocess is "Identify Question at Hand" in the Investments process. The Identify Decision_Making Concept subprocess follows it. The Identify Investment Terms subprocess completes the Investments process.

The pseudo-code for the Identify Question at Hand subprocess is listed below. As is the convention, the first line of this listing is a comment. It tells that the question belongs to one of the two main categories of Socratic Questions called "Questions that Target the Parts of Thinking." The remaining part of this first comment tells us that the question asked of the user persona is in the subcategory of "Question at Issue." This subcategory of Socratic Questions focuses on determining the main question that the user persona needs to answer. The second comment confirms this by telling us that this subprocess asks the user persona to identify the question at hand.

```
/* Questions that Target the Parts of Thinking - Question at
Issue

/* Ask user persona to identify question at hand
BEGIN Subprocess Identify_Question_At_Hand

/* Generate a Random Number Between 1 and 3 - the Possible
Forms of the Question
RandomInteger:= GenerateRandomInteger[1,3]

/* Select a Form of the Question
    CASE RandomInteger OF
    1: Question:= "So, the question at hand is " + Problem_
Description + "?"
    2: Question:= "Then, the question at hand is " + Problem_
Description + "?"
    3: Question:= "OK, the question at hand is " + Problem_
Description + "?"
    END_CASE

OUTPUT Question
```

```
INPUT Answer

User_Response:= Answer

Question:= Problem_Description

/* Understood_Response will come back as "Yes" or "No"
Natural_Language_Processor (User_Response, Understood_Response)

/* If no, then give user persona a chance to correct the
question at hand
IF Understood_Response <> "Yes" Then OUTPUT "Then what is the
question at hand?"
INPUT Answer
Question:= Answer

END_IF

/* Save Question_At_Hand to database
UPDATE Define_Problem_Table
SET
Question_At_Hand:= Question
WHERE Problem_Area = "Investments"  AND Session_ID = Current_
Session_ID

END Subprocess Identify_Question_At_Hand
```

Pseudo Code for the Identify_Question_ At_Hand Subprocess

When the Identify_Question_At_Hand subprocess runs, the first action is to generate a random integer between 1 and 3 for randomly selecting a form of the question to present to the user persona. As discussed previously, having Socrates Digital™ ask this question differently each time makes it more "natural" and "human-like" and improves the conversational interaction for the user persona.

In the investment example dialog, Socrates Digital™ selects the first form of the question and asks the user persona, "So, the question at hand is deciding whether to invest in the Rosebud Motel chain?" The CASE statement shows that this question generates from some beginning text concatenated with the string variable, Problem_Description. In our investment example dialog, Problem_Description holds the value "deciding whether to invest in the Rosebud Motel chain." In this pseudo-code, the "+" operator is the string concatenation operator. It knits together the strings "So, the question at hand is, " "deciding whether to invest in the Rosebud Motel chain," and "?," to create the question, "So, the question at hand is deciding whether to invest in the Rosebud Motel chain?"

In our investment example dialog, the user persona replies with "Yes."

Figure 5. Identify Decision-Making Concept is the Second Subprocess in the Investment Process

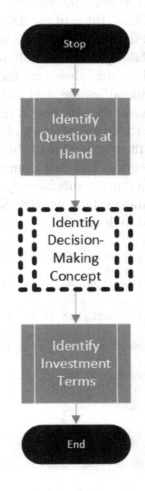

This answer is assigned to the User_Response variable. Next, the Problem_ Description is assigned to the Question variable. Afterward, the natural language processor is called and returns a "Yes" response from the user persona.

If something other than "Yes" is returned by the natural language processor, Socrates Digital™ will ask the user persona to provide the question at hand.

The last step for this subprocess is to save the value for the question at hand, provided by the user persona, to the Define_Problem_Table table in the database. Since the record's creation occurred earlier, it simply needs to be updated with the value for the Question_At_Hand field. The "UPDATE" command identifies the database table for the update, and the "SET" field command identifies the field to be updated. Together, these two commands will update the Question_At_Hand field with the value held in the Question variable in the Define_Problem_Table of the database.

Figure 5. highlights that the next subprocess in the Investments process is the "Identify Decision-Making Concept" subprocess.

Below is the pseudo-code of the subprocess Identify_Decision_Making_Concept. This subprocess identifies the decision-making concept that the user persona will use to answer the question at hand. The first comment in the subprocess tells us that the main category of Socratic Questioning that Socrates Digital™ will ask the user persona is in the "Questions that Target the Parts of Thinking" category. The first comment also tells us that the question for the user persona is in the subcategory of "Questioning Concepts and Ideas." The second comment tells us what Socrates Digital™ is after, identifying the concept used to decide.

```
/* Questions that Target the Parts of Thinking -- Questioning
Concepts and Ideas
/* Ask user persona to identify concept that will be used to
make the decision
BEGIN Subprocess Identify_Decision_Making_Concept

/* Generate a Random Number Between 1 and 3 - the Possible
Forms of the Question
RandomInteger:= GenerateRandomInteger[1,3]

/* Select a Form of the Question
    CASE RandomInteger OF
    1: Question:= "What is the main concept that you will use
to make your decision?"
    2: Question:= "To make your decision, what main concept
will you use?"
    3: Question:= "What concept will you apply to make the
decision?"
    END_CASE

OUTPUT Question
```

```
INPUT Answer

Description:= Answer

/* Call Subprocess Decision_Making_Concept_Questioning_
Relevance and Get Back an
/* Answer
Subprocess Decision_Making_Concept_Questioning_Relevance
(Answer)

Question_At_Hand:= Answer

/* Save Decision_Making_Concept_Description and
/* Decision_Making_Concept_Relates_Question_At_Hand to database
UPDATE Define_Problem_Table
SET
Decision_Making_Concept_Description:= Description
Decision_Making_Concept_Relates_Question_At_Hand:= Question_At_
Hand

WHERE Problem_Area = "Investments"  AND Session_ID = Current_
Session_ID

END Subprocess Identify_Decision_Making_Concept
```

Pseudo Code for the Identify_Decision_ Making_Concept Subprocess

Like the other subprocesses, when Identify_Decision_Making_Concept runs, the first action generates a random integer between 1 and 3 for randomly selecting a form to present the user persona. In our investment example dialog, the user persona asks, "What is the main concept you will use to make your decision?"

The user persona responded, "We need to know if the investment will boost total revenue enough to pay back the investors." This text is captured in the Answer variable with the INPUT command and stored in the Description.

Here is where the logic of our pseudo-code takes a detour from the previous subprocesses where Socrates Digital™ seeks more context around the user persona's answers. In this subprocess, Socrates Digital™ is looking for more context around the decision-making concept identified by the user persona. Specifically, Socrates Digital™ is looking for the relevance of the

117

user persona's answer. That is more information about how this concept will answer the question at hand – and be used to make the decision.

To get this information from the user persona, another subprocess, Decision_ Making_Concept_Questioning_Relevance, is called to gather this answer from the user persona. Obviously, another subprocess is not needed to gather this information from the user persona – the main subprocess could embed this code. However, as we will see shortly, it is a different kind of question that belongs to a different category of Socratic Questioning. Moreover, its focus is different. It targets the quality of reasoning and has a "natural" support role for Socratic Questioning that targets the parts of thinking.

After Decision_Making_Concept_Questioning_Relevance runs, the answer is assigned to the variable, Question_At_Hand.

This variable assignment takes us to the last step in this subprocess. This last step updates the Decision_Making_Concept_Description and the Decision_Making_Concept_Relates_Question_At_Hand fields in the Define_Problem_Table table of the database. As before, the "UPDATE" command identifies the database table for the update, and the "SET" field command identifies the fields to be updated. In this case, these two commands will update the fields Decision_Making_Concept_Description and Decision_ Making_Concept_Relates_Question_At_Hand in the Define_Problem_Table table of the database.

This update completes the Identify_Decision_Making_Concept subprocess, so we now return to the call to the Decision_Making_Concept_ Questioning_Relevance subprocess, which occurs about midway in the Identify_Decision_Making_Concept subprocess. The pseudo-code below documents this subprocess for questioning the relevance of the user persona's answer. The first comment in this subprocess tells us that the main category of Socratic Questioning that Socrates Digital™ will ask the user persona is in the "Questions that Target the Quality of Reasoning" category. More specifically, it is in the "Questioning Relevance" subcategory. The second comment tells us that this question about the quality of reasoning will ask about the relevance of the previous answer by the user persona.

```
/* Questions that Target the Quality of Reasoning --
Questioning Relevance

/* Generate Questioning Relevance question for user persona and
collect answer
BEGIN Subprocess Decision_Making_Concept_Questioning_Relevance
(Answer)
```

```
/* Generate a Random Number Between 1 and 3 - the Possible
Forms of the
/* Question
RandomInteger:= GenerateRandomInteger[1,3]

/* Select a Form of the Question
     CASE RandomInteger OF
     1: Question:= "How does it relate to the question at
hand?"
     2: Question:= "For the question at hand, how does it
relate?"
     3: Question:= "Can you tell me how it relates to the
question at hand?"
     END_CASE

OUTPUT Question

INPUT Answer

END Subprocess Decision_Making_Concept_Questioning_Relevance
```

Pseudo Code for the Decision_Making_Concept_Questioning_Relevance Subprocess

Note that this is a rather generic question that applies to many problem areas. From a software design perspective, it makes sense to place this code that asks this generic question in a subprocess that can be called by other subprocesses when asking this generic question in other contexts. This separation is good software design. However, it is more than that. This question relates to the relevance of a previous question that targeted the parts of thinking. In this case, it was a question from the subcategory of Questioning Concepts and Ideas. Placing these questions about the quality of reasoning in their own subprocesses separates them from the processes with questions that target the parts of thinking.

This separation of function is one of the design strengths of using a general-purpose programming language to implement Socrates Digital™ throughout this book. Appendix C shows an implementation of Socrates Digital™ in Microsoft's Power Virtual Agent, which provides for easy development, but does not support this separation of function between the two main categories of Socratic Questioning. Developers must embed all questions that target the quality of reasoning in the logic that presents the questions that target the parts of thinking.

As the other subprocesses, when Decision_Making_Concept_Questioning_ Relevance runs, the first action is to randomly select a form of the question for presentation to the user persona. In our investment example, Socrates Digital™ asked, "How does it relate to the question at hand?" To which the user persona replied: "We need to know if the investment will increase the total revenue for the Rosebud Motel chain so that it can repay the investment at the projected rate of return."

This user persona reply is stored in the variable answer and returned to the Identify_Decision_Making_Concept subprocess that stores the value in the database.

As highlighted in Figure 6, the third and last subprocess in the Investments process is the Identify Investment Terms subprocess.

The pseudo-code for the Identify_Investment_Terms subprocess is listed below. The first comment tells us that this subprocess presents a question from the subcategory, "Questioning Questions," that will get permission from the user persona for answering upcoming questions in the "Questions that Target the Parts of Thinking" main category. As the second comment tells us, its primary purpose is to "Ask the user persona to identify the investment terms." As we will see, the details of the investment terms need to be precise and clear, so this subprocess will call several subprocesses that ask the questions that will provide the precision and clarity needed in the user persona answers. As you might guess, these questions are answered with calls to subprocesses that target the quality of the user persona's answers.

```
/* Questions that Target the Parts of Thinking - Questioning
Questions
/* Ask user persona to identify investment terms
BEGIN Subprocess Identify_Investment_Terms

/* Generate a Random Number Between 1 and 3 - the Possible
Forms of the Question
RandomInteger:= GenerateRandomInteger[1,3]

/* Select a Form of the Question
    CASE RandomInteger OF
    1: Question:= "OK - are you ready to answer some questions
about the terms of the investment?"
    2: Question:= "How about answering questions about the
terms of the investment?"
    3: Question:= "Would you answer some questions about the
```

```
terms of the investment?"
    END_CASE

OUTPUT Question

INPUT Answer

User_Response:= Answer

/* Understood_Response will come back as "Yes" or "No"
Natural_Language_Processor (User_Response, Understood_Response)

/* If no, then give user persona a chance to correct the
question at hand
IF Understood_Response = "Yes" THEN

Rate_Of_Return_Questioning_Precision (Rate)
Investment_Amount_Questioning_Precision (Amount)
Investment_Repayment_Period_Questioning_Precision (Repay)
Investment_Purpose_Questioning_Precision (Purpose)

/* Save terms of investment to database
UPDATE Define_Problem_Table
SET
Rate_Of_Return_Questioning_Precision:= Rate
Investment_Amount_Questioning_Precision:= Amount
Investment_Repayment_Period_Questioning_Precision:= Repay
Investment_Purpose_Questioning_Precision:= Purpose

WHERE Problem_Area = "Investments"  AND Session_ID = Current_
Session_ID

ELSE

OUTPUT "OK, we will skip this for now."

END_IF

END Subprocess Identify_Investment_Terms
```

Pseudo Code for Identify_Investment_Terms Subprocess

As is our convention, when Identify_Investment_Terms runs, the first action
is to randomly select a form of the question presented to the user persona.
In our investment example dialog, the user persona asks, "What is the main
concept that you will use to make your decision?" The user persona agrees to

answer the questions by replying "Sure." This text is captured in the Answer variable with the INPUT command and stored in the User_Response variable.

Figure 6. Identify Investment Terms is the Third Subprocess in the Investment Process

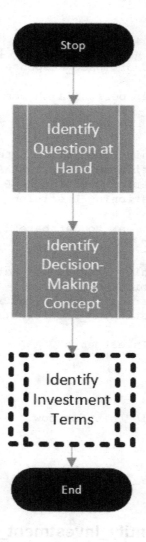

As we have seen before, the next step is to send this response by the user persona to the natural language processor. If the natural language processor identifies the user persona response as a "Yes," then it will go forward with the questions about the terms of investment. However, If the natural language processor identifies the user persona response as something other than "Yes," Socrates Digital™ outputs "OK, we will skip this for now" to the user persona.

In our investment example dialog, the user persona answered "Sure," – which the natural language processor identified as "Yes." In the next subprocess, Socrates Digital™ looks for values that define the investment terms given to the user persona. It turns out that there are four specific questions about the terms that need answers to define the investment terms. These four questions relate to the projected rate of return, investment amount, repayment period, and what the investment will be used for. Since these four questions request more information about the investment terms, separate subprocesses that target the quality of reasoning present them and return the answers to the subprocess Identify_Investment_Terms. As we will see, three of these subprocesses will relate to "precision," and one will relate to the "clarity" of the investment terms. Note that these questions are specific to the problem area of investments. However, the naming convention for the subprocesses illustrates that their names are a combination of the specific term they address and the category of Socratic Questioning in which they belong.

As the pseudo-code for Identify_Investment_Terms shows, the first subprocess that seeks an answer with precision is Rate_Of_Return_Questioning_Precision, which asks about the projected rate of return on the investment. The second subprocess, Investment_Amount_Questioning_Precision, seeks a precise answer about the amount required for the investment. The third subprocess, Investment_Repayment_Period_Questioning_Precision (and perhaps the longest subprocess name in history), seeks a precise answer about the period for repayment of the investment. Finally, the fourth subprocess, Investment_Purpose_Questioning_Precision, seeks an answer that clarifies the purpose of the investment – or, better said, what it will be used for.

Note that each of these subprocesses that focus on the quality of reasoning is specific to the problem area of investments and ensures that they capture the details needed to describe the terms of investment completely. Other problem areas may require more questions and follow-up questions to ensure that Socrates Digital™ has the details needed to define the problem the user persona is trying to solve.

After these four subprocesses have returned answers from the user persona, the Identify_Investment_Terms subprocess goes to the last step. In this step, the UPDATE and SET commands update the Rate_Of_Return_Questioning_Precision,

Investment_Amount_Questioning_Precision, Investment_Repayment_Period_Questioning_Precision, and the Investment_Purpose_Questioning_Precision fields in the Define_Problem_Table table of the database.

Below, lists the pseudo-code for three subprocesses related to the precision aspect of the quality of reasoning. The fourth subprocess also relates to the precision aspect of the quality of reasoning. As we will see, it also calls another subprocess that relates to the clarity aspect of the quality of reasoning.

```
/* Questions that Target the Quality of Reasoning --
Questioning Precision

/* Generate Questioning Precision question for user persona and
collect answer
BEGIN Subprocess Rate_Of_Return_Questioning_Precision (Answer)

Question:= "What is the projected rate of return?"

OUTPUT Question

INPUT Answer

END Subprocess Rate_Of_Return_Questioning_Precision


/* Questions that Target the Quality of Reasoning --
Questioning Precision

/* Generate Questioning Precision question for user persona and
collect answer
BEGIN Subprocess Investment_Amount_Questioning_Precision
(Answer)

Question:= "What is the investment amount?"

OUTPUT Question

INPUT Answer

END Subprocess Investment_Amount_Questioning_Precision


/* Questions that Target the Quality of Reasoning --
Questioning Precision

/* Generate Questioning Precision question for user persona and
collect answer
BEGIN Subprocess Investment_Repayment_Period_Questioning_
```

```
Precision (Answer)

Question:= "What is the repayment period?"

OUTPUT Question

INPUT Answer

END Subprocess Investment_Repayment_Period_Questioning_
Precision
```

Pseudo Code for Rate of Return, Investment Amount, and Repayment Period Subprocesses

The first subprocess, the Rate_Of_Return_Questioning_Precision subprocess, relates to precision in the quality of reasoning. We see this in the first comment, "Questions that Target the Quality of Reasoning -- Questioning Precision." Moreover, the second comment tells us that this question requires the user persona to provide precision in the answer about the rate of return. The user persona asks the question, "What is the projected rate of return?". The user persona's answer is captured in the Answer variable and returned to the subprocess that called it.

Note that only one form of the question is available to Socrates Digital™. This single option is a design decision. Since Socrates Digital™ only asks this question once a session, other forms of the question are not necessary for the user persona. As it must be evident, offering three forms of the question in the previous subprocesses is also a design choice. Three possible forms of the question were enough to make Socrates Digital™ questions seem more natural and human-like.

The second subprocess, the Investment_Amount_Questioning_Precision subprocess, also relates to the quality of reasoning. It shows in the first comment, "Questions that Target the Quality of Reasoning -- Questioning Precision." Moreover, as before, the second comment tells us that it will ask a question requiring the user persona to have precision about the investment amount. In our investment example dialog, Socrates Digital™ asks, "What is the investment amount?" To which the user persona replies, "$3,500,000." That would be three and one-half million dollars. As before, the user persona's answer is captured in the Answer variable and returned to the Identify_Investment_Terms subprocess.

The third subprocess, the Investment_Repayment_Period_Questioning_ Precision, subprocess, also relates to the quality of reasoning. (Sorry, subprocess names will not get any longer than this in this book.) The first comment tells us that this question belongs to a now-familiar main Socratic Questioning category, "Questions that Target the Quality of Reasoning," and is in the subcategory of "Questioning Precision." Furthermore, as is our convention, the second comment tells us that the purpose of this question is to collect an answer about how long it will take to recover the investment. In our investment example dialog, Socrates Digital™ asks, "What is the repayment period?" This question prompts the user persona to reply, "Five years." In what now is our familiar coding pattern, the user persona's answer is captured in the Answer variable and returned to the Identify_Investment_Terms subprocess.

The fourth subprocess has a little more logic in it than the other three subprocesses. That is because the conversation designer decided that the user persona would require a detailed answer to what the investment would be used for. Below is how this plays out in the pseudo-code.

When called, the fourth subprocess, Investment_Purpose_Questioning_ Precision, starts like the other three subprocesses. The first comment tells us that the question it will ask belongs to the main category of "Questions that Target the Quality of Reasoning" and subcategory "Questioning Precision." Furthermore, the second comment tells us that this question will require a precise answer about what the investment funds will be used for. In our investment example dialog, Socrates Digital™ asks the user persona, "What will the investment be used for?" To which, the user persona replies, "It will fund motel renovations and promotional services." The handling of the answer is different from the other three subprocesses we have examined.

```
/* Questions that Target the Quality of Reasoning --
Questioning Precision

/* Generate Questioning Precision question for user persona and
collect answer
BEGIN Subprocess Investment_Purpose_Questioning_Precision
(Answer)

Question:= "What will the investment be used for?"

OUTPUT Question
INPUT Answer

IF answer < 100 Characters THEN
Investment_Purpose_Questioning_Clarity (Clarified_Answer)
```

```
Answer:= Clarified_Answer
END_IF

END Subprocess Investment_Purpose_Questioning_Precision


/* Questions that Target the Quality of Reasoning --
Questioning Clarity

/* Generate Questioning Precision question for user persona and
collect answer
BEGIN Subprocess Investment_Purpose_Questioning_Clarity
(Answer)

Question:= "Could you elaborate further about what the
investment will be used for?"

OUTPUT Question

INPUT Answer

END Subprocess Investment_Purpose_Questioning_Clarity
```

Pseudo Code for the Investment Purpose Questioning Precision Subprocess

This fourth subprocess is different because the designer wanted to ensure that the answer for this critical question is precise and detailed enough to have clarity. The designer put in code to check if the answer was long enough to ensure it had clarity. If the answer was less than 100 characters, then another subprocess, Investment_Purpose_Questioning_Clarity, is called a follow-up question to clarify the first answer about what the investment would be used for. Note that this simplistic approach to test for clarity is replaceable by more sophisticated methods – such as text analysis – to evaluate the quality of the answer.

Note that the first comment in the subprocess, Investment_Purpose_ Questioning_Clarity, called to ensure clarity in the answer, tells us that it is "Questions that Target the Quality of Reasoning -- Questioning Clarity." The second comment tells us that this question will require a clarifying answer about what the investment funds will be used for. As seen in the other subprocesses, the user persona's answer is captured in the Answer variable and returned to the Investment_Purpose_Questioning_Precision subprocess.

With this additional question about clarity, the final answer for this critical question about the investment is precise and detailed enough to have clarity. This last step concludes the Identify_Investment_Terms process.

Figure 7 shows the Identify Vested Interest subprocess of the Define Problem process. This last subprocess of the Define Problem process asks the user persona about any vested interests in the investment opportunity under examination.

Figure 7. The Identify Vested Interest Subprocess of the Define Problem Process

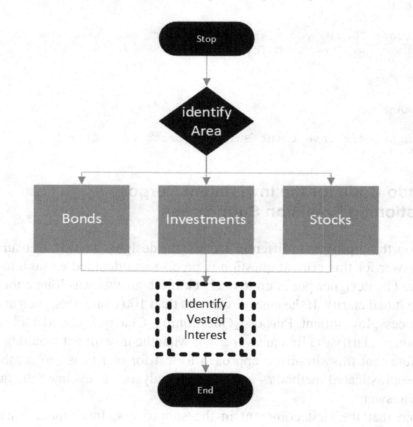

The pseudo-code for the Identify_Vested_Interest subprocess is listed below. The first comment in this subprocess, "Questions that Target the Parts of Thinking – Questioning Goals and Purposes," tells us that the question belongs to the main Socratic Questioning category about the parts of thinking. It also tells us that the subcategory is about questioning the goals and purposes of the user persona. The second comment tells us that this question will require the user persona to identify any vested interests in the business opportunity under examination.

Note that this subprocess does not ask any questions – it calls Vested_ Interest_Questioning_Fairness to ask its only question. Note that the Identfy_Vested_Interest subprocess could ask this question. However, we are following our established convention where Socrates Digital™ initially calls a subprocess that asks a question related to the main Socrates Questioning category to target the parts of thinking. This subprocess then calls other subprocesses related to the other main Socrates Questioning category that target the quality of reasoning. In our investment example dialog, Socrates Digital™ asks, "Before we get started, do you have vested interest in the question at hand? For example, you would have a vested interest in this business opportunity if the Rosebud Motel was owned by one of your relatives." To which the user persona answers, "No, I do not have a vested interest." Suppose more clarity, accuracy, precision – or any other aspect relating to the quality of reasoning were needed to ensure a satisfying answer. In that case, other additional subprocesses that target the quality of reasoning can ask follow-up questions. This convention of initially asking questions that target the parts of thinking – and using follow-up questions that target the quality of reasoning -- will ensure that the user persona's answers will be descriptive and comprehensive.

```
/* Questions that Target the Parts of Thinking – Questioning
Goals and Purposes
/* Ask user persona to identify any vested interests
BEGIN Subprocess Identify_Vested_Interest

Vested_Interest_Questioning_Fairness (Answer)

Vested_Interest_Questioning_Fairness:= Vested_Interest_
Questioning_Fairness

/* Save terms of investment to database
UPDATE Define_Problem_Table
SET
Vested_Interest_Questioning_Fairness:= Vested_Interest_
Questioning_Fairness

WHERE Problem_Area = "Investments"  AND Session_ID = Current_
Session_ID

END Subprocess Identify_Vested_Interest
```

```
/* Questions that Target the Quality of Reasoning --
Questioning Fairness

/* Ask Questioning Fairness question about vested interest of
user persona and collect answer
BEGIN Subprocess Vested_Interest_Questioning_Fairness (Answer)

Question:= "Before we get started, do you have vested interest
in the question at hand?  For example, you would have a vested
interest in this business opportunity if the Rosebud Motel were
owned by one of your relatives."

OUTPUT Question

INPUT Answer

END Subprocess Vested_Interest_Questioning_Fairness
```

Pseudo Code for Identify_Vested_Interest Subprocess

After Identify_Vested_Interest calls Vested_Interest_Questioning_Fairness to ask its only question, it uses the UPDATE and SET commands to update the Vested_Interest_Questioning_Fairness field in the Define_Problem_Table table of the database.

When the Vested_Interest_Questioning_Fairness subprocess runs, the first comment in this subprocess, "Questions that Target the Quality of Reasoning -- Questioning Fairness," tells us that the question belongs to the Socratic Questioning category about the quality of reasoning. It also tells us that the subcategory is about questioning fairness. The second comment tells us that this question will require an answer to this vested interest question. As is the convention with these subprocesses, the user persona's answer is captured in the Answer variable and returned to the Identify_Vested_Interest subprocess. This last step concludes the Identify_Vested_Interest subprocess, and consequently, the Define Problem process.

SUMMARY

In this chapter, we see that the first process that the Socrates Digital™ module calls is the "Define Problem" process. This process identifies the problem area, and the user persona provides the problem-defining information. Again, we use the investment example dialog in this chapter to show how the Define Problem process collects this information. Since this example is on reasoning about investments, the Define Problem process identifies what type of investment it is, the financial details of the investment, and whether the user group has any vested interest in the investment.

We also see in this chapter that pseudo-code describes the operation of the subprocesses that make up the processes for Socrates Digital™. The pseudo-code provides readers with enough detail to implement the logic presented in any procedural and general-purpose computer programming language. However, no-code options for providing much of this logic are available from artificial intelligence service providers, including Apple, Microsoft, Google, IBM, and Amazon. Developers can use the pseudo code provided in this book to implement the parts they choose in a general programming language.

In this chapter, we see that Socrates Digital™ needs more answers from the user persona after asking a question that targets the parts of thinking in many situations. The questions aimed at getting these answers are questions that target reasoning.

These are generic questions that apply to many problem areas. From a software design perspective, it makes sense to place the code that asks this generic question in a subprocess that can be called by other subprocesses when asking this generic question in other contexts. This separation is good software design. Placing these questions about the quality of reasoning in their own subprocesses separates them from the processes with questions that target the parts of thinking.

This separation of function is one of the design strengths of using a general-purpose programming language to implement Socrates Digital™ throughout this book. This chapter notes that no-code options for developing Socrates Digital™ applications are available from artificial intelligence service providers, including Apple, Microsoft, Google, IBM, and Amazon. However, they do not typically support this separation of function between the two main categories of Socratic Questioning.

Appendix C shows an implementation of Socrates Digital™ in Demo of Microsoft's Power Virtual Agent, which provides for easy development, but does not support this separation of function between the two main categories of Socratic Questioning. Developers must embed all questions that target the quality of reasoning in the logic that presents the questions that target the parts of thinking.

Finally, selecting a database as the external storage for session data with the investment example dialog simplified things. However, Socrates Digital™ can use other external storage choices. For example, it can use Microsoft's SharePoint, a spreadsheet, external files, or a business intelligence platform for external storage.

Chapter 7
Information, Assumptions, and Concepts:
Forming the Basis for Conclusions

ABSTRACT

This chapter shows the interrelationships between the processes to analyze information, identify assumptions, or apply concepts. This chapter uses an example to show how Socrates Digital™ examines the assumptions and the information they rest on simultaneously. If the user begins with analyzing information, then Socrates Digital™ asks the user to provide a data item that is relevant to the analysis. Next, it asks the user to identify the underlying assumptions used to analyze the data. After identifying the assumptions, Socrates Digital™ asks for the evidence that the assumption holds for a larger dataset.

INTRODUCTION

As demonstrated in the investment example dialog in Chapter 3, the user persona can analyze information, identify assumptions, or apply concepts in any order. For example, when the user persona begins by analyzing information, Socrates Digital™ asks the user persona to provide a data item that is relevant to the analysis. Next, Socrates Digital™ will ask what assumption underlies the selection of that data item. Socrates Digital™ will also follow up and ask for evidence that the assumption holds for a larger dataset. After showing

DOI: 10.4018/978-1-7998-7955-8.ch007

that the assumption does hold for a larger dataset, Socrates Digital™ asks the user persona what concepts to apply. Alternatively, the user persona can begin by identifying assumptions or applying concepts, and next choose one of the two remaining options – then go on to the last one.

WHAT TO WORK ON? DECISION PROCESS

As Figure 1 highlights, the next module after the Define Problem process in the Socrates Digital™ module is the "What to Work On?" decision process. This process is where Socrates Digital™ asks the user persona what to work on next. As the names of the modules show, the choices are to Analyze Information, Identify Assumptions, or Apply Concepts.

The pseudo-code for the What to Work On? decision process is listed below. The first comment states that the question asked by Socrates Digital™ of the user persona belongs to one of the two main categories of Socratic Questions called "Questions that Target the Parts of Thinking." The second part of this first comment, "Questioning Goals and Purposes," tells us that the question belongs to the subcategory of Socratic Questions to determine the goal, or purpose, of user persona.

```
/* Questions that Target the Parts of Thinking -- Questioning
Goals and Purposes

/* Ask user persona to what to work on - information,
assumptions, or concepts
BEGIN Subprocess What_To_Work_On

/* Generate a Random Number Between 1 and 3 - the Possible
Forms of the Question
RandomInteger:= GenerateRandomInteger[1,3]

/* Select a Form of the Question
    CASE RandomInteger OF
    1: Question:= "OK, of the following, what would you like
to work on?"
    2: Question:= "What do you want to work on from this
list?"
    3: Question:= "Given these options, what do you want to
work on?"
    END_CASE

OUTPUT Question
```

Figure 1. What to Work On? Decision Process in Socrates Digital™

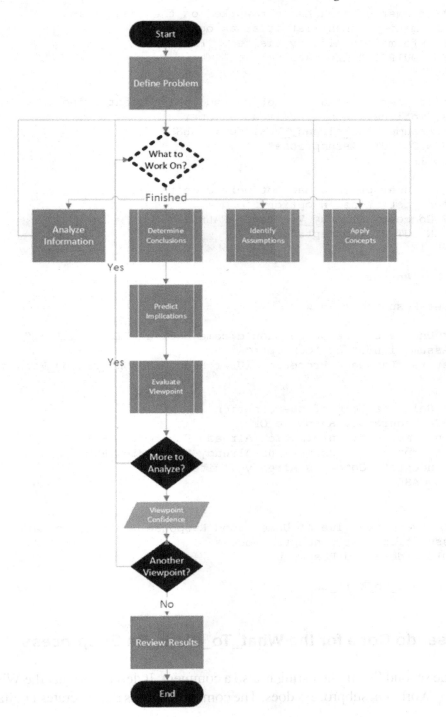

```
/* If user persona has not worked on the identifying
information, then list it as an option
IF Information_Already_Visited = FALSE
THEN OUTPUT "Information"
END_IF

/* If user persona has not worked on the identifying
assumptions, then list it as an option
IF Assumptions_Already_Visited = FALSE
THEN OUTPUT "Assumptions"
END_IF

/* If user persona has not worked on the identifying concepts,
then list it as an option
IF Concepts_Already_Visited = FALSE
THEN OUTPUT "Concepts"
END_IF

INPUT Answer

User_Response:= Answer

/* Understood_Response should come back as "Information,"
"Assumptions," or "Concepts"
Natural_Language_Processor (User_Response, Understood_Response)


/* Select a Form of the Question
CASE Understood_Response OF
"Information": Information_Already_Visited:= TRUE
"Assumptions": Assumptions_Already_Visited:= TRUE
"Concepts": Concepts_Already_Visited:= TRUE
END_CASE


/* Given the value of Understood_Response, go to information,
assumptions, or concepts process
GOTO Understood_Response

END What_To_Work_On
```

Pseudo Code for the What_To_Work_On Subprocess

The second line in the listing is also a comment. It describes what the What_To_Work_On subprocess does. The comment tells us that Socrates Digital™

will ask the user persona what to work on next – information, assumptions, or concepts.

When What_To_Work_On runs, the first action is to call a function, GenerateRandomInteger, to generate a random integer between 1 and 3 to randomly select a form of the question to present to the user persona. Right after this is output, Socrates Digital™ follows with a list of options for the user persona. In our investment example dialog, we see that the first time What_To_Work_On executes, it produces the following list of items:

- *Information*
- *Assumptions*
- *Concepts*

Three Boolean variables -- Information_Already_Visited, Assumptions_Already_Visited, and Concepts_Already_Visited -- determine which items are displayed. If they have a value of FALSE, they are displayed. Otherwise, they have a value of TRUE and are not displayed.

In one of the times our investment example dialog is run, the user persona replies with, "Information." The natural language processor returns this as "Information" and assigns the value to the string variable "Understood_Response." The GOTO statement evaluates Understood_Response and directs control to the Analyze_Information subprocess.

The last instruction in the What_To_Work_On subprocess evaluates Understood_Response in a CASE statement, then assigns the value "TRUE" to the Boolean variable indicating the choice by the user persona. In our investment example, the value of Information_Already_Visited becomes TRUE – meaning that next time it will not be listed as an option.

ANALYZE INFORMATION PROCESS

Figure 7.2 highlights that one of the processes that the user persona can select is the "Analyze Information" process. This process generates questions about information, data, and experience for the user persona. Afterward, Socrates Digital™ asks the user persona to evaluate information, data, and experience related to the question at hand.

Figure 2. The Analyze Information Process of the Socrates Digital™ Module

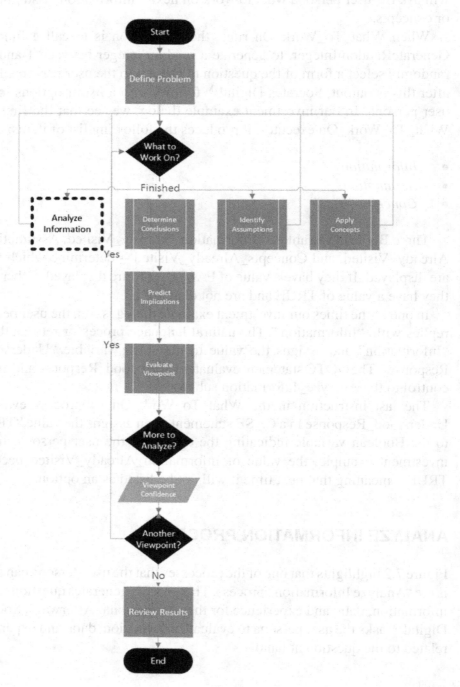

Figure 3 shows the inner workings of the Analyze Information process. The first subprocess highlighted in Figure 3, Identify Information, asks the user persona to identify the information to be analyzed. Next, the Identify Assumption subprocess asks the user persona to identify any underlying assumption used to analyze the information. Then, the third step, Analyze Dataset subprocess, asks the user persona if the assumption holds after analysis of the larger dataset.

Figure 3. The Identify Information Subprocess is First in the Analyze Information Process

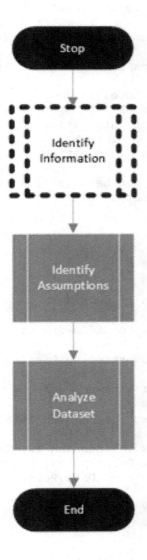

The pseudo-code for the "Identify Information" subprocess is listed below. The first comment states that the question asked by Socrates Digital™ belongs to one of the main categories of Socratic Questions called Questions that Target the Parts of Thinking. The second part of this first comment, Information, Data, and Experience, tells us that the question belongs to a subcategory of Socratic Questions to question the user persona about information, data, and experience.

```
/* Questions that Target the Parts of Thinking - Information,
Data, and Experience
/* Ask user persona to Identify Information for Analysis
BEGIN Subprocess Identify_Information

/* Generate a Random Number Between 1 and 3 - the Possible
Forms of the Question
RandomInteger:= GenerateRandomInteger[1,3]

/* Select a Form of the Question
    CASE RandomInteger OF
    1: Question:= "What information, data, or experience do
you have that supports or informs this analysis?"
    2: Question:= "What information, data, or experience do
you have?"
    3: Question:= "Do you have information, data, or
experience that illustrates this?"
    END_CASE

OUTPUT Question

INPUT Answer

Information_Description:= Answer

/* Call Subprocess Data_Point_Questioning_Clarity and Get Back
an Answer
Subprocess Data_Point_Questioning_Clarity (Answer)

Data_Point_Description:= Answer

/* Save Information_Description  and Data_Point_Description  in
database
INSERT INTO Datasets_Table (Session_ID, Information_
Description, Data_Point_Description) VALUES (Current_Session_
ID, Information_Description, Data_Point_Description)

END Subprocess Identify_Information
```

```
/* Questions that Target the Quality of Reasoning --
Questioning Clarity

/* Generate Questioning Clarity question for user persona and
collect answer
BEGIN Subprocess Data_Point_Questioning_Clarity (Answer)

/* Generate a Random Number Between 1 and 3 - the Possible
Forms of the
/* Question
RandomInteger:= GenerateRandomInteger[1,3]

/* Select a Form of the Question
    CASE RandomInteger OF
    1: Question:= "Can you give me an example data point about
this?"
    2: Question:= "Can you provide an example data point that
shows this?"
    3: Question:= "Do you have an example data item that
illustrates this?"
    END_CASE

OUTPUT Question

INPUT Answer

END Subprocess Data_Point_Questioning_Clarity
```

Pseudo Code for the Identify Information Process

The second comment describes what the Identify_Information subprocess does. It tells us that it asks the user persona to identify information to be analyzed.

As introduced last chapter, when Identify_Information runs, the first action is to call GenerateRandomInteger to generate a random integer between 1 and 3. This random integer randomly selects a form of the question to present to the user persona.

In the investment example dialog, Socrates Digital™ generates the value 1 for the random integer and selects the first form of the question. Socrates Digital™ uses this form to ask the user persona, "What information, data, or experience do you have that supports or informs this analysis?" The first time the user persona answers this question in the conversation, with this reply, "I have spreadsheet data on occupancy rates and revenue for the Rosebud Motel chain." The user persona's answer is assigned to the Information_Description variable.

Now that Socrates Digital™ has a description for the information analyzed, the next call is to a subprocess that will get some more detail, or clarity, for this information. This subprocess is the Data_Point_Questioning_Clarity subprocess.

As seen in the pseudo-code for the Data_Point_Questioning_Clarity subprocess above, the first line of this listing is a comment. It tells that the question belongs to one of the two main categories of Socratic Questions called Questions that Target the Quality of Reasoning. The remaining part of this first comment tells us that the question asked of the user persona is in the subcategory of Questioning Clarity. This subcategory of Socratic Questions focuses on clarifying or adding detail to the previous answer given by the user persona about the information that will be analyzed.

As with the other subprocesses, when Data_Point_Questioning_Clarity runs, the first action is to generate a random integer between 1 and 3 and use it to randomly select a form of the question to present to the user persona. Socrates Digital™ selects and presents the following question to the user persona in our investment example dialog: "Can you give me an example data point about this?" To which the user persona replies, "As the spreadsheet shows, the Dundalk Inn & Suites motel has low occupancy rates and low total revenue." This reply is assigned to the variable Answer and returned to the Identify_Information subprocess, where it is assigned to the variable Data_Point_Description.

Given the investment problem area, the designer of the Identify_Information subprocess decided to include a question from the subcategory Questioning Clarity from the main category of Questions that Target the Quality of Reasoning. After determining that other questions from the main category were needed to ensure the quality of reasoning, they can be added and similarly called from the Identify_Information subprocess.

In the last step of the Identify_Information subprocess, the INSERT updates the Information_Description, Data_Point_Description in the Datasets Table table of the database.

IDENTIFY ASSUMPTIONS SUBPROCESS

As Figure 4 highlights, the next step in the Analyze Information process is the Identify Assumptions subprocess.

As discussed in Chapter 5 and shown in Figure 5, the user persona can analyze information, assumptions, and concepts in any order. However, examining assumptions and the information they rest on happens at the same time. When the Analyze Information process runs, it asks the user persona

Figure 4. The Identify Assumptions Subprocess is the Second Step in the Analyze Information Process

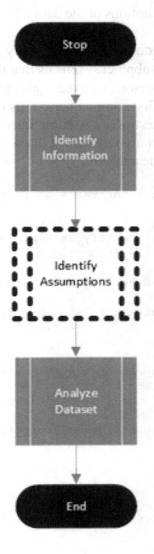

to provide an example of relevant data for the analysis. Then it asks about the underlying assumptions of the data. When the Identify Assumptions subprocess runs, it asks the user persona to identify its assumptions and then asks for information that reinforces the assumption. Figure 5 shows that the same logic shown in the Identify Assumption subprocess of Figure 4 can be accessed directly without going first to the Analyze Information process. If the Identify Assumptions subprocess is accessed directly from the What_To_Work_On? subprocess, then, later, Socrates Digital™ does not ask about the underlying assumptions of the data when the Analyze Information process runs.

Listed below is the pseudo-code for the Identify_Assumptions subprocess. The first comment in the subprocess tells us that the question which system persona will ask the user persona is in the "Questions that Target the Parts of Thinking" category. The first comment also tells us that the question for the user persona is in the "Questioning Assumptions" subcategory. The second comment tells us what Socrates Digital™ will ask the user persona to identify the assumption used for the analysis.

```
/* Questions that Target the Parts of Thinking -- Questioning
Assumptions

/* Ask user persona to Identify assumption for analysis
BEGIN Subprocess Identify_Assumptions

/* Generate a Random Number Between 1 and 3 - the Possible
Forms of the Question
RandomInteger:= GenerateRandomInteger[1,3]

/* Select a Form of the Question
     CASE RandomInteger OF
     1: Question:= "Do any of the following assumptions
underlie this observation?"
     2: Question:= "Of the following assumptions, do any
underly this observation?"
     3: Question:= "Any of these assumptions underlie this
observation?"
     END_CASE

OUTPUT Question

/* Display assumptions from the database for this session
SELECT Assumption_Description,
FROM Assumptions_Table
WHERE  Problem_Area = "Investments"
```

Figure 5. The Identify Assumptions Subprocess of the Socrates Digital™ Module

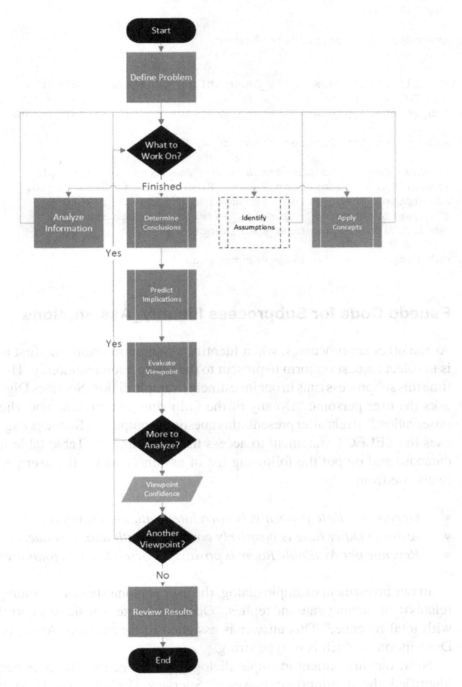

```
INPUT Answer

Assumption_Description:= Answer


/* Call Subprocess Apply_Assumptions_Questioning_Significance
and Get an Answer
Subprocess Apply_Assumptions_Questioning_Significance (Answer)

Assumption_Confidence:= Answer

/* Save Answer to Current Session Assumptions Description
INSERT INTO Assumptions_Table (Problem_Area, Session_ID,
Assumption_Description, Assumption_Confidence) VALUES
("Investment_Motel", Current_Session_ID, Assumption_
Description, Assumption_Confidence)

END Subprocess Identify_Assumptions
```

Psuedo Code for Subprocess Identify_Assumptions

As the other subprocesses, when Identify_Assumption runs, the first action is to select a question form to present to the user persona randomly. The first time this subprocess runs in our investment example dialog, Socrates Digital™ asks the user persona: "Do any of the following assumptions underlie this observation?" Right after presents this question is outputted, Socrates Digital™ uses the SELECT statement to access the Assumptions_Table table in the database and output the following list of assumptions for the user persona to choose from:

- *Occupancy Rate is positively correlated with total revenue.*
- *Average Daily Rate is positively correlated with total revenue.*
- *Revenue per Available Room is positively correlated with total revenue.*

In our investment example dialog, the user persona states the assumption relates to occupancy rate and replies, "Occupancy rate is positively correlated with total revenue." This answer is assigned to the variable Assumption_ Description – which is of type string.

Now, our investment example dialog switches gears. The user persona identified the assumption; however, Socrates Digital™ needs to know how significant this assumption is for later generating a conclusion. To determine the significance of the assumption, Socrates Digital™ calls the Apply_Assumptions_Questioning_Significance subprocess. This subprocess returns the user persona's evaluation of the significance of the assumption and stores it in the variable Assumption_Confidence – which is of type decimal.

The last step for the Identify_Assumptions process updates the Assumption_ Description and Assumption_Confidence in the Assumptions_Table table of the database with the INSERT command.

```
/* Questions that Target the Quality of Reasoning --
Questioning Significance
/* Generate Questioning Significance question for user persona
and collect answer
BEGIN Subprocess Apply_Assumptions_Questioning_Significance
(Answer)

/* Generate a Random Number Between 1 and 3 - the Possible
Forms of the Question
RandomInteger:= GenerateRandomInteger[1,3]

/* Select a Form of the Question
     CASE RandomInteger OF
     1: Question:= "Do you want to apply this assumption in
your reasoning?"
     2: Question:= "Is this the assumption you want to use
right now?"
     3: Question:= "Do you want to apply this assumption for
your thinking on this?"
     END_CASE

OUTPUT Question

OUTPUT
"Definitely Apply It
  Probably Apply It
  Maybe Apply it
  Disregard It for Now
  Delete It"

INPUT User_Response

Natural_Language_Processor (User_Response, Understood_Response)

CASE Understood_Response OF

Definitely Apply It:  Answer: = 0.75
Probably Apply It:  Answer: = 0.5
Maybe Apply it: Answer: = 0
```

```
Disregard It for Now: Answer: =    -0.5
Delete It: Answer: = -0.75

END_CASE

END Subprocess Apply_Assumptions_Questioning_Significance
```

Pseudo Code for Apply_Assumptions_ Questioning_Significance Subprocess

Listed above is the pseudo-code for the Apply_Assumptions_Questioning_ Significance subprocess. The first comment tells us that the question belongs to the main category of Socratic Questions called Questions that Target the Quality of Reasoning. The remaining part of this first comment tells us that the question asked of the user persona is in the subcategory of Questioning Significance. This subcategory of Socratic Questions focuses on the significance, or importance, of the previous answer given by the user persona about the assumption.

As is our convention, when Apply_Assumptions_Questioning_Significance runs, the first action randomly selects a form of the question to present to the user persona. In the first call of this subprocess in our investment example dialog, Socrates Digital™ asks, "Do you want to apply this assumption in your reasoning?" It follows this question with the below list of options to indicate the significance, or importance, of this assumption for analyzing the information:

- *Definitely Apply It*
- *Probably Apply It*
- *Maybe Apply it*
- *Disregard It for Now*
- *Delete It*

In our investment example dialog, the user persona answers, "Probably keep it," – which is stored in the variable User_Response and passed to the natural language processor matches to one of those responses presented in the list. In our investment example dialog, the user persona's answer matched the "Probably Apply it" option, and the Answer variable was assigned the decimal value 0.5 and returned to the subprocess Identify_Assumption.

As highlighted in Figure 6, the Analyze Dataset subprocess is the third step in the Analyze Information process.

The pseudo-code for the Analyze_Dataset subprocess is listed below. The first comment in the subprocess tells us that the question asked is in the Questions that Target the Parts of Thinking category. The first comment also tells us that the question for the user persona is in the Questioning

Figure 6. The Analyze Dataset Subprocess is the Third Step in the Analyze Information Process

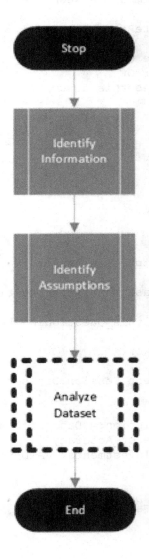

Information, Data, and Experience subcategory. The second comment tells us what Socrates Digital™ will ask the user persona if the assumption holds for the larger dataset.

```
/* Questions that Target the Parts of Thinking -- Questioning
Information, Data, and Experience

/* Ask user persona If Assumption Holds for Larger Dataset
BEGIN Subprocess Analyze_Dataset

/* Generate a Random Number Between 1 and 3 - the Possible
Forms of the Question
RandomInteger:= GenerateRandomInteger[1,3]

/* Select a Form of the Question
    CASE RandomInteger OF
    1: Question:= "Does this assumption hold for the larger
dataset?"
    2: Question:= "For the larger dataset, does this
assumption hold?"
    3: Question:= "Is this assumption true for the larger
dataset?"
    END_CASE

OUTPUT Question

INPUT Answer

Dataset_Analysis_Description:= Answer

/* Call Subprocess Dataset_Analysis_Questioning_Accuracy and
Get an Answer
Subprocess Dataset_Analysis_Questioning_Accuracy (Answer)

Dataset_Accuracy:= Answer

/* Save Answer to Current Session Datasets Description
UPDATE Datasets_Table
SET
Dataset_Analysis_Description:= Dataset_Analysis_Description
Dataset_Accuracy:= Dataset_Accuracy
WHERE Problem_Area = "Investments"  AND Session_ID = Current_
Session_ID

END Subprocess Analyze_Dataset
```

Pseudo Code for the Analyze_Dataset Subprocess

When the Analyze_Dataset subprocess runs, the first action randomly selects a form of the question to present to the user persona. In the first call of this subprocess in our investment example dialog, Socrates Digital™ asks the user persona: "Does this assumption hold for the larger dataset?" To which, the user persona replies: "Yes. As the spreadsheet scatterplot shows, the Rosebud Motel chain occupancy rate is positively correlated with total revenue." This response is assigned to the Dataset_Analysis_Description string variable.

The next step in this subprocess is to call another subprocess, Dataset_Analysis_Questioning_Accuracy. This subprocess aims to have the user persona rate the accuracy of the information in the larger dataset. That rating is returned as a decimal number to Analyze_Dataset and assigned to the variable Dataset_Accuracy.

After Analyze_Dataset calls Dataset_Analysis_Questioning_Accuracy to ask its only question, it uses the UPDATE and SET commands to update the Analyze_Dataset and Dataset_Analysis_Questioning_Accuracy fields in the Datasets_Table table of the database.

```
/* Questions that Target the Quality of Reasoning --
Questioning Accuracy
BEGIN Subprocess Dataset_Analysis_Questioning_Accuracy (Answer)

/* Generate a Random Number Between 1 and 3 - the Possible
Forms of the
/* Question
RandomInteger:= GenerateRandomInteger[1,3]

/* Select a Form of the Question
    CASE RandomInteger OF
    1: Question:= "How would you rate the accuracy of this
information?"
    2: Question:= "How accurate is this information?"
    3: Question:= "This information - how accurate is it?"
    END_CASE

OUTPUT Question

OUTPUT
"Accurate
Probably Accurate
Unknown Accuracy
Probably Not Accurate
Inaccurate"
```

```
INPUT User_Response

Natural_Language_Processor (User_Response, Understood_Response)

CASE Understood_Response OF

Accurate:  Answer: = 0.75
Probably Accurate:  Answer: = 0.5
Unknown Accuracy: Answer: = 0
Probably Not Accurate: Answer: =    -0.5
Inaccurate: = -0.75

END_CASE

END Subprocess Dataset_Analysis_Questioning_Accuracy
```

Pseudo Code for Dataset_Analysis_ Questioning_Accuracy Subprocess

Listed above is the pseudo-code for the Dataset_Analysis_Questioning_ Accuracy subprocess. The first comment tells us that the question belongs to the main category of Socratic Questions called Questions that Target the Quality of Reasoning. The remaining part of this first comment tells us that the question asked of the user persona is in the subcategory of Questioning Accuracy. This subcategory of Socratic Questions focuses on the accuracy of the previous answer given by the user persona for upholding the assumption in the larger dataset.

When Dataset_Analysis_Questioning_Accuracy runs, the first action is to randomly select a form of the question to present to the user persona. In the first call of this subprocess in our investment example dialog, the user persona is asked, "How would you rate the accuracy of this information?" A list of options immediately follows for the user persona to indicate the accuracy of the information for upholding the assumption:

- *Accurate*
- *Probably Accurate*
- *Unknown Accuracy*
- *Probably Not Accurate*
- *Inaccurate*

In our investment example dialog, the user persona answers, "I think that it is probably accurate," – which is stored in the variable User_Response. This response is passed on to the natural language processor, matching it to one of the responses in the list. In our investment example dialog, it matched "Probably Accurate," and the Answer variable was assigned the decimal value 0.5 and returned to the subprocess Analyze_Dataset. This last step concludes the Analyze_Dataset subprocess and the Analyze Information Process.

APPLY CONCEPTS PROCESS

As Figure 7 highlights, one of the processes that the user persona can select is the "Apply Concepts" process. This process is where questions about concepts are generated and presented to the user persona. In response, Socrates Digital™ asks the user persona to identify concepts and evaluate them for answering the question at hand.

The pseudo-code for the Apply_Concepts subprocess is listed below. The first comment in the subprocess tells us that the question is in the Questions that Target the Parts of Thinking category. The first comment also tells us that the question for the user persona is in the Questioning Concepts subcategory. The second comment tells us what Socrates Digital™ will ask the user persona to identify the concept used to answer the question at hand.

```
/* Questions that Target the Parts of Thinking -- Questioning
Concepts

/* Ask user persona to apply concept for analysis
BEGIN Subprocess Apply_Concepts

/* Generate a Random Number Between 1 and 3 - the Possible
Forms of the Question
RandomInteger:= GenerateRandomInteger[1,3]

/* Select a Form of the Question
    CASE RandomInteger OF
    1: Question:= "Which concept do you want to use to explain
how to answer the question at hand? " + Question_At_Hand
    2: Question:= "Of the following, which do you want to use
to answer the question at hand? " + Question_At_Hand
    3: Question:= "Which concept do you want to use for this
question at hand? "+ Question_At_Hand
    END_CASE
```

Figure 7. The Apply Concepts Subprocess of the Socrates Digital™ Process

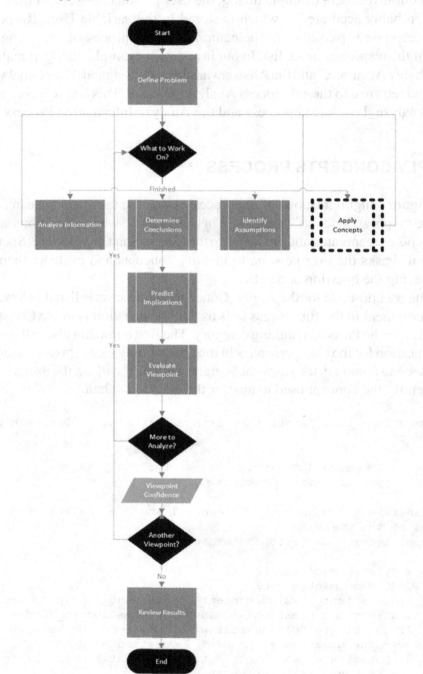

```
OUTPUT Question

/* Display concepts from the database for this session
SELECT Concept_Description,
FROM Concepts_Table
WHERE  Problem_Area = "Investments"

OUTPUT "Another Concept"

INPUT User_Response

Natural_Language_Processor (User_Response, Understood_Response)

Concept_Description:= Understood_Response

IF Concept_Description = "Another Concept" THEN
OUTPUT "What do you call this concept?"
INPUT User_Response
Natural_Language_Processor (User_Response, Understood_Response
Concept_Description:= Understood_Response
END_IF


/* Call Subprocess Apply_Concepts_Questioning_Significance and
Get an Answer
Subprocess Apply_Concepts_Questioning_Significance (Answer)

Concept_Strength:= Answer

/* Save Answer to Current Session Concepts Description
INSERT INTO Concepts_Table (Problem_Area, Session_ID, Concept_
Description, Concept_Strength) VALUES ("Investment_Motel",
Current_Session_ID, Concept_Description, Concept_Strength)

END Subprocess Apply_Concepts
```

Pseudo Code for Subprocess Apply_Concepts

As the other subprocesses, when calling Apply_Concepts, the first action is to randomly select a form of the question to present to the user persona. In the first call of this subprocess in our investment example dialog, the user persona is asked: "Which concept do you want to use to explain how to answer the question at hand? We need to know if the investment will boost total revenue enough to pay back the investors." Right after asking this question, Socrates

Digital™ outputs the following list of assumptions for the user persona to choose from:

- *Occupancy Rate – a measure of the percentage of total rooms rented*
- *Average Daily Rate – a measure of average room price*
- *Revenue per Available Room – a measure of average room price, including vacant rooms*
- *Another Concept*

In our investment example dialog, the user persona selects the concept about occupancy rate and replies, "Occupancy Rate." This answer is saved in the variable Concept_Description – which is of type string. If the user persona states, "Another concept," Socrates Digital™ asks for the concept's name, which is assigned to the variable Concept_Description.

In our investment example dialog, the user persona identified the concept. Socrates Digital™, however, needs to know how important this concept is for generating a conclusion later. It calls the Apply_Concepts_Questioning_ Significance subprocess. This subprocess returns the user persona's evaluation of the concept's significance and stores it in the decimal variable Concept_ Strength.

In the last step for the subprocess Apply_Concepts, Socrates Digital™ updates the Concept_Description and Concept_Strength in the Concepts_Table table of the database with the INSERT command.

```
/* Questions that Target the Quality of Reasoning --
Questioning Significance
/* Generate Questioning Significance question for user persona
and collect answer
BEGIN Subprocess Apply_Concepts_Questioning_Significance
(Answer)

/* Generate a Random Number Between 1 and 3 - the Possible
Forms of the
/* Question
RandomInteger:= GenerateRandomInteger[1,3]

/* Select a Form of the Question
    CASE RandomInteger OF
    1: Question:= "How well does this concept explain how to
answer the question at hand?"
    2: Question:= "For the question at hand, how well does
this concept explain how to answer it?"
    3: Question:= "How well does it explain how to answer the
```

```
question at hand?"
    END_CASE

OUTPUT Question

OUTPUT
"Always Explains
  Mostly Explains
  Sometimes Explains
  Rarely Explains
  Never Explains"

INPUT User_Response

Natural_Language_Processor (User_Response, Understood_Response)

CASE Understood_Response OF

Always Explains:  Answer:  = 0.75
Mostly Explains:  Answer:  = 0.5
Sometimes Explains: Answer: = 0
Rarely Explains: Answer: =    -0.5
Never Explains: Answer = -0.75

END_CASE

END Subprocess Apply_Concepts_Questioning_Significance
```

Pseudo Code for the Apply_Concepts_Questioning_Significance Subprocess

The pseudo-code for the Apply_Concepts_Questioning_Significance subprocess is listed above. The first comment tells us that the question belongs to one of the two main categories of Socratic Questioning called Questions that Target the Quality of Reasoning. The remaining part of this first comment tells us that the question asked of the user persona is in the subcategory of Questioning Significance. This subcategory of Socratic Questions focuses on the significance, or importance, of the previous answer given by the user persona about the concept.

When Apply_Concepts_Questioning_Significance runs, the first action is to randomly select a form of the question to present to the user persona. In the first call of this subprocess in our investment example dialog, the user persona is asked, "How well does this concept explain how to answer the question at hand?" A list of options follows this question for the user persona to indicate the significance of this concept for answering the question at hand:

- *Always Explains*
- *Mostly Explains*
- *Sometimes Explains*
- *Rarely Explains*
- *Never Explains*

In our investment example dialog, the user persona answers, "Sometimes explains," – which is stored in the variable User_Response. This variable is passed to the natural language processor, which matches it to one of those responses presented in the list. In our investment example dialog, it matched easily with "Sometimes Explains," and the Answer variable was assigned the decimal value 0.0 and returned to the subprocess that called it -- Apply_Concepts.

SUMMARY

As demonstrated in the investment example dialog in Chapter 3, the user persona can analyze information, identify assumptions, or apply concepts in any order. However, as detailed in this chapter, assumptions and the information they rest on are examined simultaneously. Socrates Digital™ asks the user persona to provide a data item relevant to the analysis when the user persona begins analyzing information. Next, it asks the user persona to identify the underlying assumptions used to analyze the data. After identifying the assumption, Socrates Digital™ asks for evidence that the assumption holds for a larger dataset. When the user persona begins identifying assumptions, Socrates Digital™ does not ask about the underlying assumptions of the data when the user persona analyzes information. Similarly, when the user persona begins by applying concepts, the user persona can next choose to analyze information or identify assumptions. As we see in the next chapter, after the user persona has analyzed the information, identified the underlying assumptions, and applied the concepts, Socrates Digital™ will guide the user persona to form a conclusion.

Chapter 8
Conclusions, Implications, and Viewpoints:
Creating a Point of View for Solving a Problem

ABSTRACT

This chapter shows how users can use Socrates Digital™ to analyze information, identify assumptions, and apply concepts to determine conclusions. After the user determines the conclusions, the next step for users is to predict the implications of those conclusions. Predicting the implications is followed by a step where the user summarizes the conclusions and implications into a viewpoint. Afterward, the user evaluates this viewpoint, and Socrates Digital™ presents the opportunity to create another viewpoint. After the user decides there is no more evidence to gather, Socrates Digital™ will calculate a score that provides a confidence level in the current viewpoint for the user.

INTRODUCTION

As demonstrated in the investment example dialog in Chapter 4, after the user persona analyzes the information, identifies the assumptions, and applies the concepts, the next step is to determine the conclusions. After determining the conclusions, the next step is predicting the implications of those conclusions. Following this step, the next step the user persona summarizes the conclusions

DOI: 10.4018/978-1-7998-7955-8.ch008

Figure 1. The Determine Conclusions Subprocess of the Socrates Digital™ Module

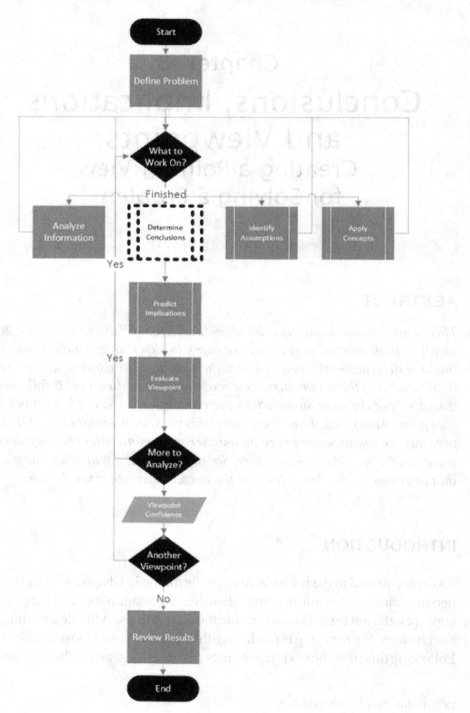

and implications into a viewpoint. Afterward, the user persona evaluates this viewpoint, and Socrates Digital™ provides the opportunity to create another viewpoint.

As Figure 1 highlights, the "Determine Conclusions" process is the next module to be executed after the user persona has completed the Analyze Information, Identify Assumptions, and Apply Concepts modules. In the Determine Conclusions process, Socrates Digital™ guides the user persona in summarizing the analyzed information, identified assumptions, and applied concepts into a conclusion. Afterward, Socrates Digital™ asks the user persona to rate the logic of this conclusion. In this process, Socrates Digital™ guides the user persona with questions from Paul and Elder's subcategory of Inferences and Conclusions that belong to their main category of Questions that Target the Quality of Elements of Thought (Paul & Elder, 2019).

INSIDE THE DETERMINE CONCLUSIONS SUBPROCESS

Below, the pseudo-code for the Determine_Conclusions subprocess is listed. The first comment in the subprocess tells us that the system persona's question will ask the user persona is in the Questions that Target the Parts of Thinking category. The first comment also tells us that the question for the user persona is in the Questioning Inferences and Conclusions subcategory. The second comment tells us that Socrates Digital™ will ask the user persona to identify the conclusion that seems most reasonable given the concepts, assumptions, and information gathered so far.

```
/* Questions that Target the Parts of Thinking - Questioning
/* Inferences and Conclusions

/* Ask user persona to Determine Conclusion of the analysis
BEGIN Subprocess Determine_Conclusions

/* Generate a Random Number Between 1 and 3 - the Possible
Forms of the /* Question
RandomInteger:= GenerateRandomInteger[1,3]

/* Select a Form of the Question
    CASE RandomInteger OF
    1: Question:= "Given these concepts, assumptions, and
information, what is the most reasonable conclusion?"
    2: Question:= "What is the most reasonable conclusion with
these concepts, assumptions, and information?"
```

```
    3: Question:= "With these concepts, assumptions, and
information, what is the best conclusion?"
    END_CASE

OUTPUT Question

INPUT Answer

Conclusion_Description: = Answer

/* Call Subprocess Determine_Conclusion_Questioning_Inferences
and Get
/* an Answer
Subprocess Determine_Conclusion_Questioning_Inferences (Answer)

Conclusion_Logic: = Answer

/* Save Answer to Current Session Data Point Description
INSERT INTO Conclusions_Table (Session_ID, Conclusion_
Description, Conclusion_Logic) VALUES (Current_Session_ID,
Conclusion_Description, Conclusion_Logic)

END Subprocess Determine_Conclusions
```

Pseudo Code for Subprocess Determine_Conclusions

Consistent with the other subprocesses, when Determine_Conclusion executes, the first action randomly selects a question form to present to the user persona. In the first call of this subprocess in our investment example dialog, Socrates Digital™ asks, "Given these concepts, assumptions, and information, what is the most reasonable conclusion?"

The user persona answers this question with the following reply, "Raising the occupancy rate for all the motels in the Rosebud Motel chain would raise total revenue for the chain." This answer is assigned to the variable Conclusion_Description – which is of type string.

The next step in the Determine_Conclusions subprocess is to call another subprocess, Determine_Conclusion_Questioning_Inferences, which will ask the user persona to rate the logic of the conclusion. This rating is assigned to a decimal variable named Conclusion_Logic.

The last step for the subprocess Determine_Conclusions is to update the Conslusion_Description and Conclusion_Logic values in the Conclusions_ Table table of the database.

```
/* Questions that Target the Quality of Reasoning --
Questioning Logic

/* Ask user persona to rate how logical the conclusion is
BEGIN Subprocess Determine_Conclusion_Questioning_Inferences
(Answer)

/* Generate a Random Number Between 1 and 3 - the Possible
Forms
/* of the Question
RandomInteger:= GenerateRandomInteger[1,3]

/* Select a Form of the Question
     CASE RandomInteger OF
     1: Question:= "Given this is all the evidence that
you currently have, how would you rate the logic of this
conclusion?"
     2: Question:= "Given all this evidence, how would you rate
this logic ?"
     3: Question:= "How would you rate this logic, given this
evidence?"
     END_CASE

OUTPUT Question

OUTPUT
"Very Logical
Probably Logical
Unknown How Logical
Probably Not Logical
Illogical"
INPUT User_Response

Natural_Language_Processor (User_Response, Understood_Response)

CASE Understood_Response OF

Very Logical:  Answer: = 0.75
Probably Logical:  Answer: = 0.5
Unknown How Logical: Answer: = 0
Probably Not Logical: Answer: =    -0.5
Illogical: = -0.75

END_CASE

END Subprocess Determine_Conclusion_Questioning_Inferences
```

Pseudo Code for the Determine_Conclusion_ Questioning_Inferences Subprocess

Listed Above is the pseudo-code for the Determine_Conclusion_Questioning_ Inferences subprocess. The first comment tells us that the question belongs to one of the two main categories of Socratic Questioning called Questions that Target the Quality of Reasoning. The remaining part of this first comment tells us that the question asked of the user persona is in the subcategory of Questioning Logic. This subcategory of Socratic Questions focuses on rating the logic of the previous conclusion provided by the user persona.

When run, the first action for Determine_Conclusion_Questioning_ Inferences is to randomly select a question form for presenting to the user persona. In the first call of this subprocess in our investment example dialog, Socrates Digital™ asks the user persona: "Given this is all the evidence that you currently have, how would you rate the logic of this conclusion?" After this question is output, the following list of options for the user persona to rate the logic of the conclusion is displayed:

- *Very Logical*
- *Probably Logical*
- *Unknown How Logical*
- *Probably Not Logical*
- *Illogical*

In our investment example dialog, the user persona answers, "I would say that it is probably logical," – which is stored in the variable User_Response. The natural language processor receives this variable and tries to match it to one of those responses presented in the list. Our investment example dialog matches it to "Probably Logical," and the Answer variable is assigned the decimal value 0.5 and returned to the subprocess Determine_Conclusions.

PREDICT IMPLICATIONS

As Figure 2 shows, the following process to be called after the Determine Conclusions subprocess is the "Predict Implications" subprocess. This process asks the user persona about the implications of the conclusion determined in the Determine Conclusions subprocess. The second part of the Predict

Implications subprocess asks the user persona to rate the confidence in the implications of the conclusion.

The pseudo-code for the Predict_Implications subprocess is listed below. The first comment in the subprocess tells us that the system persona's question will ask the user persona is in the Questions that Target the Parts of Thinking category. The first comment also tells us that the question for the user persona is in the Questioning Implications and Consequences subcategory. The second comment tells us that Socrates Digital™ will ask the user persona to predict the implications of the conclusion determined in the previous Determine_Conclusions subprocess.

```
/* Questions that Target the Parts of Thinking -- Questioning
Implications and Consequences

/* Ask user persona to Predict Implications of a Conclusion
BEGIN Subprocess Predict_Implications

/* Generate a Random Number Between 1 and 3 - the Possible
Forms of the Question
RandomInteger:= GenerateRandomInteger[1,3]

/* Select a Form of the Question
    CASE RandomInteger OF
    1: Question:= "What are the implications of this
conclusion?"
    2: Question:= "For this conclusion, what do you think are
the implications?"
    3: Question:= "Can you explain the implications of this
conclusion?"
    END_CASE

OUTPUT Question

INPUT Answer

Implication_Description: = Answer

/* Call Subprocess Predict_Implications_Questioning_Breadth and
Get an Answer
Subprocess Predict_Implications_Questioning_Breadth (Answer)

Implication_Evidence: = Answer

/* Save Answer to Current Session Data Point Description
INSERT INTO Implications_Table (Session_ID, Implication_
Description, Implication_Evidence) VALUES (Current_Session_ID,
```

Figure 2. The Predict Implications Subprocess of the Socrates Digital™ Module

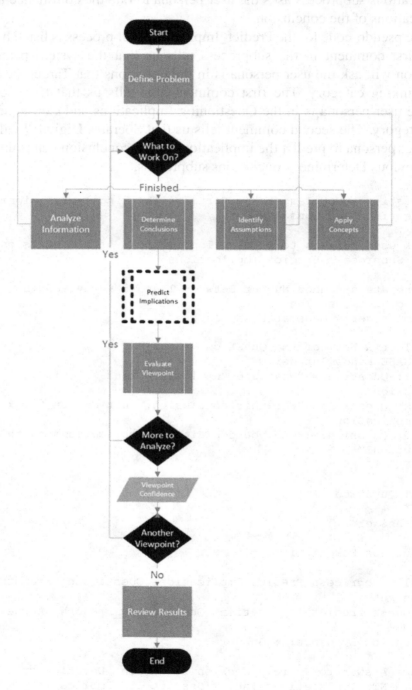

```
Implication_Description, Implication_Evidence)

END Subprocess Predict_Implications
```

Pseudo Code for Subprocess Predict_Implications

The first action that Predict_Implications will do is to randomly select a form of the question to present to the user persona. In the first call of this subprocess in our investment example dialog, Socrates Digital™ asks, "What are the implications of this conclusion?"

The user persona answers this question with the following reply, "Increased marketing can raise the occupancy rate and total revenue for motels in the Rosebud Motel chain." This answer is saved in the string variable Implication_Description.

The next step in the Predict_Implications subprocess is to call the Predict_Implications_Questioning_Breadth subprocess, which will ask the user persona to rate the confidence in the implications of this conclusion. This rating is saved and returned in a decimal variable named Implication_Evidence.

The last step for the subprocess Predict_Implications is to update the Implication_Description and Implication_Evidence values in the Implications_Table table of the database.

```
/* Questions that Target the Quality of Reasoning --
Questioning Breadth

/* Ask user persona to rate the implications of this conclusion
BEGIN Subprocess Predict_Implications_Questioning_Breadth
(Answer)

/* Generate a Random Number Between 1 and 3 - the Possible
Forms of the Question
RandomInteger:= GenerateRandomInteger[1,3]

/* Select a Form of the Question
    CASE RandomInteger OF
    1: Question:= "How would you rate your confidence in the
implications of this conclusion?"
    2: Question:= "For this implication of the conclusion, how
would you rate your confidence?"
    3: Question:= "How confident are you in this implication
of the conclusion?"
    END_CASE
```

```
OUTPUT Question

OUTPUT
"Highly Justified
   Probably Justified
   Insufficient Evidence to Judge
   Not Justified by the Evidence
   Refuted by the Evidence"
INPUT User_Response

Natural_Language_Processor (User_Response, Understood_Response)

CASE Understood_Response OF

Highly Justified:  Answer: = 0.75
Probably Justified:  Answer: = 0.5
Insufficient Evidence to Judge: Answer: = 0
Not Justified by the Evidence: Answer: =    -0.5
Refuted by the Evidence: = -0.75

END_CASE

END Subprocess Predict_Implications_Questioning_Breadth
```

Pseudo Code for the Predict_Implications_ Questioning_Consequences Subprocess

The pseudo-code for the Predict_Implications_Questioning_Consequences subprocess is listed above. The first comment tells us that the question belongs to one of the two main categories of Socratic Questioning called Questions that Target the Quality of Reasoning. The remaining part of this first comment tells us that the question asked of the user persona is in the subcategory of Questioning Breadth. In this case, this subcategory of Socratic Questions focuses on having the user persona identify the level of confidence in the implications stated for the previous conclusion.

When it runs, the first action for the Predict_Implications_Questioning_ Consequences subprocess is randomly selecting a question form for presenting to the user persona. In the first call of this subprocess in our investment example dialog, the user persona is asked, "How would you rate your confidence in the implications of this conclusion?" Socrates Digital™ follows this question with options for the user persona to rate the confidence in the implications of this conclusion:

- *Highly Justified*
- *Probably Justified*
- *Insufficient Evidence to Judge*
- *Not Justified by the Evidence*
- *Refuted by the Evidence*

In our investment example dialog, the user persona answers, "Insufficient evidence to judge," – which is stored in the string variable User_Response. This variable is passed to the natural language processor, matching it with one of the responses presented in the list. Our investment example dialog matched "Insufficient Evidence to Judge," and the Answer variable was assigned the decimal value 0.0 and returned to the subprocess Predict_Implications.

EVALUATE VIEWPOINT

As Figure 3 highlights, the next process after the Predict Implications subprocess is the "Evaluate Viewpoint" subprocess. This process is where Socrates Digital™ asks the user persona to restate the implications of the current conclusions to answer the question at hand. The second part of the Evaluate Viewpoint subprocess calculates the Viewpoint_Confidence score for the current viewpoint from the adjusted average values of the dataset, concept, assumption, conclusion, and implications scores.

Listed below is the pseudo-code for the Evaluate_Viewpoint subprocess. The first comment in the subprocess tells us that Socrates Digital™ will ask the user persona a question in the Questions that Target the Parts of Thinking category. The first comment also tells us that the question for the user persona is in the Questioning Viewpoints and Perspectives subcategory. The second comment tells us that Socrates Digital™ will ask the user persona to restate implications as a viewpoint and evaluate it -- then the system will calculate a confidence level for it

```
/* Questions that Target the Parts of Thinking - Questioning
/* Viewpoints and Perspectives

/* Ask user persona to restate implications as a viewpoint and
/* evaluate it - then system will calculate a confidence level
for it
BEGIN Subprocess Evaluate_Viewpoint
```

Figure 3. The Evaluate Viewpoint Subprocess of the Socrates Digital™ Process

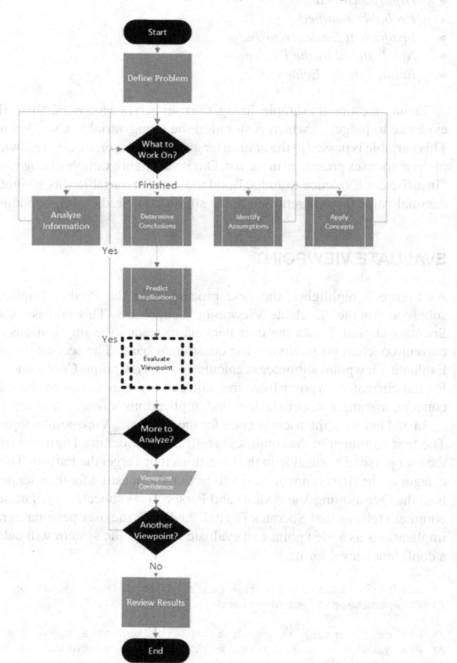

```
/* Generate a Random Number Between 1 and 3 - the Possible
Forms
/* of the Question
RandomInteger:= GenerateRandomInteger[1,3]

/* Select a Form of the Question
     CASE RandomInteger OF
     1: Question:= "Can you restate the implications of the
current conclusions, listed below, as a viewpoint for answering
the question at hand?"
     2: Question:= "Can you state a viewpoint for answering
the question at hand by using the implications of the current
conclusions, listed below?"
     3: Question:= "Can you rephrase these current
implications, listed below, into a viewpoint?"
     END_CASE

OUTPUT Question

/* Display implications from the database for this session
SELECT Implication_Description, Implication_Confidence
FROM Implication_Table
WHERE Problem_Area = "Investments"  AND Session_ID = Current_
Session_ID

INPUT Answer

Viewpoint_Description:= Answer

/* Calculate Viewpoint_Confidence from the Dataset, Concept,
Assumption, Conclusion, and Implications scores
Subprocess Evaluate_Viewpoint_Questioning_Depth (Answer)

Viewpoint_Confidence:= Answer

/* Save Viewpoint_Description and Viewpoint_Confidence to
Viewpoints_Table table in the database
INSERT INTO Viewpoints_Table (Session_ID, Viewpoint_
Description, Viewpoint_Confidence) VALUES (Current_Session_ID,
Viewpoint_Description, Viewpoint_Confidence)

END Subprocess Evaluate_Viewpoint
```

Pseudo Code for Subprocess Evaluate_Viewpoint

As is our convention, the first action for Evaluate_Viewpoint is randomly selecting a question form to present to the user persona. In the first call of this subprocess in our investment example dialog, Socrates Digital™ asks: "Can you restate the implications of the current conclusions, listed below, as a viewpoint for answering the question at hand?" Shown below, Socrates Digital™ follows this request with a list of all the implications made so far for the current question at hand:

- *Increased marketing can raise the occupancy rate and total revenue for motels in the Rosebud Motel chain.*
- *Increased marketing is needed to raise the total revenue for motels in the Rosebud Motel chain.*
- *A viewpoint such as increasing marketing is needed to increase revenue per available room for motels in the Rosebud Motel chain.*

The user persona answers this question with the following reply, "The viewpoint is focused on increasing marketing to raise occupancy rates, average daily rates, and revenue per available room to increase total revenue for motels in the Rosebud Motel chain." This answer was saved in the string variable Viewpoint_Description.

The next step in the Evaluate_Viewpoint subprocess is to call the Evaluate_Viewpoint_Questioning_Depth subprocess, which will calculate the Viewpoint_Confidence from the Dataset, Concept, Assumption, Conclusion, and Implications scores. This confidence score in the viewpoint is saved in a decimal variable named Viewpoint_Confidence and returned to the Evaluate_Viewpoint subprocess.

In the last step for the subprocess Evaluate_Viewpoint, INSERT updates the Viewpoint_Description and Viewpoint_Confidence values in the Viewpoints_Table table of the database.

```
/* Questions that Target the Quality of Reasoning --
Questioning Depth

/* Calculate the Viewpoint_Confidence in this viewpoint (values
range
/* between 0 and 1).  A value of 0 is no confidence; 1 is high
/* confidence
BEGIN Subprocess Evaluate_Viewpoint_Questioning_Depth (Answer)
```

```
/* Count the number of datasets in the current session
Number_Of_Datasets:= SELECT COUNT (Dataset_Accuracy)
 FROM Dataset_Table
 WHERE  Session_ID = Current_Session_ID

/* Calculate the average confidence score across the datasets
/* used in the current session
Dataset_Average:= SELECT AVG (Dataset_Accuracy)
        FROM Dataset_Table
        WHERE  Session_ID = Current_Session_ID

/* Increase the average confidence score for each additional
/* dataset to add more confidence
Dataset_Accuracy_Adjusted_Ave:= Dataset_Average + ((Dataset_
Average * (Number_Of_Datasets * Additional_Dataset_
Multiplier)))

/* If dataset average confidence score is over 1, then set to 1
IF Dataset_Accuracy_Adjusted_Ave > 1.0 THEN Dataset_Accuracy_
Adjusted_Ave:= 1.0

/***************

/* Also do this same count, average, and increase average
scores
/* for concepts, assumptions, conclusions, and implications
/* See the complete pseudo-code listing for the subprocess
/* Evaluate_Viewpoint_Questioning_Depth in Appendix B


/***************

/* Calculate Viewpoint_Confidence from the adjusted average
/* values for datasets, concepts, assumptions, conclusions, and
/* implications

Viewpoint_Confidence:= (Dataset_Accuracy_Adjusted_Ave *
Dataset_Weight)+
(Concept_Strength_Adjusted_Ave * Concept_Weight)+
(Assumption_Confidence_Adjusted_Ave * Assumption_Weight)+
(Conclusion_Logic_Adjusted_Ave * Conclusion_Weight)+
(Implication_Evidence_Adjusted_Ave * Implication_Weight)


/* Return Viewpoint_Confidence as the decimal value between 0
and
/* 1 that reflects the total confidence in the viewpoint
Answer:= Viewpoint_Confidence
```

```
END Subprocess Evaluate_Viewpoint_Questioning_Depth
```

Pseudo Code for the Evaluate_Viewpoint_Questioning_Depth Subprocess

The pseudo-code for the Evaluate_Viewpoint_Questioning_Depth subprocess is listed above. The first comment tells us that the question belongs to one of the two main categories of Socratic Questioning called Questions that Target the Quality of Reasoning. The remaining part of this first comment tells us that the question asked of the user persona is in the subcategory of Questioning Depth. In this case, this subcategory of Socratic Questions focuses on calculating the Viewpoint_Confidence from the Dataset, Concept, Assumption, Conclusion, and Implications scores. It will calculate a value between 0 and 1. A value of 0 shows no confidence, while a value of 1 shows high confidence in the viewpoint. This calculation answers the user persona's implied question about the viewpoint's confidence as a whole.

The first group of three calculations counts the number of datasets in the current session, calculates the average score, and increases the average confidence score for each additional dataset. This approach comes from social science research, where triangulated results provide more confidence than results from a single observation (Russ-Eft & Preskill, 2009). The effect is that confidence in the findings increases with each additional dataset.

In the first statement, the SELECT statement is used alongside the COUNT statement to count the number of datasets in the database for the current session. The FROM statement connects to the Dataset_Table table, and the WHERE statement ensures that the only entries counted are from the current session.

In the second statement, the SELECT statement is used alongside the AVG statement to average the dataset scores in the database that are part of the current session. As in the first statement, the FROM statement connects to the Dataset_Table table; the WHERE statement ensures that the only entries averaged from the table are from the current session.

The third statement calculates an adjusted average for the dataset accuracy scores. This calculation is a central feature for Socrates Digital™. Nevertheless, first, let us look at the numbers that will go into this calculation. Remember, the purpose of this subprocess is to calculate a confidence score for a particular viewpoint. As we have seen in our investment example dialog, several dataset scores may be associated with one or more assumptions, concepts, conclusions, and implications scores combined into a confidence score for that viewpoint.

The natural thing to do is to average the dataset scores to show, on average, how the dataset scores contribute to the confidence score of the viewpoint. Socrates Digital™ takes a different path from this in two ways. One way is that it adjusts the average upward with each added dataset that supports the viewpoint. The idea behind this is that the average is not a good measure of the influence of additional dataset scores on the confidence score. The average dataset score underrepresents the influence of the additional dataset scores on the confidence score for that viewpoint.

However, it is difficult to know how much the average dataset score underrepresents the influence of the additional dataset scores. This underrepresentation is especially true with other problem areas where the influence of additional datasets may be different. Socrates Digital™ applies user-assigned variables to weigh how much each additional dataset score influences the confidence score for a viewpoint to address this. These multiplier values can be adjusted empirically to find the average dataset score adjustment that makes sense for a problem area.

Precisely, the adjusted dataset average (Dataset_Accuracy_Adjusted_Ave) is calculated by taking the dataset average (Dataset_Average) times the number of datasets (Number_Of_Datasets) times the additional dataset multiplier (Additional_Dataset_Multiplier). The default value in the investment example dialog for the additional dataset multiplier is 0.1 (Additional_Dataset_Multiplier:= 0.1). In fact, all of the additional multipliers used in the investment example dialog are 0.1, as seen below. These multipliers, of course, can be adjusted for problem areas as needed.

Additional_Dataset_Multiplier:= 0.1
Additional_ Concept_Multiplier:= 0.1
Additional_ Assumption_Multiplier:= 0.1
Additional_ Conclusion_Multiplier:= 0.1
Additional_ Implication_Multiplier:= 0.1

The line with the IF, THEN statement, "Dataset_Accuracy_Adjusted_Ave > 1.0 THEN Dataset_Accuracy_Adjusted_Ave:= 1.0," is a safeguard so that the Dataset_Accuracy_Adjusted_Ave does not increase over the value of 1.0. It is easy to see that with many dataset scores, the adjusted dataset average could increase to over 1.0, thereby skewing the average too far upward.

These three calculations that 1) count the number of datasets in the current session, 2) calculates the average score for the datasets, and 3) increases the average confidence score for each additional dataset repeat for concepts, assumptions, conclusions, and implications. See the complete pseudo-code listing for the subprocess Evaluate_Viewpoint_Questioning_Depth in Appendix B.

The last step in the Evaluate_Viewpoint_Questioning_Depth subprocess is to calculate the Viewpoint_Confidence score. Socrates Digital™ calculates the Viewpoint_Confidence score by taking the adjusted average for each factor and multiplying it by its weight. For example, Socrates Digital™ multiplies Dataset_Accuracy_Adjusted_Ave by Dataset_Weight. Listed below are the default weights assigned to the factors in the investment example dialog.

Dataset_Weight:= 0.3
Concept_Weight:= 0.1
Assumption_Weight:= 0.1
Conclusion_Weight:= 0.2
Implication_Weight:= 0.3

The idea is that for the investment example dialog, Datasets and Implications are more critical than the other factors. They are followed in importance by Conclusions, with Concepts and Assumptions being the least important for calculating the Viewpoint_Confidence score.

As with the multiplier values for adjusting the average scores discussed above, it is not easy to know how much to weigh the individual factors compared to one another. Socrates Digital™ addresses this weighting issue by adjusting the factor weights empirically to find the right balance between the factors that make sense for a problem area.

The last step in calculating the Viewpoint_Confidence score is to add the values for all the factors. This resulting score is a decimal between 0 and 1. Listed below are the categories and their values for Viewpoint_Confidence in the investment example dialog.

Great Confidence (1.0)
Good Confidence (0.75)
Some Confidence (0.5)
Little Confidence (0.25)
No Confidence (0.0)

MORE TO ANALYZE DECISION PROCESS

As Figure 4 highlights, the next module after the Evaluate Viewpoint subprocess in the Socrates Digital™ module is the "More to Analyze?" decision process.

This process is where Socrates Digital™ asks the user persona if more information, assumptions, or concepts need examination.

The pseudo-code for the "More to Analyze?" decision process is listed below. The first comment states that the question asked by Socrates Digital™ belongs to the category of Socratic Questions called Questions that Target the Parts of Thinking. The second part of this first comment, Questioning Goals and Purposes, tells us that the question belongs to a subcategory of Socratic Questions aimed at determining the goals and purposes of the user persona. As seen in the second comment, Socrates Digital™ asks the user persona if there is more data to examine.

```
/* Questions that Target the Parts of Thinking -- Questioning
Goals and Purposes

/* Ask user persona if more confirming evidence is available
BEGIN Subprocess More_To_Analyze

/* Generate a Random Number Between 1 and 3 - the Possible
Forms
/* of the Question
RandomInteger:= GenerateRandomInteger[1,3]

/* Select a Form of the Question
    CASE RandomInteger OF
    1: Question:= "Can we get more confirming evidence about
this?"
    2: Question:= "Is there more information that supports
this?"
    3: Question:= "Can you provide more data that backs this
     up?"
    END_CASE

OUTPUT Question
INPUT Answer

Problem_Description:= Answer

User_Response:= Answer

/* Understood_Response should come back as "Yes " or "No"
Natural_Language_Processor (User_Response, Understood_Response)

IF Understood_Response <>  "Yes" OR "No" THEN
OUTPUT "Sorry I didn't understand you. Is it yes or no that
you have more confirming evidence?"
INPUT Answer
```

Figure 4. The More to Analyze? Subprocess of the Socrates Digital™ Module

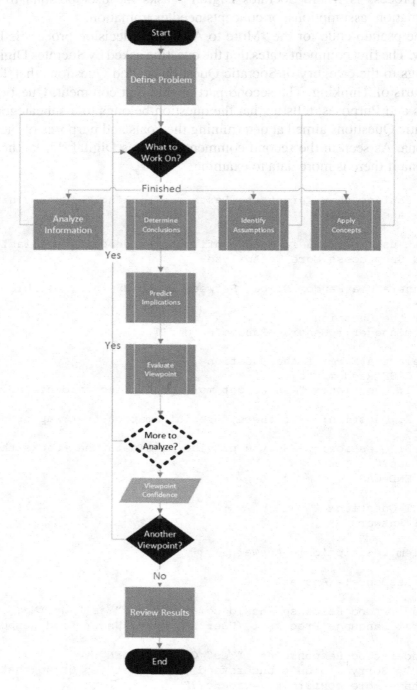

```
User_Response:= Answer
END_IF

IF Understood_Response    = "Yes"   THEN
GOTO WHAT_TO_WORK_ON
END_IF

END Subprocess More_To_Analyze
```

The Pseudo Code for the More to Analyze? Subprocess

When More_To_Analyze executes, the first action is to randomly select a form of the question to present to the user persona. The first time this subprocess is called in our investment example dialog, the user persona asks, "Can we get more confirming evidence about this?"

The user persona replies, "Yes, I believe we can." Socrates Digital™ sends this reply to the natural language processor, which returns a value of "Yes" as the understood response. The next step is an "IF" statement that tests whether the user persona's answer is "Yes." Since it is in our investment example dialog, the user persona has more evidence to examine, and a "GOTO" statement sends control of the program to the "WHAT_TO_WORK_ON" decision process. If the user persona's answer is "No," then control of the program goes to the next subprocess, which is the Viewpoint_Confidence output process for this problem area.

VIEWPOINT CONFIDENCE OUTPUT PROCESS

After the More to Analyze? the decision process completes, the "Viewpoint Confidence" output process is the next process to execute. As Figure 5 shows, it lies between a decision icon process for processing more information and a decision icon process for looking at another viewpoint.

```
/* Questions that Target the Quality of Reasoning --
Questioning Depth
```

Figure 5. The Viewpoint Confidence Process in the Socrates Digital™ Module

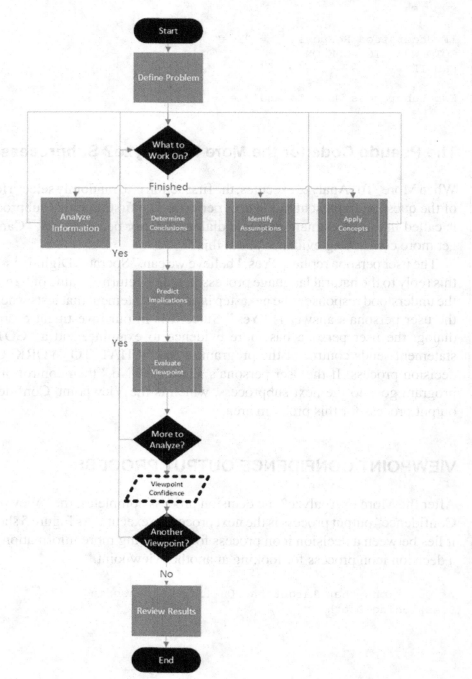

```
/* Tell user persona the confidence (between 0 and 1) in the
viewpoint and the description of the viewpoint
BEGIN Subprocess Viewpoint_Confidence

OUTPUT User_Persona_Identity " has expressed an overall
confidence of " + Viewpoint_Confidence + " for the following
viewpoint " + Viewpoint_Description
END Subprocess Viewpoint_Confidence
```

Pseudo Code for the Viewpoint Confidence Subprocess

Listed above is the pseudo-code for the Viewpoint Confidence subprocess. It asks and answers the implied question about the user persona's description and level of confidence in the current viewpoint under consideration. The first line of this listing is a comment which tells that the implied question belongs to the category of Socratic Questions called Questions that Target the Quality of Reasoning. The rest of this first comment tells us that the implied question of the user persona is in the subcategory of Questioning Depth. This subcategory of Socratic Questions focuses on providing additional depth for a previous answer. In this case, it is the confidence the user persona has in the current viewpoint. The second comment confirms this by stating it will output the confidence level (between 0 and 1) in the viewpoint and the description of the viewpoint for the user persona.

ANOTHER VIEWPOINT? DECISION PROCESS

The next module after the Viewpoint Confidence subprocess in the Socrates Digital™ module, shown in Figure 6, is the "Another Viewpoint?" decision process. This next process is where Socrates Digital™ asks the user persona if there is any more information, assumptions, or concepts to examine for creating another viewpoint.

The pseudo-code for the "Another Viewpoint?" decision process is listed below. The first comment states that the question asked by Socrates Digital™ belongs to the category of Socratic Questions called Questions that Target the Parts of Thinking. The second part of this first comment, Questioning Goals and Purposes, tells us that the question belongs to a subcategory of Socratic Questions aimed at determining the goals and purposes of the user

Figure 6. The Another Viewpoint? Subprocess of the Socrates Digital™ Module

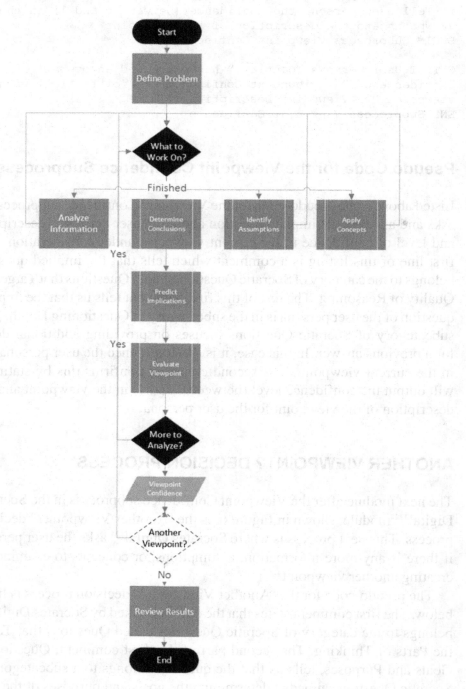

persona. As seen in the second comment, Socrates Digital™ will ask the user persona if another viewpoint is needed.

```
/* Questions that Target the Parts of Thinking -- Questioning
Goals and
/* Purposes

/* Ask user persona if another viewpoint that should be
considered
BEGIN Subprocess Another_Viewpoint

/* Generate a Random Number Between 1 and 3 - the Possible
Forms
/* of the Question
RandomInteger:= GenerateRandomInteger[1,3]

/* Select a Form of the Question
   CASE RandomInteger OF
   1: Question:= "Is there another viewpoint that should be
considered?"
   2: Question:= "Should we consider another viewpoint?"
   3: Question:= "At this time, is there another viewpoint we
should look at?"
   END_CASE

OUTPUT Question

INPUT Answer

Problem_Description:= Answer

User_Response:= Answer

/* Understood_Response should come back as "Yes " or "No"
Natural_Language_Processor (User_Response, Understood_Response)

IF Understood_Response <> "Yes" OR "No" THEN
OUTPUT "Sorry I didn't understand you. Is it yes or no that
another viewpoint that should be considered?"
INPUT Answer
User_Response:= Answer
END_IF

IF Understood_Response   = "Yes"  THEN
GOTO WHAT_TO_WORK_ON
END_IF

END Subprocess Another_Viewpoint
```

The Pseudo Code for the Another Viewpoint? Subprocess

When Another_Viewpoint runs, the first action is to randomly select a form of the question to present to the user persona. In the first call of this subprocess in our investment example dialog, the user persona is asked, "Is there another viewpoint that should be considered?"

During the investment example dialog, the second user group (UP2) replies, "Yes, come to think of it, we know that price is only one of the influencing factors for customers of motel rooms. For example, customers are influenced by clean rooms in good repair, friendly staff, and complimentary gifts." In this case, Socrates Digital™ sends this to the natural language processor, which returns a value of "Yes" as the understood response. The next step is an "IF" statement that tests whether the user persona's answer is "Yes." Since it is, the user persona does have more evidence to examine, and a "GOTO" statement sends control of the program to the "WHAT_TO_WORK_ON" decision process. If the user persona's answer is "No," then control of the program goes to the Review Results process.

REVIEW RESULTS PROCESS

As Figure 7 highlights, the next module after the Another Viewpoint? decision subprocess in the Socrates Digital™ module is the "Review Results" process. This process is where Socrates Digital™ presents the results for a particular question at hand.

Figure 8 shows the insides of the Review Results process. The first subprocess highlighted, Report Results, asks the user persona if there is a need to see all the viewpoints and their confidence levels for this session. Next, Answer Question at Hand subprocess asks the user persona if the session results helped answer the question at hand. The third subprocess, State the Decision, asks the user persona if a decision has been made about the question at hand. Then, the fourth step, Identify Decision Implications subprocess, asks the user persona about the implications of the decision.

Below, the pseudo-code for the "Report_Results" subprocess is listed. The first comment states that the question asked by Socrates Digital™ belongs to the category of Socratic Questions called Questions that Target the Parts of Thinking. The second part of this first comment, Questioning Viewpoints and Perspectives, tells us that the question belongs to the subcategory of

Figure 7. The Review Results Process of the Socrates Digital™ Module

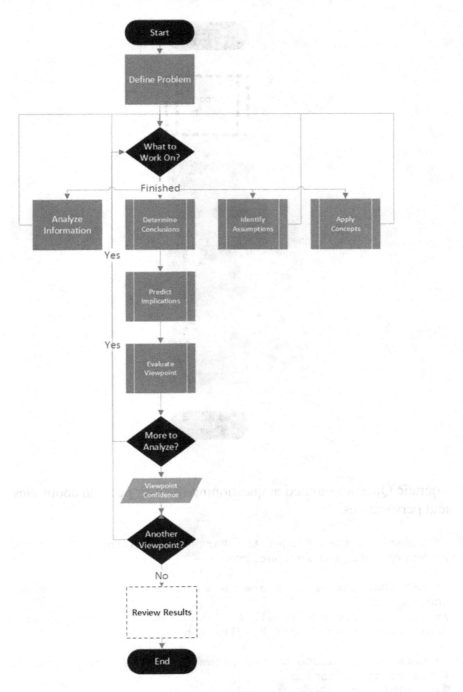

Figure 8. The Report Results Subprocess of the Review Results Process

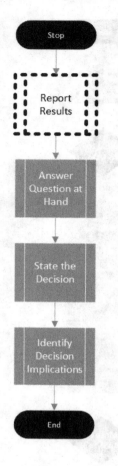

Socratic Questions aimed at questioning the user persona about viewpoints and perspectives.

```
/* Questions that Target the Parts of Thinking - Questioning
/* Viewpoints and Perspectives

/* Ask user person if there is a need to see all the viewpoints
and
/* their confidence levels for answering the question at hand
BEGIN Subprocess Report_Results (Answer)

/* Generate a Random Number Between 1 and 3 - the Possible
Forms of the Question
RandomInteger:= GenerateRandomInteger[1,3]
```

```
/* Select a Form of the Question
     CASE RandomInteger OF
     1: Question:= "Would you like to see all the viewpoints
and their confidence levels for answering the question at
hand?"
     2: Question:= "Display all the viewpoints and their
confidence levels for answering the question at hand?"
     3: Question:= "Show all the viewpoints and confidence
levels for answering the question at hand?"
     END_CASE

OUTPUT Question

INPUT Answer

User_Response:= Answer


Natural_Language_Processor (User_Response, Understood_Response)

IF Understood_Response = "Yes" THEN

/* Display viewpoints from the database for this question /* at
hand
SELECT User_Persona_Identity, Viewpoint_Description, Viewpoint_
Confidence
FROM Viewpoint_Table
WHERE Problem_Area = "Investments"  AND Session_ID =
Current_Session_ID

END_IF

/* Save the user persona's Viewed_Viewpoints answer to database
UPDATE Define_Problem_Table
SET
User_Persona_Identity:= User_Persona_Identity
Viewed_Viewpoints:= Understood_Response
WHERE Problem_Area = "Investments"  AND Session_ID =
Current_Session_ID

END Subprocess Report_Results
```

Pseudo Code for the Report_Results Subprocess

The second comment describes what the Report_Results subprocess does. It asks the user persona if they want a recap on all the viewpoints for this session.

When Report_Results executes, it randomly selects a form of the question to present to the user persona. In our investment example dialog, it asks the user persona: "Would you like to see all the viewpoints and their confidence levels for this question at hand?"

To this question, the user persona replies: "Yes." The natural language processor confirms this answer, and all the viewpoints and their confidence levels are provided for this question at hand by the SELECT, FROM, and WHERE statements.

The last step of Report_Results uses the UPDATE and SET commands to update the Viewed_Viewpoints field in the Define_Problem_Table table of the database.

Figure 9. The Answer Question at Hand Subprocess of the Review Results Process

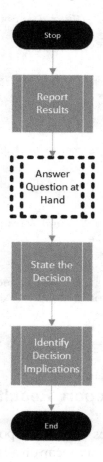

Figure 9 shows that the Answer Question at Hand subprocess is the next step in the Review Results Process.

The pseudo-code for the Answer_Question_At_Hand subprocess is listed below. The comment in the first line tells us that the question belongs to the category of Socratic Questions called Questions that Target the Parts of Thinking. The remaining part of this first comment tells us that the question is in the subcategory of Question at Issue. This subcategory of Socratic Questions relates to answering the question at hand.

```
/* Ask user persona to identify question at hand
BEGIN Subprocess Answer_Question_At_Hand

/* Generate a Random Number Between 1 and 3 - the Possible
Forms
/* of the Question
RandomInteger:= GenerateRandomInteger[1,3]

/* Select a Form of the Question
    CASE RandomInteger OF
    1: Question:= "Does this help answer the question at hand
about " + Question_At_Hand + "?"
    2: Question:= "Is the question at hand answered -- " +
Question_At_Hand + "?"
    3: Question:= "Does this answer the question at hand -- "
+ Question_At_Hand + "?"
    END_CASE

OUTPUT Question

INPUT Answer

User_Response:= Answer

/* Understood_Response will come back as "Yes" or "No"
Natural_Language_Processor (User_Response, Understood_Response)

/* If no, then give user persona a chance to correct the
question
/* at hand
IF Understood_Response = "No" THEN OUTPUT "Then, it looks
unresolved for now"
END_IF

/* Save Answer_Question_At_Hand to database
UPDATE Define_Problem_Table
SET
```

```
Answer_Question_At_Hand:= Understood_Response
WHERE Problem_Area = "Investments"  AND Session_ID =
Current_Session_ID

END Subprocess Answer_Question_At_Hand
```

Pseudo Code for the Answer_Question_ At_Hand Subprocess

When Answer_Question_At_Hand runs, the first action is to randomly select a form of the question to present to the user persona. In our investment example dialog, Socrates Digital™ selects and presents the following question to the user persona, "Does this help answer the question at hand about deciding whether to invest in the Rosebud Motel chain?"

The natural language processor examines the user persona's response and returns either a "Yes" or a "No." In our investment example dialog, the user persona replied, "Yes." If the answer had been "No," Socrates Digital™ would have output a response that said, "Then, it looks unresolved for now."

The last step of Answer_Question_At_Hand uses the UPDATE and SET commands to update the Answer_Question_At_Hand field in the Define_ Problem_Table table of the database.

Figure 10 shows that the State The Decision subprocess is the next step in the Review Results Process.

Below, the pseudo-code for the State_The_Decision subprocess is listed. The comment in the first line tells that the question belongs to the category of Socratic Questions called Questions that Target the Parts of Thinking. The remaining part of this first comment tells us that the question asked is in the subcategory of Questioning Goals and Purposes. This subcategory of Socratic Questions relates to the decision to be made. For the investment example dialog, it is deciding on investing in the Rosebud Motel chain.

```
/* Questions that Target the Parts of Thinking -- Questioning
Goals and Purposes

/* Ask user persona to state the decision
BEGIN Subprocess State_The_Decision

/* Generate a Random Number Between 1 and 3 - the Possible
Forms
/* of the Question
RandomInteger:= GenerateRandomInteger[1,3]
```

Figure 10. The State the Decision Subprocess of the Review Results Process

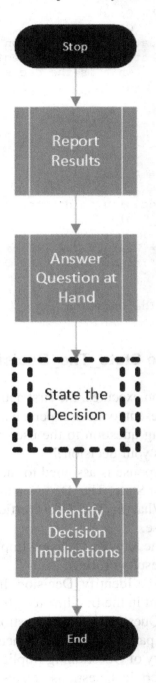

```
/* Select a Form of the Question
    CASE RandomInteger OF
    1: Question:= "What is your decision?"
    2: Question:= "What have you decided?"
    3: Question:= "So, what is the decision?"
    END_CASE

OUTPUT Question

INPUT Answer

What_Is_The_Decision:= Answer

/* Save What_Is_The_Decision to database
UPDATE Define_Problem_Table
SET
What_Is_The_Decision:= What_Is_The_Decision
WHERE Problem_Area = "Investments"  AND Session_ID =
Current_Session_ID

END Subprocess State_The_Decision
```

Pseudo Code for the State_The_Decision Subprocess

When State_The_Decision executes, the first action is to randomly select a form of the question to present to the user persona. Socrates Digital™ selects and presents the following question to the user persona in our investment example dialog: "What is your decision?"

The user persona's response is assigned to the variable "What_Is_The_Decision." The last step of State_The_Decision uses the UPDATE and SET commands to update the What_Is_The_Decision field in the Define_Problem_Table table of the database.

Figure 11 shows that the Identify Decision Implications subprocess is the last step in the Review Results Process.

The pseudo-code for the Identify_Decision_Implications subprocess is listed below. The comment in the first line tells that the question belongs to the category of Socratic Questions called Questions that Target the Parts of Thinking. The remaining part of this first comment tells us that the question asked is in the subcategory of Questioning Implications and Consequences. This subcategory of Socratic Questions relates to the implications and consequences of the decision. The investment example dialog shows the planned expectations for the investment in the Rosebud Motel chain.

```
/* Ask User Persona to identify the implications of the
decision
BEGIN Subprocess Identify_Decision_Implications

/* Generate a Random Number Between 1 and 3 - the Possible
Forms
/* of the Question
RandomInteger:= GenerateRandomInteger[1,3]

/* Select a Form of the Question
     CASE RandomInteger OF
     1: Question:= "What are the implications of this
decision?"
     2: Question:= "For this decision, what are the
implications?"
     3: Question:= "So, what do you think are the implications
of this decision?"
     END_CASE

OUTPUT Question

INPUT Answer

Decision_Implications:= Answer


/* Save Decision_Implications to database
UPDATE Define_Problem_Table
SET
Decision_Implications:= Decision_Implications

WHERE Problem_Area = "Investments"  AND Session_ID =
Current_Session_ID

OUTPUT "OK, that completes this session."

END Subprocess Identify_Decision_Implications
```

Figure 11. The Identify Decision Implications Subprocess of the Review Results Process

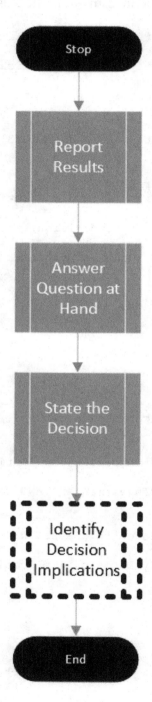

Pseudo Code for the State the Identify_ Decision_Implications Subprocess

When Identify_Decision_Implications executes, the first action is to randomly select a form of the question to present to the user persona. Socrates Digital™ selects and presents the following question to the user persona in our investment example dialog, "What are the implications of this decision?"

In our investment example dialog, as the following shows, the user persona response expresses almost a mini-business plan as the implications of deciding to invest in the Rosebud Motel:

"If Rosebud Motels uses its investment funds for marketing and make the motel renovations it did with Saint Ola for all its motels, it would increase the Rosebud Motel chain revenue by $2,000,000 in the first year. This mini-business plan would make it easily possible to repay the $4,800,000 for the loan over five years. It would provide a good return for investors at 10% and increase revenues for the Rosebud Motel chain in the future."

The user persona's response is assigned the variable "Decision_ Implications." The second to last step of Identify_Decision_Implications uses the UPDATE and SET commands to update the Decision_Implications field in the Define_Problem_Table table of the database.

The last step for the Identify_Decision_Implications subprocess is to output to the user persona this sign-off message: "OK, that completes this session."

SUMMARY

As shown in this chapter, after the user persona analyzes the information, identifies the assumptions, and applies the concepts, the next step is to determine the conclusions. Predicting the implications of those conclusions is the next step for the user persona. Summarizing the conclusions and implications into a viewpoint comes next. Afterward, the user persona evaluates this viewpoint. Socrates Digital™ follows the user persona's evaluation by presenting the opportunity to create another viewpoint. After the user persona decides there are no more viewpoints to consider, Socrates Digital™ calculates a score that provides a confidence level in the current viewpoint. Finally, Socrates Digital™ presents the user persona with the opportunity to view all the viewpoints and their confidence levels for the question at hand.

REFERENCES

Paul, R., & Elder, L. (2019). *The thinker's guide to Socratic questioning: Based on critical thinking concepts and tools.* Rowan & Littlefield.

Russ-Eft, D., & Preskill, H. (2009). *Evaluation in organizations: A systematic approach enhancing learning, performance, and change* (2nd ed.). Basic Books.

Chapter 9
Dialog Development Manager:
Managing the System Design and Development Process

ABSTRACT

This chapter shows how software development professionals use the provided flow charts and pseudo-code to create the Dialog Development Manager. Analysts then use the Dialog Development Manager to create the problem-specific knowledge needed by a natural language processor to support the conversation between Socrates Digital™ and end users. The Dialog Development Manager guides the analysts through design and development of the Understand, Explore, Materialize, and Realize phases to create the conversational interface for Socrates Digital™.

INTRODUCTION

As we have seen, Socrates Digital™ serves two audiences – software development professionals and end-users. The software development professionals can use the flow charts and pseudo-code to create a Socrates Digital™ system for end-users to engage. In our investment example dialog, end-users, as analysts, engage with a Socrates Digital™ system to analyze investment opportunities. What is different in this chapter is that analysts in a new role use the Dialog Development Manager. These developer analysts use the Dialog Development Manager to create the problem-specific knowledge

DOI: 10.4018/978-1-7998-7955-8.ch009

needed by the natural language processor to support the conversation between Socrates Digital™ and the end-users solving a problem. The Dialog Development Manager engages these developer analysts in conversation to create this problem-specific knowledge. As you might guess, the software development professionals create the questions/answers file for the natural language processor to have this conversation with the developer analysts. In this way, a Socrates Digital™ system helps create and manage the conversational knowledge needed for solving problems in a specific area such as investment opportunities.

As described in Chapter 4, Socrates Digital™ leverages artificial intelligence services to process natural human language. That leaves the book's principal focus on the design and development process of the conversational user experience. The approach for this book borrows heavily from the YouTube video created by Jeff Humble of CareerFoundry (Humble, 2019) for the first three phases. The last phase, Realize, was added for the implementation phase of a Socrates Digital™ system.

As shown in Figure 1, the Dialog Development Manager provides a submit, review, and approval process for all the steps – Understand, Explore, Materialize, and Realize – of the dialog development process described in Chapter 4. The result of this dialog development process is a file of question/answer pairs that the developer uploads to a natural language processor. The Dialog Development Manager guides analysts through this dialog development process and makes all the artifacts available to the analysts that created them and other organizational members. These other organizational members will apply lessons learned from previous efforts to develop their questions/answers files to complete the phases.

Figure 1. The Dialog Development Manager Process

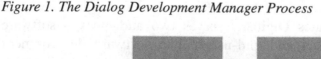

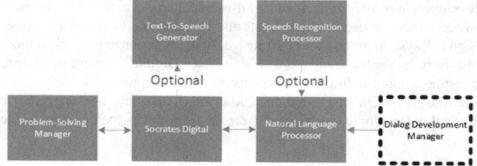

INSIDE THE DIALOG DEVELOPMENT MANAGER PROCESS

In Figure 2, we see that the first step to the Dialog Development Manager process is the Understand subprocess.

The pseudo-code for the Understand subprocess is listed below. The first comment tells us that this subprocess presents a question from the subcategory, Questioning Questions, that will get permission from the user persona to answer upcoming questions in the Questions that Target the Parts of Thinking category. As the second comment tells us, its primary purpose is to create a user persona profile, define Socrates Digital™ behavior, and identify user journey mapping. As we will see, the details collected by the Understand subprocess need to be precise, so this subprocess will call several subprocesses to ask the questions that will provide the precision needed in the user persona answers. As we have seen before, Socrates Digital™ will answer these questions with calls to subprocesses that target the quality of the user persona's answers.

```
/* Questions that Target the Parts of Thinking - Questioning
Questions
/* Ask the analyst to create a user persona profile, define
system
/* persona behavior, and identify user journey mapping
BEGIN Subprocess Understand

Question:= "Are you ready to answer some questions about the
user persona profile, Socrates Digital™ behavior, and user
journey mapping?"

OUTPUT Question

INPUT Answer

User_Response:= Answer

/* Understood_Response will come back as "Yes" or "No"
Natural_Language_Processor (User_Response, Understood_Response)

/* If no, then give the analyst an opportunity to skip this.
IF Understood_Response = "Yes" THEN

Subprocess Create_Profile_Questioning_Precision (ProfileFile)
Subprocess Define_Behavior_Questioning_Precision (BehaviorFile)
Subprocess Identify_Journey_Questioning_Precision (MappingFile)
```

Figure 2. The Understand Subprocess in the Dialog Development Manager Process

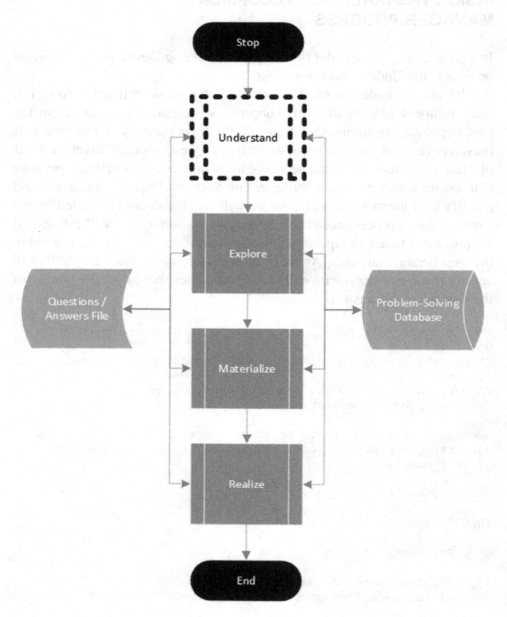

```
/* Save Understand phase answers to database
UPDATE Understand_Table
SET
Create_Profile:= ProfileFile
Define_Behavior:= BehaviorFile
Identify_Journey:= MappingFile

WHERE Problem_Area = "Investments"

ELSE

OUTPUT "OK, we will skip this for now."

END_IF

END Subprocess Understand
```

Pseudo Code for the Understand Subprocess

When the Understand subprocess runs, the first action is to present a question to the user persona, who is a developer analyst. In our investment example dialog, the analyst is asked, "Are you ready to answer some questions about the user persona profile, Socrates Digital™ behavior, and user journey mapping?" The analyst's answer is captured in the Answer variable with the INPUT command and stored in the User_Response variable. Note that only one form of the question is available for Socrates Digital™ to present to the analyst. Since Socrates Digital™ asks this question once a session, other forms of the question will not be needed. This simplification also makes it simpler for the software development professional to create the answers/questions file for the natural language processor.

The next step is to send the response by the analyst to the natural language processor. If the natural language processor identifies the analyst's response as a "Yes," it will go forward with the questions about the Understand process. However, If the natural language processor identifies the analyst's response as something other than "Yes," then Socrates Digital™ outputs "OK, we will skip this for now" to the analyst.

In the Understand process, three specific questions need to be answered by the analyst to complete the process. These three questions relate to the user persona profile, Socrates Digital™ behavior, and user journey mapping. Since these three questions request more information about the Understand process, Socrates Digital™ presents them in separate subprocesses that target the quality of reasoning. These three subprocesses relate to the quality – more specifically, the "precision" -- of the analyst's answers in the Understand subprocess.

As the pseudo-code for Understand shows, the first subprocess that seeks an answer with precision, is the subprocess, Create_Profile_Questioning_ Precision, which asks the analyst to provide a profile of the user persona. The second subprocess, Define_Behavior_Questioning_Precision, seeks a precise answer about how Socrates Digital™ will behave. The third subprocess, Identify_Journey_Questioning_Precision, seeks a precise answer that shows how the key conversational interactions play out.

After these three subprocesses have returned answers from the analyst, Socrates Digital™ performs the last step of the Understand subprocess. In this step, the UPDATE and SET commands update the Create_User_Persona_ Profile, Define_System_Persona_Behavior, and the Identify_User_Journey_ Mapping fields in the Understand_Table table of the database.

The pseudo-code is listed below for the Create_Profile_Questioning_ Precision subprocess.

```
/* Questions that Target the Quality of Reasoning --
Questioning Precision

/* Generate Questioning Precision question for user persona and
/* collect answer
BEGIN Subprocess Create_Profile_Questioning_Precision (Answer)

Question:= "How would you describe the profile of your user
persona?  You should include what the problem area is and the
level of experience of the user persona.  For example, you
could describe the user persona as a member of an investment
firm considering investing in a commercial real estate
opportunity. After you have completed your user persona
profile, upload the file so it can be found with the click of a
mouse."

OUTPUT Question

UPLOAD_FILE Answer

Subprocess Provide_Initial_Background

END Subprocess Create_Profile_Questioning_Precision
```

Pseudo Code for Create_Profile_ Questioning_Precision Subprocess

As we see in this pseudo-code for the Create_Profile_Questioning_Precision subprocess, the first comment tells us that the questioning done by this subprocess belongs to the Questioning Precision subcategory in the Questions that Target the Quality of Reasoning category. It begins with a lengthy question to get the analyst to provide a detailed profile for the user persona. Noted as necessary in the question is the inclusion of the problem area and level of experience of the user persona in the analyst's answer. After the analyst has completed the user persona profile, the analyst uploads the file where it is returned in the variable "Answer" to the Understand subprocess.

```
,
/* Questions that Target the Parts of Thinking - Questioning
Questions
/* Ask user persona to provide some initial information,
concepts, and
/* assumptions to start the learning and problem-solving
process for the
/* user persona
BEGIN Subprocess Provide_Initial_Background


Question:= "It's important to provide some initial information,
concepts, and assumptions to start the learning and problem-
solving process for the user persona of the system.

Do you want to provide some initial information, concepts, and
assumptions to start the learning and problem-solving process
for the user persona."

OUTPUT Question

INPUT Answer

User_Response:= Answer

/* Understood_Response will come back as "Yes" or "No"
Natural_Language_Processor (User_Response, Understood_Response)

/* If no, then give the analyst an opportunity to skip this.
IF Understood_Response = "Yes" THEN

Subprocess Provide_Initial_Information
```

```
Subprocess Provide_Initial_Concepts
Subprocess Provide_Initial_Assumptions

ELSE

OUTPUT "OK, we will skip this for now."

END_IF

END Subprocess Provide_Initial_Background
```

Pseudo Code for Provide_Initial_Background Subprocess

In the pseudo-code for the Provide_Initial_Background subprocess, the first comment tells us that the questioning done by this subprocess belongs to the Questioning Questions subcategory in the Questions that Target the Parts of Thinking category. It begins by providing a lengthy explanation about the importance of providing some initial information, concepts, and assumptions to start the learning and problem-solving process for the user persona. Socrates Digital™ follows this explanation with a question that asks if the user persona wants to provide these initial resources at this time. If the natural language processor determines the answer is "yes," then three subprocesses (Provide_Initial_Information, Provide_Initial_Concepts, and Provide_Initial_Assumptions) are called to gather the initial information, concepts, and assumptions. Otherwise, if the natural language processor determined the user persona said "no," then it outputs the text, "OK, we will skip this for now."

```
/* Questions that Target the Quality of Reasoning --
Questioning Precision

/* Generate Questioning Precision question for user persona to
provide
/* initial information and update database

BEGIN Subprocess Provide_Initial_Information


Question:= "Let's start with information. Do you want to add a
source of information for the user persona?"

OUTPUT Question
```

```
INPUT User_Response
/* Send off to natural language processor to determine yes/no
answer
Natural_Language_Processor (User_Response, Understood_Response)

If Understood_Response = "Yes"

WHILE Understood_Response = "Yes"
OUTPUT "How would describe the information?"
INPUT Information_Description
OUTPUT "What is the URL for the information?"
INPUT Information_URL
/* Save Information Description and URL Information Table
/* in Database
INSERT INTO Information_Table (Problem_Area, Information_
Description, Information_URL, VALUES("Investment_Motel",
Information_Description, Information_URL)
OUTPUT "Do you want to add another source of information for
the user persona?"
INPUT User_Response
/* Send off to natural language processor to determine
/* yes/no answer
Natural_Language_Processor (User_Response, Understood_Response)

END WHILE

END Subprocess Provide_Initial_Information
```

Pseudo Code for Provide_Initial_Information Subprocess

The first comment in this pseudo-code for the Create_Profile_Questioning_ Precision subprocess tells us that the questioning done by this subprocess belongs to the Questioning Precision subcategory in the Questions that Target the Quality of Reasoning category. It first asks, "Do you want to add a source of information for the user persona?" If the natural language processor determines that the analyst's answer is "yes," the subprocess goes into a WHILE loop to gather the information sources. In this WHILE loop, Socrates Digital™ asks the analyst to describe the information source and its URL. During the WHILE loop, the application inserts the description and URL of the information resource into the Information_Table table of the database. At the end of the WHILE loop, Socrates Digital™ asks the analyst if there is another information source to add. Suppose the natural language processor determines that the answer is "yes" from the analyst. In that case, the subprocess goes back to the top of the WHILE loop to gather another information resource. If the natural language processor determines that the analyst's answer is "no," it exits the WHILE loop and completes the subprocess.

```
/* Questions that Target the Quality of Reasoning --
Questioning Precision

/* Generate Questioning Precision question for user persona to
provide
/* initial concepts and update database

BEGIN Subprocess Provide_Initial_Concepts


Question:= "Let's start with concepts. Do you want to add a
concept for the user persona?"

OUTPUT Question

INPUT User_Response
/* Send off to natural language processor to determine yes/no
answer
Natural_Language_Processor (User_Response, Understood_Response)

If Understood_Response = "Yes"

WHILE Understood_Response = "Yes"
OUTPUT "What is the name for the concept?"
INPUT Concept_Name
OUTPUT "How would describe the concept?"
INPUT Concept_Description
/* Save concept name and description in Concepts Table in
database
INSERT INTO Concepts_Table (Problem_Area, Concept_Name,
Concept_Description, VALUES("Investment_Motel", Concept_Name,
Concept_Description)
OUTPUT "Do you want to add another concept for the user
persona?"
INPUT User_Response
/* Send off to natural language processor to determine yes/no
answer
Natural_Language_Processor (User_Response, Understood_Response)

END WHILE

END Subprocess Provide_Initial_Concepts
```

Pseudo Code for Provide_Initial_Concepts Subprocess

The first comment in this pseudo-code for the Provide_Initial_Concepts subprocess tells us that the questioning done by this subprocess belongs to the Questioning Precision subcategory in the Questions that Target the Quality of Reasoning category. The Provide_Initial_Concepts subprocess is similar to the Provide_Initial_Information subprocess, as shown in its first question, "Do you want to add a concept for the user persona?" If the natural language processor determines that the answer is "yes," then the subprocess goes into a WHILE loop to gather the concepts. In this WHILE loop, Socrates Digital™ asks the analyst to provide the concept's name and description. In the WHILE loop, the application inserts the concept's name and description into the Concepts_Table table of the database. At the end of the WHILE loop, Socrates Digital™ asks the analyst if there is another concept to add. If the natural language processor determines that the answer is "yes," then the subprocess returns to the top of the WHILE loop to gather another concept from the analyst. If the natural language processor determines that the analyst's answer is "no," it exits the WHILE loop and completes the subprocess.

```
/* Questions that Target the Quality of Reasoning --
Questioning Precision

/* Generate Questioning Precision question for user persona to
provide
/* initial assumptions and update database

BEGIN Subprocess Provide_Initial_Assumptions


Question:= "Let's turn to assumptions. Do you want to add an
assumption for the user persona?"

OUTPUT Question

INPUT User_Response
/* Send off to natural language processor to determine yes/no
answer
Natural_Language_Processor (User_Response, Understood_Response)

If Understood_Response = "Yes"

WHILE Understood_Response = "Yes"
OUTPUT "What is the name for the assumption?"
INPUT Assumption_Name
```

```
OUTPUT "How would describe the assumption?"
INPUT Assumption_Description
/* Save assumption name and description in Assumptions Table in
database
INSERT INTO Assumptions_Table (Problem_Area, Assumption_Name,
Assumption_Description, VALUES("Investment_Motel", Assumption_
Name, Assumption_Description)
OUTPUT "Do you want to add another assumption for the user
persona?"
INPUT User_Response
/* Send off to natural language processor to determine yes/no
answer
Natural_Language_Processor (User_Response, Understood_Response)

END WHILE

END Subprocess Provide_Initial_Assumptions
```

Pseudo Code for Provide_Initial_ Assumptions Subprocess

The Provide_Initial_Assumptions subprocess is similar to the other two subprocesses called from the Provide_Initial_Background subprocess. The first comment in the pseudo-code tells us that the questioning done by this subprocess belongs to the Questioning Precision subcategory in the Questions that Target the Quality of Reasoning category. It starts by asking, "Do you want to add an assumption for the user persona?" According to the natural language processor, if the answer is "yes," then the subprocess goes into a WHILE loop to gather the assumptions the user persona can use from the start. In this WHILE loop, Socrates Digital™ asks the user persona to provide the name of the assumption and its description. Next, in the WHILE loop, the application inserts the name of the assumption and its description into the Assumptions_Table table of the database. At the end of the WHILE loop, the application asks if the user persona wants to add another assumption. If the natural language processor determines that the answer is "yes," then the subprocess goes back to the top of the WHILE loop to gather another assumption from the analyst. If the natural language processor determines that the analyst's answer is "no," it exits the WHILE loop and completes the subprocess.

```
/* Questions that Target the Quality of Reasoning --
Questioning Precision

/* Generate Questioning Precision question for user persona and
collect
/* answer
BEGIN Subprocess Define_Behavior_Questioning_Precision(Answer)

Question:= "What is the behavior of Socrates Digital™? In other
words, how does it help the user persona solve a problem?  The
overall behavior should guide the user persona in conversation
to analyze the information, concepts, and assumptions of the
problem, then to the discover the conclusions, identify the
implications of those conclusions, and how all of this forms
a viewpoint about how to solve the problem. The behavior of
Socrates Digital™ should describe how it does this within the
problem area. Afterward, upload the file so it can be found
with the click of a mouse."

OUTPUT Question

UPLOAD_FILE Answer

END Subprocess Define_Behavior_Questioning_Precision
```

Pseudo Code for Define_Behavior_ Questioning_Precision Subprocess

The first comment in the pseudo-code for the Define_Behavior_Questioning_ Precision subprocess tells us that the questioning done by this subprocess belongs to the Questioning Precision subcategory in the Questions that Target the Quality of Reasoning category. It begins with a long and detailed question to get the analyst to describe how the system will guide the user persona in solving a problem. Precisely, how will it guide the user persona in conversation to analyze the problem's information, concepts, and assumptions, discover the conclusions, identify the implications of those conclusions, and how all of this forms a viewpoint about how to solve the problem. This answer is uploaded as a file to the database.

```
/* Questions that Target the Quality of Reasoning --
Questioning Precision

/* Generate Questioning Precision question for user persona and
```

```
collect answer
BEGIN Subprocess Identify_Journey_Questioning_Precision
(Answer)

Question:= "User journey mapping begins by deciding what are
the most important parts of the conversation that Socrates
Digital™ and user persona will have.  These important parts
are then scripted for Socrates Digital™ and user persona to
ensure that Socrates Digital™ provides the user persona what it
needs to decide about the problem at hand.  The next step is to
document this journey mapping in a file. Afterward, upload the
file so it can be found with the click of a mouse."

OUTPUT Question

UPLOAD_FILE Answer

END Subprocess Identify_Journey_Questioning_Precision
```

Pseudo Code for Identify_Journey_ Questioning_Precision Subprocess

In the pseudo-code for the Define_Behavior_Questioning_Precision subprocess, the first line tells us that the questioning done by this subprocess belongs to the Questioning Precision subcategory in the Questions that Target the Quality of Reasoning category. The rest of the pseudo-code begins with a long and detailed question. It asks the analyst to identify the essential parts of the conversation between Socrates Digital™ and the user persona. Then it asks the analyst to document that Socrates Digital™ provides the user persona what it needs to decide about the problem at hand. Afterward, the analyst uploads the file, and it is returned in the variable "Answer" to the Understand subprocess.

In Figure 3, we see that the second step to the Dialog Development Manager process is the Explore subprocess.

The pseudo-code for the Explore subprocess is listed below. The first comment tells us that this subprocess presents a question from the subcategory, Questioning Questions, that will get permission from the user persona for answering upcoming questions in the Questions that Target the Parts of Thinking main category. As the second comment tells us, its primary purpose is to create a sample dialog, perform a table reading, and conduct Wizard of Oz testing. As we will see, the details collected by the Explore subprocess

Figure 3. The Explore Subprocess in the Dialog Development Manager Process

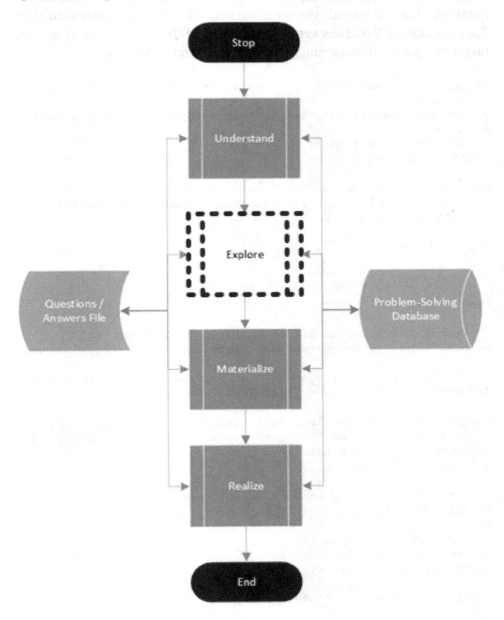

need to be precise, so this subprocess will call several subprocesses to ask the questions that will provide the precision needed in the user persona answers. Socrates Digital™ will answer these questions with calls to subprocesses that target the quality of reasoning in the user persona's answers.

```
/* Questions that Target the Parts of Thinking - Questioning
Questions
/* Ask the analyst to create a sample dialog, perform a table
reading
/* and conduct Wizard of Oz testing.
BEGIN Subprocess Explore

Question:= "Are you ready to answer some questions about
creating a sample dialog, performing a table reading, and
conducting Wizard of Oz testing?"

OUTPUT Question

INPUT Answer

User_Response:= Answer

/* Understood_Response will come back as "Yes" or "No"
Natural_Language_Processor (User_Response, Understood_Response)

/* If no, then give the analyst an opportunity to skip this.
IF Understood_Response = "Yes" THEN

Subprocess Create_Sample_Questioning_Precision (SampleFile)
Subprocess Perform_Reading_Questioning_Precision (ReadingFile)
Subprocess Conduct_Wizard_Test_Questioning_Precision
(WizardFile)

/* Save Explore phase answers to database
UPDATE Explore_Table
SET
Create_Sample:= SampleFile
Perform_Reading:= ReadingFile
Conduct_Wizard_Test:= WizardFile

WHERE Problem_Area = "Investments"

ELSE

OUTPUT "OK, we will skip this for now."

END_IF
```

```
END Subprocess Explore
```

Pseudo Code for the Explore Subprocess

When the Explore subprocess executes, the first action is to present a question to the user persona. In our investment example dialog, the analyst is asked, "Are you ready to answer some questions about creating a sample dialog, performing a table reading, and conducting Wizard of Oz testing?" The analyst's answer is captured in the Answer variable with the INPUT command and stored in the User_Response variable. As with the Understand subprocess, the application offers only one form of the question since it is asked once in a session.

As with the Understand subprocess, the next step is to send the response by the analyst to the natural language processor. If the natural language processor identifies the analyst's response as a "Yes," it will go forward with the questions about the Explore process. However, If the natural language processor identifies the analyst's response as something other than "Yes," then Socrates Digital™ outputs "OK, we will skip this for now" to the analyst.

Three questions need answers in the Explore process. They relate to creating a sample dialog, performing a table reading, and conducting Wizard of Oz testing. Since these three questions request more information about the Explore process, Socrates Digital™ presents them in separate subprocesses that target the quality of reasoning related to the "precision" of the analyst's answers in the Explore subprocess.

As the pseudo-code for Explore shows, the first subprocess that seeks an answer with precision is Create_Sample_Questioning_Precision, which asks the analyst to create a sample dialog for the user persona. The second subprocess, Perform_Reading_Questioning_Precision, seeks a precise answer for conducting a table reading. The third subprocess, Conduct_Wizard_Test_Questioning_Precision, seeks a precise answer for conducting Wizard of Oz testing.

After these three subprocesses have returned answers from the analyst, the application performs the last step of the Explore subprocess. In this step, the UPDATE and SET commands update the Create_Sample, Perform_Reading, and the Conduct_Wizard_Test fields in the Explore_Table table of the database.

Below, the pseudo-code is listed for the Create_Sample_Questioning_Precision subprocess.

```
/* Questions that Target the Quality of Reasoning --
Questioning Precision

/* Generate Questioning Precision question for user persona and
collect
/* answer
BEGIN Subprocess Create_Sample_Questioning_Precision (Answer)

Question:= "For the sample dialog, take those conversations
identified from the journey mapping step in the Understand
subprocess and flesh them out into conversations.  These
conversations use the 'happy path' approach that assumes
there are not any misunderstandings in the conversations
between Socrates Digital™ and the user persona. This keeps the
conversations simple and allows the designers to focus on the
information that will be exchanged in the conversation.

For all Socrates Digital™ systems, this sample dialog should
guide the user persona through the steps to identify the
information the user persona will examine, what concepts it
will use to make sense of the information, and what assumptions
underlie the analysis of the data.

The sample dialog should conclude by guiding the user persona
to make a conclusion and identify the implications of that
conclusion.  Finally, the sample dialog should guide the
user into taking all the information, concepts, assumptions,
conclusions, and implications into account to create a
viewpoint to solving the problem at hand.

The next step is to document this sample dialog in a file.
Afterward, upload this file so it can be found with the click."

OUTPUT Question

UPLOAD_FILE Answer

END Subprocess Create_Sample_Questioning_Precision
```

Pseudo Code for Create_Sample_ Questioning_Precision Subprocess

As we see in this pseudo-code for the Create_Sample_Questioning_Precision subprocess, the first comment tells us that the questioning done by this subprocess belongs to the Questioning Precision subcategory in the Questions that Target the Quality of Reasoning category. It begins with a lengthy question to get the analyst to create a sample dialog between Socrates Digital™ and the user persona. As described in the question, the analyst is given specific instructions for including details showing how Socrates Digital™ will guide the user persona in examining the information, concepts, assumptions, conclusions, and implications that make up a viewpoint for solving a problem. Finally, the analyst documents the sample dialog in a file. The analyst uploads the file, and it is returned in the variable "Answer" to the Explore subprocess.

Below, the pseudo-code is listed for the Perform_Reading_Questioning_Precision subprocess.

```
/* Questions that Target the Quality of Reasoning --
Questioning Precision

/* Generate Questioning Precision question for user persona and
collect
/* answer
BEGIN Subprocess Perform_Reading_Questioning_Precision (Answer)

Question:= "In this next step of the Explore Phase, volunteers
are used as actors to see if the sample dialog created in
the previous step captures the important things for the user
persona to solve the problem. Have one volunteer read Socrates
Digital™ part and another volunteer read the user persona part.

Afterward, conduct a debrief where you ask both volunteers for
their impressions of Socrates Digital™. Specifically, ask
them if Socrates Digital™ asked the right questions - and in
the right way. Ask them if some questions were missing.  The
most important aspect of the debrief is to have your volunteer
actors look at the line of reasoning to see if it makes sense.

The last thing to do in this step is to take this feedback and
use it to update the sample dialog so that it represents a
clear and logical progression from reasoning about information
to constructing a viewpoint for solving the problem at hand.

Afterward, document this sample dialog in a file and upload
it."

OUTPUT Question

UPLOAD_FILE Answer

END Subprocess Perform_Reading_Questioning_Precision
```

Pseudo Code for Perform_Reading_ Questioning_Precision Subprocess

As we see in this pseudo-code for the Perform_Reading_Questioning_ Precision subprocess, the first comment tells us that the questioning done by this subprocess belongs to the Questioning Precision subcategory in the Questions that Target the Quality of Reasoning category. It begins with a long question that asks the analyst to use volunteers as actors to see if the sample dialog created in the previous step captures the essential things for the user persona to solve the problem. The analyst is given specific instructions for including details showing how Socrates Digital™ will guide the user persona in examining the information, concepts, assumptions, conclusions, and implications that make up a viewpoint for solving a problem. Finally, the analyst documents the sample dialog in a file and uploads it.

The pseudo-code for the Conduct_Wizard_Test_Questioning_Precision subprocess is listed below.

```
/* Questions that Target the Quality of Reasoning --
Questioning Precision

/* Generate Questioning Precision question for user persona and
collect answer
BEGIN Subprocess Conduct_Wizard_Test_Questioning_Precision
(Answer)

Question:= "After the updates to the sample dialog during the
Table Reading step, this is the next step called Wizard of Oz
Testing.  The idea with this step is to have an actor play
the role of the user persona and have that person communicate
with the unseen Socrates Digital™, who is in another room.  It
provides a way to test the sample dialog in a setting that
more closely represents how communication will occur between
Socrates Digital™ and the user persona.

The first thing to do in this step is to have your volunteers
go through the sample dialog.  As before, you will be looking
to see if the sample dialog represents a clear and logical
progression from reasoning about information to constructing
a viewpoint for solving the problem at hand.  As before, you
are looking for weak spots where the reasoning makes too big
of a leap, such as a conclusion based on shaky concepts or
assumptions. Make revisions as needed.

Afterward, provide the revisions of the sample dialog in a new
```

```
file and upload it."

OUTPUT Question

UPLOAD_FILE Answer

END Subprocess Conduct_Wizard_Test_Questioning_Precision
```

Pseudo Code for Conduct_Wizard_Test_ Questioning_Precision Subprocess

As we see in this pseudo-code for the Conduct_Wizard_Test_Questioning_ Precision subprocess, the first comment tells us that the questioning done by this subprocess belongs to the Questioning Precision subcategory in the Questions that Target the Quality of Reasoning category. It begins with a long question that asks the analyst to have an actor play the role of the user persona and have that person communicate with the unseen actor playing Socrates Digital™ in another room. The analyst is given specific instructions for how the volunteers go through the sample dialog. As before, the analyst will be looking to see if the sample dialog represents a clear and logical progression from reasoning about information to constructing a viewpoint for solving the problem at hand. Socrates Digita guides the analyst to make revisions as necessary.

Finally, Socrates Digita asks the analyst to revise the sample dialog in a new file and upload it.

In Figure 4, we see that the third step in the Dialog Development Manager process is the Materialize subprocess.

The pseudo-code for the Materialize subprocess is listed below. The first comment tells us that this subprocess presents a question from the subcategory, Questioning Questions, that will get permission from the user persona for answering upcoming questions in the Questions that Target the Parts of Thinking main category. As the second comment tells us, it will ask the analyst to create user flow charts, voice scripts, and defining multimodal interactions. As we will see, the details collected by the Materialize subprocess need to be precise, so this subprocess will call several subprocesses to ask the questions that will provide the precision needed in the user persona answers. These questions will be answered with calls to subprocesses that target the quality of the user persona's answers.

Figure 4. The Materialize Subprocess in the Dialog Development Manager Process

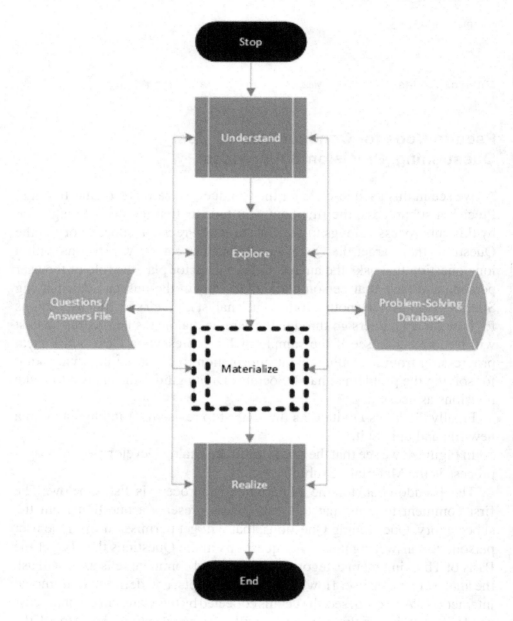

```
/* Questions that Target the Parts of Thinking - Questioning
Questions
/* Ask the analyst to create user flow charts, voice scripts,
and define
/* multimodal interactions.
BEGIN Subprocess Materialize

Question:= "Are you ready to answer some questions about
creating user flow charts, voice scripts, and defining
multimodal interactions?"

OUTPUT Question

INPUT Answer

User_Response:= Answer

/* Understood_Response will come back as "Yes" or "No"
Natural_Language_Processor (User_Response, Understood_Response)

/* If no, then give the analyst an opportunity to skip this.
IF Understood_Response = "Yes" THEN

Subprocess Create_FlowCharts_Questioning_Precision (ChartsFile)
Subprocess Develop_Scripts_Questioning_Precision (ScriptsFile)
Subprocess Define_Multimodal_Questioning_Precision
(MultimodalFile)

/* Save Materialize phase answers to database
UPDATE Materialize_Table
SET
Create_FlowCharts:= ChartsFile
Develop_Scripts:= ScriptsFile
Define_Multimodal:= MultimodalFile

WHERE Problem_Area = "Investments"

ELSE

OUTPUT "OK, we will skip this for now."

END_IF

END Subprocess Materialize
```

Pseudo Code for the Materialize Subprocess

When the Materialize subprocess runs, the first action is to present a question to the user persona. In our investment example dialog, the analyst is asked, "Are you ready to answer some questions about creating user flow charts, voice scripts, and defining multimodal interactions?" The analyst's answer is captured in the Answer variable with the INPUT command and stored in the User_Response variable. As with the Understand and Explore subprocesses, Socrates Digital™ presents only one question form since this question will only be asked once in a session.

As with the Understand and Explore subprocesses, the next step is to send the response by the analyst to the natural language processor. If the natural language processor identifies the analyst's response as a "Yes," it will go forward with the questions about the Materialize process. However, If the natural language processor identifies the analyst's response as something other than "Yes," then Socrates Digital™ outputs "OK, we will skip this for now" to the analyst.

Three questions need to be answered in the Materialize subprocess -- as with the Understand and Explore subprocesses. They relate to creating user flow charts, voice scripts, and defining multimodal interactions. Since these three questions request more information about the Materialize subprocess, the application presents them in separate subprocesses that target the quality of reasoning related to the "precision" of the analyst's answers in the Materialize subprocess.

As the pseudo-code for Materialize shows, the first subprocess that seeks an answer with precision, is the subprocess, Create_FlowCharts_Questioning_Precision, which asks the analyst to create flow charts that map the flow of control for Socrates Digital™. The second subprocess, Develop_Scripts_Questioning_Precision, seeks a precise answer for developing a detailed script from the earlier sample dialogs. The third subprocess, Define_Multimodal_Questioning_Precision, seeks a precise answer for how the developer plans to integrate Socrates Digital™ with visualizations, charts, and other multimedia content.

After these three subprocesses have returned answers from the analyst, the application performs the last step of the Materialize subprocess. In this step, the UPDATE and SET commands update the Create_FlowCharts, Develop_Scripts, and the Define_Multimodal fields in the Materialize_Table table of the database.

Below, the pseudo-code is listed for the Create_FlowCharts_Questioning_ Precision subprocess.

```
/* Questions that Target the Quality of Reasoning --
Questioning Precision

/* Generate Questioning Precision question for user persona and
collect answer
BEGIN Subprocess Create_FlowCharts_Questioning_Precision
(Answer)

Question:= "This first step of the Materialize phase is to
create the user flow charts for the subprocesses that capture
answers with questions that make up the parts of thinking. The
subprocesses that capture answers with questions that make up
the parts of the quality of reasoning are not seen in the flow
charts.  That is because they are called from the subprocesses
that focus on the parts of thinking.

As shown in the previous chapters of this book, using the
sample dialog that resulted from the Wizard of Oz testing and
revision, the details of the flow of control are defined so
that all the possible user persona's responses are addressed.

After the flow charts have been created, the last step is to
place the flowcharts in a file and upload the file so it can be
found with the other design documentation."

OUTPUT Question

UPLOAD_FILE Answer

END Subprocess Create_FlowCharts_Questioning_Precision
```

Pseudo Code for Create_FlowCharts_ Questioning_Precision Subprocess

As we see in this pseudo-code for the Create_FlowCharts_Questioning_ Precision subprocess, the first comment tells us that the questioning done by this subprocess belongs to the Questioning Precision subcategory in the Questions that Target the Quality of Reasoning category. It begins with a detailed question to get the analyst to create flow charts of the dialog between Socrates Digital™ and the user persona. As described in the question, the analyst is given detailed instructions for the flow of control to address all the possible user persona's responses. Finally, Socrates Digital™ asks the analyst to place all the flow charts in a file. The analyst uploads the file, and it is returned in the variable "Answer" to the Materialize subprocess.

The pseudo-code for the Develop_Scripts_Questioning_Precision subprocess is listed below.

```
/* Questions that Target the Quality of Reasoning --
Questioning Precision

/* Generate Questioning Precision question for user persona and
collect answer
BEGIN Subprocess Develop_Scripts_Questioning_Precision (Answer)

Question:= "In this step of the Materialize Phase, all
questions and possible responses are documented in a word
processing document or spreadsheet application.  Since most
natural language processing services can process single
question/answer pairs, there is a temptation to skip this step.
It turns out that there are two good reasons to document the
question/answer pairs and upload them as a file to a natural
language processing service.

The first reason is that with a documented "knowledge base" of
question/answer pairs, designers can easily see what needs to
be changed, make those changes, and upload the question/answer
pairs as a batch to make those systematic changes.

The second reason to put the question/answer pairs in a file is
to have a way to divide up the work.  The upfront design work
described in these first three phases of design and development
can be done by a designer.  Then, the file containing the
knowledge base of questions and answer pairs can be handed off
to a programmer for the Realize Phase.

The last thing to do in this step is to take this file and
upload it."

OUTPUT Question

UPLOAD_FILE Answer

END Subprocess Develop_Scripts_Questioning_Precision
```

Pseudo Code for Develop_Scripts_ Questioning_Precision Subprocess

As we see in this pseudo-code for the Develop_Scripts_Questioning_Precision subprocess, the first comment tells us that the questioning done by this subprocess belongs to the Questioning Precision subcategory in the Questions that Target the Quality of Reasoning category. It begins with a detailed question that asks the analyst to use the sample dialogs that have been revised in the table reading and Wizard of Oz steps and develop a list of question/answer pairs that cover all the possible interactions between Socrates Digital™ and the user persona. Finally, the program asks the analyst to document the question/answer pairs in a file and upload it.

Below, the pseudo-code is listed for the Define_Multimodal_Questioning_ Precision subprocess.

```
/* Questions that Target the Quality of Reasoning --
Questioning Precision

/* Generate Questioning Precision question for user persona and
collect answer
BEGIN Subprocess Define_Multimodal_Questioning_Precision
(Answer)

Question:= "In this third step of the Materialize Phase, the
possible multimodal interactions between the system and user
personas are examined. In the investment dialog example, the
user persona interacts with data sources such as spreadsheets,
databases, and business intelligence platforms at the same
time the user persona is interacting with Socrates Digital™.
However, Socrates Digital™ is not integrated with the data
sources.  Socrates Digital™ relies on the user persona to
provide the requested values from the data sources to it.

If Socrates Digital™ is expected to interact directly with the
data sources during its conversation with the user persona,
that would be addressed here.  For example, when Socrates
Digital™ asks the user persona if a correlation found in an
individual data item holds for the larger dataset, Socrates
Digital™ could interact with the data source, run the
correlation, and present the results to the user to evaluate.
This level of interaction between the Socrates Digital™, user
persona, and the data sources would require additional design,
development, and system user testing to ensure the system works
as envisioned.
```

```
After these multimodal aspects of the design have been
addressed and stored in a file, then upload the file."

OUTPUT Question

UPLOAD_FILE Answer

END Subprocess Define_Multimodal_Questioning_Precision
```

Pseudo Code for Define_Multimodal_ Questioning_Precision Subprocess

As we see in this pseudo-code for the Define_Multimodal_Questioning_ Precision subprocess, the first comment tells us that the questioning done by this subprocess belongs to the Questioning Precision subcategory in the Questions that Target the Quality of Reasoning category. It begins with a lengthy discussion that asks the analyst to address the multimodal aspects of the final system. The program gives the analyst specific instructions about describing the integration of multimodal displays in the system. These instructions point out that the more tightly the integration between Socrates Digital™ and multimodal displays, the more work will be needed in the design, development, and system user testing to ensure the system works as designed.

Finally, the analyst addresses these multimodal aspects of design in a document and uploads it.

In Figure 5, we see that the fourth step in the Dialog Development Manager process is the Realize subprocess.

The pseudo-code for the Realize subprocess is listed below. The first comment tells us that this subprocess presents a question from the subcategory, Questioning Questions, that will get permission from the user persona for answering upcoming questions in the Questions that Target the Parts of Thinking main category. As the second comment tells us, it will ask the analyst to create vocabulary, develop implementation logic, and set calculation weights. As we will see, the details collected by the Realize subprocess need to be precise, so this subprocess will call several subprocesses to ask the questions that will provide the precision needed in the user persona answers. As is our convention, these questions will be answered with calls to subprocesses that target the quality of the user persona's answers.

Figure 5. The Realize Subprocess in the Dialog Development Manager Process

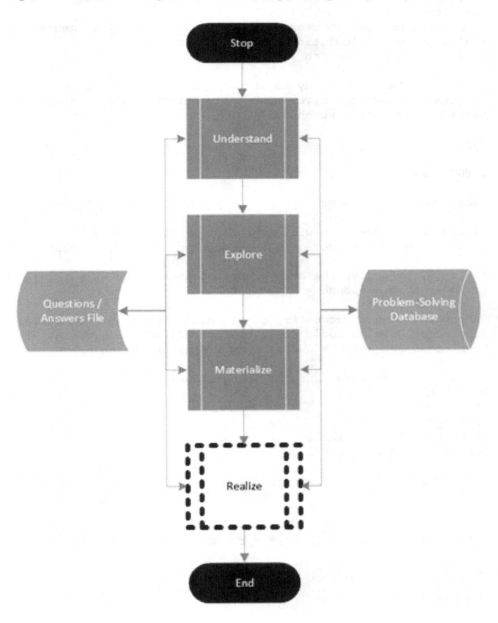

```
/* Questions that Target the Parts of Thinking - Questioning
Questions
/* Ask the analyst to create vocabulary, develop implementation
logic, and set calculation weights.
BEGIN Subprocess Realize

Question:= "Are you ready to answer some questions about
creating vocabulary, developing implementation logic, and
setting calculation weights?"

OUTPUT Question

INPUT Answer

User_Response:= Answer

/* Understood_Response will come back as "Yes" or "No"
Natural_Language_Processor (User_Response, Understood_Response)

/* If no, then give the analyst an opportunity to skip this.
IF Understood_Response = "Yes" THEN

Subprocess Create_Vocabulary_Questioning_Precision (VocabFile)
Subprocess Develop_Logic_Questioning_Precision (LogicFile)
Subprocess Set_Weights_Questioning_Precision (WeightsFile)

/* Save Realize phase answers to database
UPDATE Realize_Table
SET
Create_Vocabulary:= VocabFile
Develop_Logic:= LogicFile
Set_Weights:= WeightsFile

WHERE Problem_Area = "Investments"

ELSE

OUTPUT "OK, we will skip this for now."

END_IF

END Subprocess Realize
```

Pseudo Code for the Realize Subprocess

When the Realize subprocess executes, the first action is to present a question to the user persona. In our investment example dialog, the analyst is asked, "Are you ready to answer some questions about creating vocabulary, developing implementation logic, and setting calculation weights?" The analyst's answer is captured in the Answer variable with the INPUT command and stored in the User_Response variable. As with the other subprocesses, the program offers only one form of the question since it is asked once in a session.

As with the subprocesses in the design and development process, the next step is to send the response by the analyst to the natural language processor. If the natural language processor identifies the analyst's response as a "Yes," it will go forward with the questions about the Realize process. However, If the natural language processor identifies the analyst's response as something other than "Yes," then Socrates Digital™ outputs "OK, we will skip this for now" to the analyst.

As with the other subprocesses, three questions need answers in the Realize subprocess. They relate to creating vocabulary, developing implementation logic, and setting calculation weights. Since these three questions request more information about the Realize process, Socrates Digital™ will present them in separate subprocesses that target the quality of reasoning related to the "precision" of the analyst's answers in the Realize subprocess.

As the pseudo-code for the Realize subprocess shows, the first subprocess that seeks an answer with precision is the Create_Vocabulary_Questioning_Precision, which asks the analyst to create a vocabulary for uploading into the natural language processor. The second subprocess, Develop_Logic_Questioning_Precision, seeks a precise answer for developing implementation logic for Socrates Digital™. The third subprocess, Set_Weights_Questioning_Precision, seeks a precise answer for setting the calculation weights of Socrates Digital™.

After these three subprocesses have returned answers from the analyst, the program performs the last step of the Realize subprocess. In this step, the UPDATE and SET commands update the Create_Vocabulary, Develop_Logic, and the Set_Weights fields in the Realize_Table table of the database.

The pseudo-code for the Create_Vocabulary_Questioning_Precision subprocess is listed below.

```
/* Questions that Target the Quality of Reasoning --
Questioning Precision
```

```
/* Generate Questioning Precision question for user persona to
create vocabulary file
BEGIN Subprocess Create_Vocabulary_Questioning_Precision
(Answer)
```

Question:= "In this first step of the Realize phase, the
vocabulary is built for the natural language processing
service. This is typically a simple, straightforward, and
well-documented process. This process to create the vocabulary
for the natural language processing service is similar across
artificial intelligence service providers such as Apple,
Microsoft, Google, and Amazon.

Creating a vocabulary for a natural language processing service
typically has the following steps:

1) Create an account with the artificial intelligence service
provider.
2) Create an entity that will process the string of words that
you send it. These are usually called something like a "bot,"
"agent," or similar name.
3) Upload the knowledge base of question/answer pairs.
4) Train the bot on the knowledge base.
5) Test the bot to see if it answers the questions in the way
you expect.
6) Revise the question/answer pairs.
7) Publish the bot.
8) Access the bot from the Socrates Digital™ system. This is
usually done by using the published endpoint of the bot.

After the vocabulary for a natural language processing service
has been created and saved in a file, the last step is to
upload the file to the natural language processor for it to use
in recognizing answers by the user persona during a session
with Socrates Digital™. In addition, upload the file to
Socrates Digital™ for safekeeping in the Dialog Manager."

```
OUTPUT Question

UPLOAD_FILE Answer

END Subprocess Create_Vocabulary_Questioning_Precision
```

Pseudo Code for Create_Vocabulary_ Questioning_Precision Subprocess

As we see in this pseudo-code for the Create_Vocabulary_Questioning_ Precision subprocess, the first comment tells us that the questioning done by this subprocess belongs to the Questioning Precision subcategory in the Questions that Target the Quality of Reasoning category. It begins with a detailed question to get the analyst to create the vocabulary for the natural language processing service. As the detailed instructions state, this is typically a simple, straightforward, and well-documented process. This process to create the vocabulary for the natural language processing service is similar across artificial intelligence service providers such as Apple, Microsoft, Google, and Amazon.

Finally, the program asks the analyst to place vocabulary in a file. The analyst uploads the file to the natural language processor service for it to use in recognizing answers by the user persona during a session with Socrates Digital™. In addition, the analyst uploads the file to Socrates Digital™, and it is returned in the variable "Answer" to the Realize subprocess to be managed by the Dialog Development Manager.

Below, the pseudo-code is listed for the Develop_Logic_Questioning_ Precision subprocess.

```
/* Questions that Target the Quality of Reasoning --
Questioning Precision

/* Generate Questioning Precision question for user persona to
develop implementation logic
BEGIN Subprocess Develop_Logic_Questioning_Precision (Answer)

Question:= "In this second step of the Realize phase, the
implementation logic is developed for the Socrates Digital™
system.  This can be done in more than one way and your choice
will depend on several factors.  One factor is concerns which
artificial intelligence service provider is selected.  Some
have no code application programming interfaces (APIs) while
others have APIs that can only be accessed by a general
programming language such as Java, C, or Python.

This book presents the pseudo-code for developing most of the
logic in a general programming language. Developers can then
use this pseudo-code to implement the parts they choose in a
general programming language.
```

By the time this book is published, there will be many options to develop implementation logic across all of the artificial intelligence service providers, including Apple, Microsoft, Google, IBM, and Amazon.
The last thing to do in this step is to put this implementation logic to use for your Socrates Digital™ system. In addition, take this file
and upload it to Socrates Digital™ to be managed by the Dialog Development Manager."

```
OUTPUT Question

UPLOAD_FILE Answer

END Subprocess Develop_Logic_Questioning_Precision
```

Pseudo Code for Develop_Logic_ Questioning_Precision Subprocess

As we see in this pseudo-code for the Develop_Logic_Questioning_Precision subprocess, the first comment tells us that the questioning done by this subprocess belongs to the Questioning Precision subcategory in the Questions that Target the Quality of Reasoning category. It begins with a detailed question that asks the analyst to develop implementation logic for the Socrates Digital™ system. The analyst is instructed that this can be done in more than one way, and the choice will depend on several factors. One factor concerns which artificial intelligence service provider is selected. Some have no code application programming interfaces (APIs) while others have APIs that can only be accessed by a general programming language such as Java, C, or Python.

The program instructs the user persona to put this implementation logic to use for the Socrates Digital™ system. In addition, the program tells the user persona to take this file and upload it to Socrates Digital™ to be managed by the Dialog Development Manager.

Below, the pseudo-code is listed for the Set_Weights_Questioning_ Precision subprocess.

```
/* Questions that Target the Quality of Reasoning --
Questioning Precision

/* Generate Questioning Precision question for user persona to
set calculation weights
```

```
BEGIN Subprocess Set_Weights_Questioning_Precision (Answer)

Question:= "The last step in the Realize Phase is setting the
numerical weights for the calculations in the implementation
logic.

As presented in Chapter 8, they are used to empirically adjust
the Viewpoint Confidence according to the problem area.

/* Set Multiplier for each factor - investment example dialog
/* shown

Additional_Dataset_Multiplier:= 0.1
Additional_ Concept_Multiplier:= 0.1
Additional_ Assumption_Multiplier:= 0.1
Additional_ Conclusion_Multiplier:= 0.1
Additional_ Implication_Multiplier:= 0.1

/* Set Weight for each factor - investment example dialog shown
Dataset_Weight:= 0.3
Concept_Weight:= 0.1
Assumption_Weight:= 0.1
Conclusion_Weight:= 0.2
Implication_Weight:= 0.3

First, set these multipliers and weights for all the factors
in the implementation logic of your Socrates Digital™ system.
Second, upload a copy of the settings in a file to Socrates
Digital™ for safekeeping in the Dialog Development Manager."

OUTPUT Question

UPLOAD_FILE Answer

END Subprocess Set_Weights_Questioning_Precision
```

Pseudo Code for Set_Weights_ Questioning_Precision Subprocess

As we see in this pseudo-code for the Set_Weights_Questioning_Precision subprocess, the first comment tells us that the questioning done by this subprocess belongs to the Questioning Precision subcategory in the Questions that Target the Quality of Reasoning category. The second comment tells the user persona to set calculation weights

This subprocess begins with a discussion that asks the analyst to set the numerical weights for the calculations in the implementation logic. The program instructs the analyst about setting the weights in the context of determining the overall Viewpoint_Confidence. The additional multiplier values discussed in Chapter 8 add additional confidence to information, concepts, assumptions, conclusions, or implications. The factor weights have to do with the importance of the factor in determining the Viewpoint_Confidence. For example, analysts may set the Dataset_Weight higher in some problem areas due to the importance of data for solving the problem.

The program instructs the user persona to set these multipliers and weights for all the factors in the implementation logic of the Socrates Digital™ system. Afterward, the program instructs the user persona to upload a copy of the settings in a file for safekeeping in the Dialog Development Manager.

SUMMARY

This chapter shows how software development professionals can use the provided flow charts and pseudo-code to create the Dialog Development Manager. Analysts then use the Dialog Development Manager to create the problem-specific knowledge needed by a natural language processor to support the conversation between Socrates Digital™ and the end-users solving a problem. For the Dialog Development Manager to have this conversation with the developer analysts, software development professionals need to create the questions/answers file for the natural language processor. In this way, the Dialog Development Manager helps analysts create and manage the conversational knowledge needed for solving problems in a specific area, such as investment opportunities.

The Dialog Development Manager provides a submit, review, and approval process for all the steps – Understand, Explore, Materialize, and Realize – of the dialog development process described in Chapter 4. The purpose of the questions by the Dialog Development Manager in the Understand phase is to create a user persona profile, define Socrates Digital™ behavior, and identify user journey mapping. In the Explore phase, the Dialog Development Manager asks questions of the user persona to create a sample dialog, perform a table reading, and conduct Wizard of Oz testing. The Dialog Development Manager will ask analysts to create user flow charts, voice scripts, and define multimodal interactions in the Materialize phase. Furthermore, in the Realize phase, the Dialog Development Manager will ask analysts to create vocabulary, develop implementation logic, and set calculation weights for Socrates Digital™. As we saw in this chapter, the details collected in each of these phases need to be precise, so Socrates Digital™ calls several subprocesses to ask the questions that provide the precision needed in the user persona answers.

REFERENCES

Humble, J. (2019). *The Voice Design Process For Voice User Interfaces (VUIs)*. CareerFoundry [YouTube channel]. Retrieved November 22, 2019, from https://www.youtube.com/watch?v=8OXN0ZDpwrM&t=1s

Chapter 10
Problem–Solving Manager:
Creating an Innovative Learning Organization

ABSTRACT

The Problem-Solving Manager makes the approved best practices available across the organization. This chapter presents the flow charts and pseudo-code for developing the Problem-Solving Manager. This chapter also shows that this additional role for the Problem-Solving Manager enables an innovative learning (iLearning) organization. Innovative learning begins with all team members having access to the same knowledge for the current "best way" of solving a problem. This knowledge is where the lessons learned from the past meet the best thinking of the present to learn how to do things better – innovative learning.

INTRODUCTION

From what we have seen so far, Socrates Digital™ uses the Problem-Solving Manager as storage during the development of viewpoints. We remember that a viewpoint comprises information analysis, concept application, assumption identification, conclusion development, and implication prediction from previous chapters. When Socrates Digital™ needs one of these viewpoint components for the user persona, the Problem-Solving Manager retrieves it and passes it back to Socrates Digital™ for presentation.

DOI: 10.4018/978-1-7998-7955-8.ch010

As shown in Figure 1, the Problem-Solving Manager also provides a submit, review, and approval process of a viewpoint to become a "best practice" for an organization to solve a particular problem. The Problem-Solving Manager makes these approved best practices available across the organization.

Figure 1. The Problem-Solving Manager Process

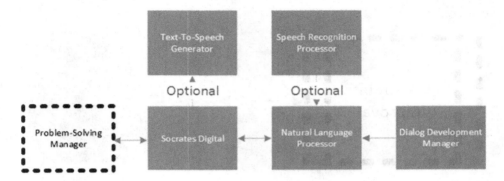

INSIDE THE PROBLEM-SOLVING MANAGER PROCESS

As we saw in Chapter 5, Socrates Digital™ interacts directly with the Problem-Solving Database, a part of the Problem-Solving Manager. As we are discovering in this chapter, the Problem-Solving Manager also manages viewpoints for the organization. In Figure 2, we see the Viewpoint_Approval subprocess of the Problem-Solving Manager that manages the submit, review, and approval process for viewpoints.

The pseudo-code for the Viewpoint_Approval subprocess is listed below. The first comment tells us that this subprocess presents a question from the subcategory, Questioning Questions, that will get permission from the user persona to answer upcoming questions in the Questions that Target the Parts of Thinking category. As the second comment tells us, its primary purpose is to ask analysts if they have a viewpoint to submit for approval as a best practice for the organization.

Figure 2. The Viewpoint_Approval Subprocess of the Problem-Solving Manager Process

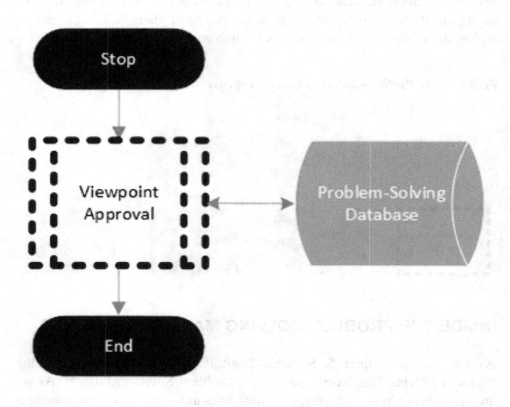

```
/* Questions that Target the Parts of Thinking - Questioning
Questions
/* Ask the analyst if there is a viewpoint to submit for
approval
/* as a best practice for the organization
BEGIN Subprocess Viewpoint_Approval

Question:= "Do you want to submit a viewpoint used in a
problem-solving session to be considered as a "best practice"
for the organization?"

OUTPUT Question

INPUT Answer

User_Response:= Answer

/* Understood_Response will come back as "Yes" or "No"
```

```
Natural_Language_Processor (User_Response, Understood_Response)

/* If no, then give the analyst an opportunity to skip this.
IF Understood_Response = "Yes" THEN

Question:= "What is the ID number of this viewpoint?"

OUTPUT Question

INPUT Answer

User_Response:= Answer

/* Understood_Response will come back as a number
Natural_Language_Processor (User_Response, Understood_Response)

ID:= Understood_Response

Subprocess Submitted_Questioning_Precision (Submittal_
Rationale)
Subprocess Reviewed_Questioning_Precision (ID, Reviewed,
Opinion)
Subprocess Approved_Questioning_Precision (ID, Approved,
Reason)

/* Save Understand phase answers to database
UPDATE Approved_Viewpoints_Table
SET
Submitted_Viewpoint:= Submittal_Rationale

Reviewed_Viewpoint:= Reviewed
Reviewed_Opinion:= Opinion

Approved_Viewpoint:= Approved
Approved_Reason:= Reason

WHERE Viewpoint_ID = Viewpoint_ID_Number

ELSE

OUTPUT "OK, we will skip this."

END_IF

END Subprocess Viewpoint_Approval
```

Pseudo Code for the Viewpoint_Approval Subprocess

When the Viewpoint_Approval subprocess runs, the first action is to present a question to the analyst. The analyst is asked, "Do you want to submit a viewpoint used in a problem-solving session to be considered as a "best practice" for the organization?" The analyst's answer is captured in the Answer variable with the INPUT command and stored in the User_Response variable. Note that since Socrates Digital™ asks this question only once a session – there is only one form of the question.

The next step is to send the response by the analyst to the natural language processor. If the natural language processor identifies the analyst's response as a "Yes," it will go forward with the questions about the Viewpoint_Approval. However, If the natural language processor identifies the analyst's response as something other than "Yes," then the system persona outputs "OK, we will skip this." to the analyst.

Four questions need answers to complete the Viewpoint_Approval process. The first question asked is, "What is the ID number of this viewpoint?" Since the following three questions request more information about the Viewpoint_Approval subprocess, Socrates Digital™ presents them in separate subprocesses that target the quality of reasoning and are called from the subprocess Viewpoint_Approval. These subprocesses relate to the "precision" of the analyst's answers in the Viewpoint_Approval subprocess. The first subprocess, Submitted_Questioning_Precision, asks the user persona, a submitter, why the organization should consider it a best practice. The second subprocess, Reviewed_Questioning_Precision, asks the user persona, a reviewer, the same question. Furthermore, the third subprocess, Approved_Questioning_Precision, asks the user persona, an approver, to approve, or disapprove, the viewpoint as a best practice.

After the subprocesses have returned answers from the different user personas, the last step of the Viewpoint_Approval subprocess is to use the UPDATE and SET commands to update the Submitted_Viewpoint, Reviewed_Viewpoint, Reviewed_Opinion, Approve_Viewpoint, and Approved_Reason fields in the Approved_Viewpoints_Table table of the database.

Below, the pseudo-code is listed for the Submitted_Questioning_Precision subprocess.

```
/* Questions that Target the Quality of Reasoning --
Questioning Precision
```

```
/* Generate Questioning Precision question for user persona and
/* collect answer
BEGIN Subprocess Submitted_Questioning_Precision (Answer)

Question:= "Why are you submitting this viewpoint for
consideration as a 'best practice' for our organization?"

OUTPUT Question

INPUT Answer


END Subprocess Submitted_Questioning_Precision
```

Pseudo Code for Submitted_Questioning_ Precision Subprocess

As we see in this pseudo-code for the Submitted_Questioning_Precision subprocess, the first comment tells us that the questioning done by this subprocess belongs to the Questioning Precision subcategory in the Questions that Target the Quality of Reasoning category. It presents the analyst with a pointed question, "Why are you submitting this viewpoint for consideration as a "best practice" for our organization?" The answer will provide the next analyst with some rationale for reviewing it as a best practice and returning in the Answer variable.

```
/* Questions that Target the Quality of Reasoning --
Questioning Precision

/* Generate Questioning Precision question for user persona and
collect
/* answer
BEGIN Subprocess Reviewed_Questioning_Precision (ID, Answer,
Opinion)

SELECT Viewpoint_Description, Viewpoint_Confidence
FROM Viewpoints_Table
WHERE Viewpoint_ID = ID


Question:= "Please review this viewpoint.  In your opinion,
should it become a best practice for our organization"

OUTPUT Question
```

```
INPUT Opinion

Answer:= "yes"

END Subprocess Reviewed_Questioning_Precision
```

Pseudo Code for Reviewed_Questioning_ Precision Subprocess

The first comment in the pseudo-code for the Reviewed_Questioning_Precision subprocess tells us that the questioning done by this subprocess belongs to the Questioning Precision subcategory in the Questions that Target the Quality of Reasoning category. It begins by displaying the viewpoint from the database. Then it asks the reviewer for an opinion as to whether the viewpoint should become a best practice for the organization. After collecting the opinion in the variable "Opinion," the Answer variable is assigned the value "yes" to indicate a completed review of the viewpoint.

```
/* Questions that Target the Quality of Reasoning --
Questioning Precision

/* Generate Questioning Precision question for user persona and
collect answer
BEGIN Subprocess Approved_Questioning_Precision  (ID, Answer,
Reason)

SELECT Viewpoint_Description, Viewpoint_Confidence
FROM Viewpoints_Table
WHERE Viewpoint_ID = ID

Question:= "Do you want to approve this viewpoint as a best
practice?"

OUTPUT Question

INPUT Answer

User_Response:= Answer

/* Understood_Response will come back as "yes" or "no"
Natural_Language_Processor (User_Response, Understood_Response)

Answer:= Understood_Response
```

240

```
Question:= "What is the reason behind your answer for
approval?"

OUTPUT Question

INPUT Reason

END Subprocess Approved_Questioning_Precision
```

Pseudo Code for Approved_Questioning_ Precision Subprocess

In the pseudo-code for the Approved_Questioning_Precision subprocess, the first line tells us that the questioning done by this subprocess belongs to the Questioning Precision subcategory in the Questions that Target the Quality of Reasoning category. The rest of the pseudo-code begins by asking the reviewer if the viewpoint should become a best practice for the organization. After collecting the yes/no answer in the variable "Answer," the next question collects the reasons behind the approval ruling and returns them in the variable, "Reason."

ENABLING INNOVATIVE LEARNING

The Problem-Solving Manager enables an innovative learning (iLearning) organization. (See Salisbury, 2009, for a detailed explanation of how to create an innovative learning organization.) Innovative learning begins with all team members having access to the same knowledge for the current "best way" of solving a problem. A way to provide this knowledge is through the information, concepts, assumptions, conclusions, and implications of a problem's viewpoint. Knowing what they know, the team is now prepared to look at innovative ways to solve the current problem. This knowledge is where the lessons learned from the past meet the best thinking of the present to learn how to do things better -- innovative learning.

Growing and Sharing Knowledge in Organizations

Organizations that grow and share their knowledge have harnessed the ongoing life cycle of knowledge – its creation, preservation, dissemination, and application. The first phase, creating new knowledge, occurs when members of the organization solve a new unique problem or solve smaller parts of a larger problem such as those generated by an ongoing project. The next phase is the preservation of this newly created knowledge. It includes recording the description of the problem as well as its new solution. This phase feeds the next one, the dissemination and application of this new knowledge. The dissemination and application phase involves sharing this new knowledge with the membership of the organization. Disseminated knowledge then becomes an input for solving new problems in the following knowledge creation phase. In this way, each knowledge life cycle phase provides input for the following phrase -- creating an ongoing cycle. Since this cycle continues to build upon itself, it becomes a knowledge spiral in the organization, as described by Nonaka and Takeuchi (1995).

While the growth and sharing of knowledge are recognized as one of the essential elements in becoming a learning organization (Easterby-Smith, 1997; Marsick & Watkins, 1994; Senge, 1990), what has been missing, according to many researchers and practitioners in the field, is the development of a cohesive theory for describing how people learn and share in an organization (Raybould, 1995; Salisbury, 2000; Salisbury, 2003). Today's organizations need this cohesive theory to avoid developing technological solutions that do not support their entire life cycle of knowledge (Plass & Salisbury, 2002). Salisbury and Plass developed a cohesive theory for creating innovative learning to address this situation (Salisbury & Plass, 2001; Salisbury, 2009, Salisbury 2010). It describes how learning can take place with one individual, be preserved, transferred to other individuals, and built upon in an organizational setting

Theory for Creating an Innovative Learning Organization

As described in Chapter 1, a revision of Bloom's Taxonomy (Bloom, 1956) developed by Anderson and his colleagues to represent the complexity of problem-solving knowledge was used to create this theory for innovative learning (Anderson et al., 1998). As shown in Figure 3, one of the significant differences in Anderson and his colleagues' revised taxonomy is identifying knowledge as a separate dimension that describes it as factual, conceptual, procedural, and metacognitive. Another significant difference is that Anderson and colleagues recast Bloom's other categories into a "process dimension," which describes the learner's cognitive processes when processing knowledge of that category. Anderson and colleagues also renamed these process dimension categories from Bloom's original "knowledge, comprehension, application, analysis, synthesis, and evaluation" to "remember, understand, apply, analyze, evaluate, and create." As introduced in Chapter 1, Anderson and colleagues place "create" as the highest level of cognition; it describes individuals putting elements together to form a novel coherent whole or make an original product.

Anderson et al. (1998) describe factual knowledge as terminology, specific details, and elements. Conceptual knowledge relates to theories, models, principles, and generalizations. Procedural knowledge includes skills, algorithms, techniques, and other methods that are specific to a product or process. Anderson and colleagues added metacognitive knowledge to Bloom's Taxonomy. It is "knowledge about knowledge" and involves general learning, thinking, and problem-solving strategies. Metacognitive knowledge also includes knowledge concerning the appropriate contexts and conditions for the use of the strategies themselves. Additionally, it includes the "heuristics" or "rules of thumb" that experts use to solve problems.

At the individual level, the innovative learning theory has elements of situated cognition as described by Brown, Collins & Duguid (1989). The theory supports learning in the context of the work– creating an "authentic context" for learning. Problem-solvers can access knowledge – and other people -- to learn how to construct solutions to pressing organizational problems in a just-in-time manner. Furthermore, the theory supports situated cognition for learners with differing cognitive needs by providing different types of knowledge as defined by Anderson and his colleagues (1998) in their revision to Bloom's Taxonomy (factual, conceptual, procedural, and metacognitive.

At the team level, innovative learning theory extends the theory of distributed cognition. (See Salomon, 1996 for an overview of distributed cognition.) One of the best-documented examples of distributed cognition in a work environment is by Edwin Hutchins in his book "Cognition in the Wild" (Hutchins, 1996). Hutchins studied how a crew collaborated to operate a large ship at sea. According to his description of the theory of distributed cognition, cognition is distributed across individuals. No one individual has complete knowledge of accomplishing a complex task such as operating a large ship. Hutchins also describes that cognition is distributed across the artifacts of an organization's work. On the ship, that means the instruments provide critical decision-making information to the crew members.

Furthermore, according to the theory of distributed cognition, cognition is in the history of those artifacts. On the ship, the previous version of an instrument gives a context for the present version. In an office environment, artifacts are the "intermediate products" of a larger process, such as a viewpoint. These intermediate products are analysis of information, application of concepts, identification of assumptions, development of conclusions, and prediction of implications. The theory of innovative learning extends the theory of distributed cognition to involve different types of knowledge as defined by Anderson and his colleagues (1998) in their revision to Bloom's Taxonomy (factual, conceptual, procedural, and metacognitive). These different types of knowledge are present in the distribution of cognition across individuals, their artifacts, and the history of their artifacts.

Innovative learning theory extends Nonaka and Takeuchi's (1995) description of creating a knowledge spiral in an organization at the organizational level. In Nonaka and Takeuchi's knowledge creation process, transferring knowledge from one organizational member to another begins by the first member converting tacit knowledge (intuitions, unarticulated mental models, and embodied technical skills) into explicit knowledge (a meaningful set of information articulated in clear language including numbers or diagrams). The first member passes this explicit knowledge to another member of the organization -- who must convert it into tacit knowledge (internalization) before using it. Again, the theory of innovative learning extends this description of knowledge creation by identifying the different categories of knowledge as defined by Anderson and his colleagues (1998) -- factual, conceptual, procedural, and metacognitive -- involved in the knowledge creation and transfer process. (See Kim, 1993 for an overview of the link between individual learning and organizational learning.)

The Distributed Nature of Problem-Solving

According to the theory of distributed cognition (Solomon, 1996, Hutchins, 1996), all the subtleness of a problem-solving process does not reside in the head of one individual. While each member of the organization knows how to do the member's part of the process, the larger process is known only collectively – the ability to make informed decisions within the process is distributed across all people who work the problem-solving process.

The second aspect of the theory of distributed cognition is that cognition is distributed in the artifacts of a collaborative problem-solving process. Artifacts capture decisions and information about problem-solving. For example, information analysis, concept application, assumption identification, conclusion development, and implications predication are artifacts of a collaborative problem-solving process in an office setting. They each have embedded knowledge about decisions that concern a unique aspect of the problem-solving process; they also represent a subset of the cognition needed to complete the entire problem-solving process. (See Nemeth, Cook, O'Connor, & Klock, 2004 for an overview on the importance of cognitive artifacts to the theory of distributed cognition.)

The third aspect of the theory of distributed cognition is that the history of an artifact reveals the context for decisions and information about the process over time. Take, for example, that organizational members update the conclusions of a problem-solving session. The history of changes in an artifact tells the reasons "why" those changes were made. Frequently, it turns out that artifacts are historically related to one another. For example, when the conclusions are updated, the implications probably need updating as well. In this way, the histories of artifacts provide critical reasoning about their present form.

The Knowledge that Problem-Solvers Seek

Figure 3 shows how Socratic problem-solving has stretched Anderson and his colleagues' (1998) revision of Bloom's Taxonomy (1956) even further. In Socratic problem-solving, factual knowledge aligns with information, conceptual knowledge with concepts, and procedural knowledge aligns with assumptions. Metacognitive knowledge aligns with conclusions, implications, and the viewpoint that pulls them together to solve a problem. As shown in the cognitive dimension of Figure 3, learners can remember, understand, apply, analyze, evaluate, and create these different types of knowledge.

Figure 4 shows how the four different types of knowledge taken from the revisionBloom's taxonomy (Bloom, 1956), developed by Anderson et al. (1998), is used for problem-solving in an organizational setting without Socrates Digital™. Using Nonaka and Takeuchi's knowledge creation process, we see that most of the four types of knowledge are tacit rather than explicit. This use of tacit knowledge means that organizational members mostly use intuitions, unarticulated mental models, and embodied technical skills to

Figure 3. Revision of the Taxonomy of Anderson and Colleagues for Socratic Problem-Solving

Cognitive Dimension	Knowledge Dimension					
	Factual	Conceptual	Procedural	Metacognitive		
	Information	Concepts	Assumptions	Conclusions	Implications	Viewpoint
Create	✓	✓	✓	✓	✓	✓
Evaluate	✓	✓	✓	✓	✓	✓
Analyze	✓	✓	✓	✓	✓	✓
Apply	✓	✓	✓	✓	✓	✓
Understand	✓	✓	✓	✓	✓	✓
Remember	✓	✓	✓	✓	✓	✓

Figure 4. Without Socrates Digital™, Organizational Knowledge is Tacit

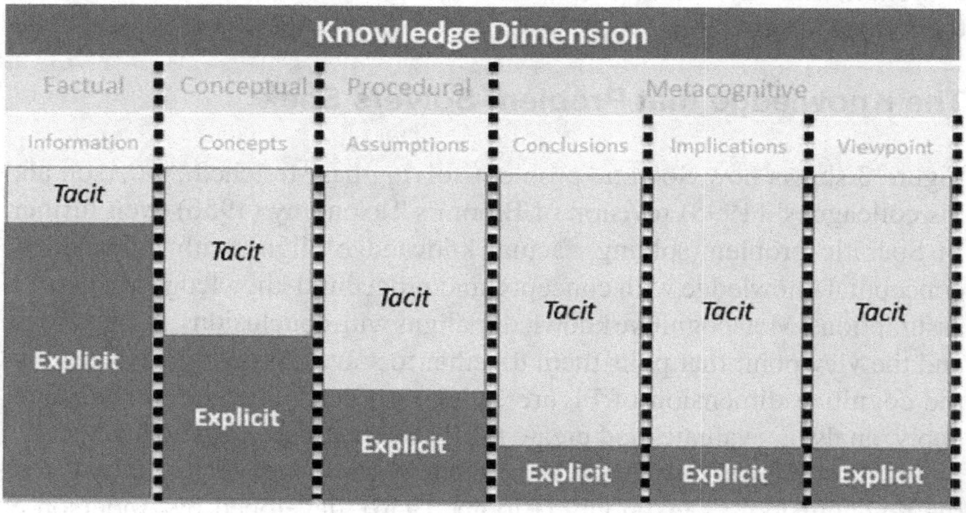

Knowledge Dimension					
Factual	Conceptual	Procedural	Metacognitive		
Information	Concepts	Assumptions	Conclusions	Implications	Viewpoint
Tacit	Tacit	Tacit	Tacit	Tacit	Tacit
Explicit	Explicit	Explicit	Explicit	Explicit	Explicit

solve problems. Furthermore, it also means that much of the logic for solving problems is unarticulated and, hence, unrecorded and is unavailable for other organizational members to know how the problem was solved.

Since most organizational knowledge remains tacit, it does not grow as a knowledge spiral as Nonaka and Takeuchi (1995) describe. While solving a new problem creates new tacit knowledge, solving a similar problem recreates old tacit knowledge not made explicit. This recreation of knowledge is the "reinventing the wheel" syndrome where knowledge growth in organizations stagnates. Nonaka and Takeuchi's knowledge spiral lacks growth since organizational members do not make tacit knowledge explicit and transfer it to other members to internalize and apply as tacit knowledge

Figure 5. With Socrates Digital^TM, Most Problem-Solving Knowledge is Explicit

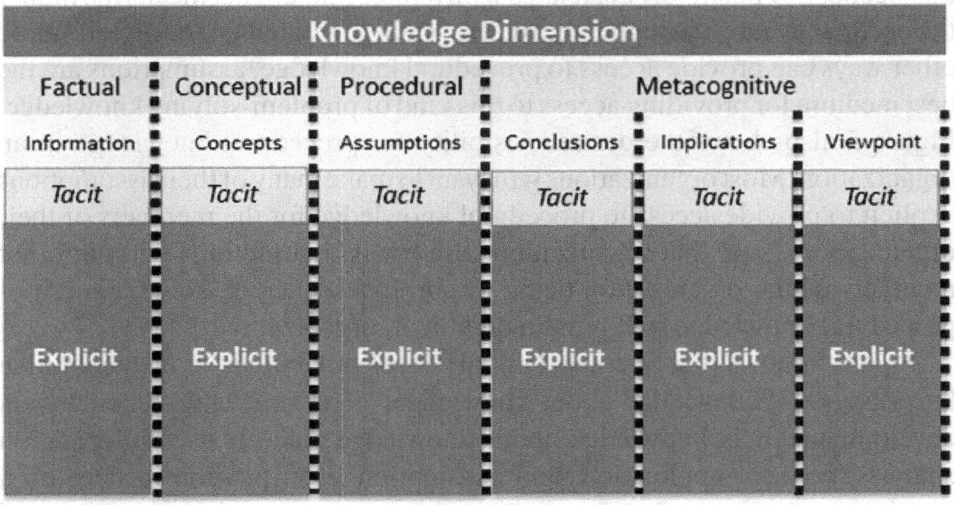

Knowledge Dimension					
Factual	Conceptual	Procedural	Metacognitive		
Information	Concepts	Assumptions	Conclusions	Implications	Viewpoint
Tacit	Tacit	Tacit	Tacit	Tacit	Tacit
Explicit	Explicit	Explicit	Explicit	Explicit	Explicit

Figure 5 shows how Socrates Digital™ addresses stagnating growth of problem-solving knowledge in organizations. We note that information analysis provides access to factual knowledge for problem-solvers using Socrates Digital™. While there are other ways to capture factual knowledge, information analysis is the most well-known and used method for capturing and disseminating factual knowledge (i.e., terminology, specific details, and elements) for problem-solving. Figure 5 shows that it would be desirable for most organizations to have most factual knowledge reside in an explicit form.

That is, most organizations would not want most of their factual knowledge floating around in their members' heads. However, note that not all factual knowledge can be made explicit.

In addition, Figure 5 shows that concept application provides access to conceptual knowledge for problem-solvers. As with factual knowledge, other resources can provide access to conceptual knowledge, but concept application provides the best medium for capturing and disseminating this kind of knowledge (i.e., general principles and concepts). As for desired visibility, the same idea is true for conceptual knowledge and factual knowledge. However, as with factual knowledge, not all conceptual knowledge can be made explicit.

Also illustrated in Figure 5, assumption identification provides access to procedural knowledge for problem-solvers. Assumptions drive expectations when concepts are applied. For example, if an analyst applies the concept of occupancy to determine the financial health of a motel, then the assumption is that occupancy positively correlates with total revenue. That means the higher the occupancy rate, the higher the total revenue generated for the motel. While other ways can provide access to procedural knowledge, assumptions are the best medium for providing access to this kind of problem-solving knowledge. Figure 5 also shows the desired visibility for procedural knowledge in an organization. Most organizations will want to make many of their assumptions explicit to provide access to procedural knowledge for the members of their organization. Note that organizations use many assumptions without other members of the organization being aware. Consequently, some amount of procedural knowledge will remain tacit in an organization.

Figure 5 shows that Socrates Digital™ uses three kinds of metacognitive knowledge -- "knowledge about knowledge." The first kind is conclusion development. It is knowledge about knowledge since it uses information analysis, concept application, and assumption identification to develop a conclusion. As Figure 5 shows, an organization that uses Socrates Digital™ will have much of its metacognitive knowledge captured in conclusions made explicit to the problem-solvers and other members of the organization.

The second kind of metacognitive knowledge is implication prediction. It is also knowledge about knowledge since it predicts the implications of acting on the conclusion. As Figure 5 shows, an organization using Socrates Digital™ will have additional metacognitive knowledge captured in implications and made explicit to the problem-solvers and other organization members.

The third kind of metacognitive knowledge is viewpoint construction. It is also knowledge about knowledge since it combines information analysis, concept application, assumption identification, conclusion development, and implication prediction into a cohesive viewpoint for solving a problem. For an organization that uses Socrates Digital™, additional metacognitive knowledge will be captured from a cohesive viewpoint and made explicit to the problem-solvers and other organization members.

Note, that as with the other types of knowledge, it will not be possible – nor desirable -- to make all metacognitive knowledge explicit. There will always be conclusions, implications, and viewpoints which are in development. As so, they will be formulating inside someone's head until Socrates Digital™ elicits it from them so it can become explicit and sharable with the other problem-solvers of the organization.

The Cognitive Processing Needs of Learners and Problem-Solvers

Figure 6. The Cognitive Processing Needs of Learners and Problem-Solvers

		Knowledge Dimension					
Cognitive Dimension		Factual	Conceptual	Procedural		Metacognitive	
		Information	Concepts	Assumptions	Conclusions	Implications	Viewpoint
Experts	Create	✓	✓	✓	✓	✓	✓
	Evaluate	✓	✓	✓	✓	✓	✓
Practitioners	Analyze	✓	✓	✓	✓	✓	✓
	Apply	✓	✓	✓	✓	✓	✓
Novices	Understand	✓	✓	✓	✓	✓	✓
	Remember	✓	✓	✓	✓	✓	✓

Figure 6 shows that when Anderson and colleagues revised Bloom's taxonomy, they recast Blooms' other categories into a "cognitive dimension," which describes the learner's cognitive processes when solving a problem in that category. Figure 10.6 also shows that novices are usually working at the level of trying to understand and remember. This level of cognitive processing is why it takes novices so long to get anything done. They are really "stuck" at the level of just trying to "get what is going on" and put it to memory. Also, Figure 6 shows that practitioners are usually working at the level of analyzing the situation and applying knowledge for a solution. They already understand what to do and remember how to do it. Give them a problem similar to one they have solved before, and they will quickly analyze the problem and take a previous solution, adapt it, and apply it to their new problem. Finally, Figure 6 shows that experts should evaluate solutions and create new and unique ones. The word "should" is put in this explanation because if an organization uses its experts like practitioners – doing the everyday work – then the organization is not getting the most from its experts. If the organization's experts spend all their time on the day's work, the opportunity is lost for better ways to do tomorrow's work.

Figure 6 also illustrates how to provide learners with an appropriate artifact. Of course, an appropriate artifact depends on the type of knowledge that they seek. Novices use the system to become practitioners, practitioners use the system to become experts, and experts utilize the system to create new knowledge.

In the process of becoming practitioners, novices seek to understand and remember the different types of knowledge. For example, novices can access an information analysis to understand how to conduct one and remember how to do it. They can also access a concept application to understand, remember, and apply it. The same is true for the other types of knowledge – assumptions, conclusions, implications, and viewpoints.

In the process of becoming experts, practitioners analyze and apply the different types of knowledge. For example, practitioners can assess an information analysis to analyze and apply the best practices for their information analysis. Furthermore, this is true for the other types of knowledge as well.

Experts create and evaluate the different types of knowledge. For example, experts can create and evaluate a new way to conduct an information analysis. They can then share this new way to conduct an information analysis with the other organizational members. Experts can create and evaluate other types of knowledge, too. In this way, experts create and evaluate the different types of knowledge for others in the organization.

Single-Loop and Double-Loop Learning

Single-loop learning is the most natural way to approach a problem (Argyris & Schön, 1996). It is learning the best-known method for solving the problem. Novices will know little about the problem and the possible solutions. They require access to conceptual knowledge for them to understand the problem and formulate a solution. Therefore, novices are seeking to understand and remember a way to solve the problem. Practitioners have solved similar problems before – they require access to procedural knowledge. They seek to analyze and apply an example – to adapt as a solution to the current problem. Experts may not know how to solve a problem immediately, but they can quickly assess what kind of problem and what solutions may work to solve it. Experts have metacognitive knowledge – knowledge about knowledge – and can provide access to it in the form of expert advice for novices and practitioners to learn how to apply the best-known method for solving the problem. Improving single-loop learning at the team level means decreasing the team's time to bring the best-known solution to a current problem. Direct access to appropriate artifacts and other people with tacit knowledge of the problem is required for teams to decrease the time to the best-known solution for a current problem.

Double-loop learning is an innovative way to solve a problem (Argyris & Schön,1996). Typically, it involves a different way of seeing a problem – a different viewpoint (Argyris, 2010). It is applying a new principle or a unique way of applying a general principle to a problem. The result of double-loop learning is a fundamental change in accomplishing work. Innovation at the team level begins with all team members having access to the different types of knowledge – factual, conceptual, procedural, and metacognitive – so the current "best way" of solving a problem is known to all team members. Knowing what they know, the team is now prepared to look at innovative ways to solve the current problem. This sharing of knowledge is where the best thinking of the past meets the best thinking of the present to create the best solution for the current problem. Innovation requires a team to build off what it knows – otherwise, the team will reinvent the exact solutions repeatedly. This knowledge building is the essence of innovative learning. Furthermore, Socrates Digital™ can significantly assist organizations in building off what they know by providing access to their artifacts during problem-solving.

SUMMARY

Chapter 4 and the following chapters describe the Problem-Solving Manager as a storage unit during the development of viewpoints. We noted that a viewpoint comprises information analysis, concept application, assumption identification, conclusion development, and implication prediction. When Socrates Digital™ marks these viewpoint components completed, it passes them to the Problem-Solving Manager for storage. When needed, the Problem-

Solving Manager retrieves these components and passes them back to Socrates Digital™ for presentation to the user persona.

This chapter shows that the Problem-Solving Manager also provides a submit, review, and approval process of a viewpoint to become a "best practice" for an organization to solve a particular problem. The Problem-Solving Manager makes these approved best practices available across the organization. This chapter provides the flow charts and pseudo-code for developing the Problem-Solving Manager.

This chapter also shows that this additional role for the Problem-Solving Manager enables an innovative learning (iLearning) organization. Innovative learning begins with all team members having access to the same knowledge for the current "best way" of solving a problem. A way to provide this knowledge is through the information, concepts, assumptions, conclusions, and implications of a problem's viewpoint. Knowing what they know, problem-solvers are now prepared to look at innovative ways to solve the current problem. This knowledge comes from where the lessons learned from the past meet the best thinking of the present to learn how to do things better -- innovative learning.

As first described in Chapter 1, a revision of Bloom's Taxonomy developed by Anderson and his colleagues represents the complexity of problem-solving knowledge to create this theory for innovative learning. Anderson and his colleagues' revised taxonomy identifies knowledge as a separate dimension that describes it as factual, conceptual, procedural, and metacognitive. Another significant difference is that Anderson and colleagues recast Bloom's other categories into a "cognitive dimension," which describes the learner's cognitive processes when processing knowledge of that category. Anderson and colleagues also renamed these process categories from Bloom's original "knowledge, comprehension, application, analysis, synthesis, and evaluation" to "remember, understand, apply, analyze, evaluate, and create."

Socratic problem-solving has stretched the revision by Anderson and his colleagues of Bloom's Taxonomy even further. In Socratic problem-solving, factual knowledge aligns with information, conceptual knowledge with concepts, and procedural knowledge aligns with assumptions. Metacognitive knowledge aligns with conclusions, implications, and the viewpoint that pulls them together to solve a problem. In the cognitive dimension, learners can remember, understand, apply, analyze, evaluate, and create these different types of knowledge.

Socratic problem-solving with Socrates Digital™ enables innovative ways to solve a problem. Using double-loop learning provides different ways of seeing a problem – different viewpoints. This double-loop learning with Socrates Digital™ begins with problem-solvers having access to the different types of knowledge – factual, conceptual, procedural, and metacognitive – so the current "best way" of solving a problem is known to the problem-solvers. Knowing what they know, the team is now prepared to look at innovative ways to solve the current problem. This sharing of knowledge is where the best thinking of the past meets the best thinking of the present to create the best solution for the current problem. This is the essence of innovative learning.

REFERENCES

Anderson, L., Krathwohl, D., Airasian, P., Cruikshank, K., Mayer, R., Pintrich, P., Raths, J., & Wittrock, M. (1998). *Taxonomy for learning, teaching and assessing: A revision of Bloom's taxonomy of educational objectives.* Longman.

Argyris, C. (2010). *Organizational traps: Leadership, culture, organizational design.* Oxford University Press. doi:10.1093/acprof:o so/9780199586165.001.0001

Argyris, C., & Schön, D. (1996). *Organizational learning II: Theory, method and practice.* Addison Wesley.

Bloom, B. (1956). *Taxonomy of behavioral objectives. Handbook I: Cognitive Domain.* David McKay.

Brown, J. S., Collins, A., & Duguid, P. (1989). Situated cognition and the culture of learning. *Educational Researcher, 18*(1), 32–42. doi:10.3102/0013189X018001032

Easterby-Smith, M. (1997). Disciplines of organizational learning: Contributions and critiques. *Human Relations, 50*(9), 1085–1113. doi:10.1177/001872679705000903

Hutchins, E. (1996). *Cognition in the wild.* MIT press. doi:10.7551/mitpress/1881.001.0001

Marsick, V., & Watkins, K. (1994). The learning organization: An integrative vision for HRD. *Human Resource Development Quarterly, 5*(4), 353–360. doi:10.1002/hrdq.3920050406

Nonaka, I., & Takeuchi, H. (1995). *The knowledge-creating company.* Oxford University Press.

Plass, J., & Salisbury, M. (2002). A living system approach to the development of knowledge management systems. *Educational Technology Research and Development*, *50*(1), 35–57. doi:10.1007/BF02504960

Raybould, B. (1995). Performance support engineering: An emerging development methodology for enabling organizational learning. *Performance Improvement Quarterly*, *8*(1), 7–22. doi:10.1111/j.1937-8327.1995.tb00658.x

Salisbury, M. (2000). Creating a process for capturing and leveraging intellectual capital. *Performance Improvement Quarterly*, *13*(3), 202–219. doi:10.1111/j.1937-8327.2000.tb00182.x

Salisbury, M. (2003). Putting theory into practice to build knowledge management systems. *Journal of Knowledge Management*, *7*(2), 128–141. doi:10.1108/13673270310477333

Salisbury, M. (2009). iLearning: How to Create an Innovative Learning Organization. New York: Wiley.

Salisbury, M. (2010). Creating an Innovative Learning Organization. *International Journal on E-Learning*, *9*(1), 115–128.

Salisbury, M., & Plass, J. (2001). A conceptual framework for a knowledge management system. *Human Resource Development International*, *4*(4), 451–464. doi:10.1080/13678860010016913

ADDITIONAL READING

Kim, D. (1993). The link between individual and organizational learning. *Sloan Management Review*, *35*(1), 37–50.

Nemeth, C., Cook, R., O'Connor, M., & Klock, P. (2004). Using cognitive artifacts to understand distributed cognition. *IEEE Transactions on Systems, Man, and Cybernetics*, *34*(6), 726–735. doi:10.1109/TSMCA.2004.836798

Salomon, G. (1996). *Distributed cognitions*. Cambridge University Press.

Chapter 11
The Road Ahead:
Enhancing Socrates Digital™

ABSTRACT

This chapter notes that most discussions around critical thinking and Socratic problem solving before this book was published described interactions between humans. However, as shown in this chapter, computers can not only automate the Socratic problem-solving process but can enhance its advantages for individuals, teams, and organizations in ways that only a computer can do. This chapter looks at eight ways that Socrates Digital™ can be enhanced to create better solutions for problem solvers in less time.

INTRODUCTION

Before this book was published, most discussions around critical thinking and Socratic problem-solving described interactions between humans. However, computers can automate the Socratic problem-solving process and enhance its advantages for individuals, teams, and organizations. As discussed in Chapter 2, it is challenging to learn how to facilitate Socratic problem-solving. It also takes much planning ahead of time and considerable guidance to keep it on track with a group of learners and problem-solvers. In addition, it is labor-intensive to document the outcome of a Socratic problem-solving session and make those results available to the participants and any larger audience.

Computer systems can help meet all of these challenges. Like an expert teacher in Socratic problem-solving, a computer can guide the conversation

DOI: 10.4018/978-1-7998-7955-8.ch011

to answer all the important questions to solve the problem. With a computer-based Socratic problem-solving system, users can immediately jump in and solve problems without much training. Also, a computer-based system can use knowledge management techniques to capture results during problem-solving sessions and make those results immediately available to participants and others.

A computer-based Socratic problem-solving system can also enhance problem-solving effectiveness in ways that only a computer can do. It can assist human problem-solvers in determining a numerical value for their level of confidence in a single step in a session – such as how much confidence they have in the information analysis step. A computer-based Socratic problem-solving system can also combine the confidence levels from several steps into an overall confidence level for the solution produced in the session.

FUTURE ENHANCEMENTS TO SOCRATES DIGITAL™

From all the previous chapters, we see that Socrates Digital™ has a conversation with the user persona to solve a problem. The resulting solution is a viewpoint for solving the problem. It comprises information analysis, concept application, assumption identification, conclusion development, and implication prediction – the artifacts that resulted from the conversation.

This chapter looks at ways this conversation between Socrates Digital™ and human users can be improved to create better solutions in less time. The first way to enhance Socrates Digital™ is to provide a spoken interface between it and the human users. The second way is to integrate Socrates Digital™ with the data sources that the user persona is analyzing. A third way is to provide a capability for consolidating concepts, assumptions, conclusions, and implications so that each is a unique entry in the database. A fourth way to enhance Socrates Digital™ is to identify and manage "favorites" viewpoints for solving particular problems. A fifth way is to use natural language processing to select viewpoints from the database used to solve similar previous problems and the current problem. A sixth way to enhance Socrates Digital™ is to use a selected viewpoint for solving a previous problem to make suggestions for information analysis, concept application, assumption identification, conclusion development, and implication prediction for solving a current problem. A seventh way to enhance Socrates Digital™ is to let it conduct – on its own -- the information analysis, concept application, assumption identification, conclusion development, and implication prediction to solve a problem. Socrates Digital™ then puts them together into a viewpoint and calculates a confidence level to solve the problem. This enhancement is the most automated and ambitious enhancement to Socrates Digital™. Finally, an eighth way that Socrates Digital™ can be enhanced is by making more world knowledge accessible to it.

Note that the role that Socrates Digital™ plays with the human problem-solvers does not change with these enhancements. Socrates Digital™ still plays the role of a human Socrates in guiding human problem-solvers to take a disciplined approach – that is explainable – in solving complex problems. The difference between these enhancements is the level of autonomy granted to Socrates Digital™. However, with all these enhancements, the human users can adjust or change any actions by Socrates Digital™.

SPOKEN LANGUAGE CONVERSATIONAL INTERFACE

Figure 1. Adding Speech Recognition Processor and Text-to-Speech Generator

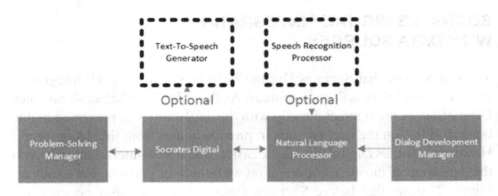

Figure 1 shows that developers can add an optional speech recognition processor and text-to-speech generator to Socrates Digital™. These two added capabilities will provide Socrates Digital™ with a spoken language conversational interface. As discussed in Chapter 4, this can make Socrates Digital™ more accessible with some devices such as smartphones. Since Socrates Digital™ uses a natural language processing cloud-based service, adding a speech recognition processor and text-to-speech generator is straightforward. Most cloud-based providers of natural language processing also provide these services as well.

Apple, Microsoft, Google, IBM, and Amazon are among these providers. For the most part, their speech recognition and text-to-speech generator services "bolt" on to their natural language processing service.

Developers can mix these artificial intelligence services for a Socrates Digital™ system. For example, the natural language processing service could be Microsoft's Power Virtual Agent, and the user persona could be interacting with Socrates Digital™ on an Apple iPhone. On an Apple iPhone, users can easily activate voice to recognize the spoken language from the user persona. Technically, the recognized text is passed to Virtual Agent – running in the cloud -- for natural language processing. In responding to the user persona, Virtual Agent produces text displayed on the iPhone display where it can read aloud by Apple's built-in text-to-speech feature. Users can even choose the language and type of voice they hear and the rate of speech. Speech recognition and text-to-speech generator services provide a "hands-free" spoken language interface for human users. See Appendix C for an overview of developing a Socrates Digital™ application with Demo of Microsoft's Power Virtual Agent.

SOCRATES DIGITAL™ INTEGRATION WITH DATA SOURCES

The second way that Socrates Digital™ can be enhanced is by integrating it with the user persona's data sources. As described in Chapter 4, Socrates Digital™ does not interact directly with the data sources as presented in this book. It relies on the user persona to provide values from the data sources. However, Socrates Digital™ could be easily enhanced to interact directly with the data sources during a conversation with the user persona. For example, Figure 2 shows that before Socrates Digital™ asks the user persona if a relation between data items holds for the larger dataset, Socrates Digital™ could interact with the data source, run the correlation, and present the results to the user persona to evaluate. This enhancement can be accomplished by connecting Socrates Digital™ through an Application Programming Interface (API) to the data source and running the correlation function.

Suppose that developers create a Socrates Digital™ no-code solution with one of the vendors that provide artificial intelligence services (i.e., Apple, Microsoft, IBM, or Amazon). In that case, integrating Socrates Digital™ directly with data sources can be even more straightforward. For example, consider a developer who used Microsoft Power Automate (formally called Flow) to create Socrates Digital™. In that case, the developer could use no-code logic to make calls to Microsoft Power BI to analyze data. To get the results shown in Figure 2, this means a developer could make a few clicks to set up the logic for Power Automate to call Power BI to run a correlation that shows the relationship between data items holds for a larger dataset. This event could trigger before asking this question, "Does this assumption hold for the larger dataset?"

Figure 2. Enhancing Socrates Digital™ to Run the Correlation and Display Results

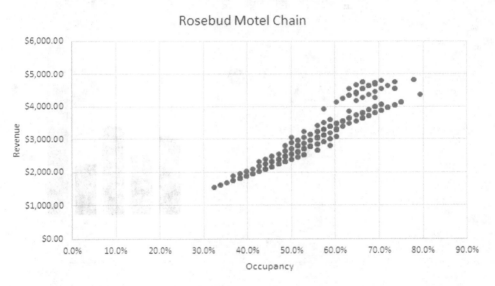

Integrating Socrates Digital™ with a data source can also provide access to advanced data analysis techniques. For example, as introduced in Chapter 3 and shown in Figure 3, Socrates Digital™ could leverage the "Key Influencers" analysis in Microsoft Power BI. From the field of artificial intelligence, Socrates Digital™ could call this analysis to help answer questions about information analysis, concept application, assumption identification, conclusion development, and implication prediction. An excerpt from the investment example dialog, presented in Chapter 3, shows how Socrates Digital™ can use the Key Influencer analysis to show that the assumption is true -- customer experience influences total revenue in the larger dataset.

SP: Is this assumption true for the larger dataset? (Questions that Target the Parts of Thinking -- Questioning Information, Data, and Experience)

UP2: Yes. In the Rosebud Motel chain, an analysis of key influencers shows that customer experience influences total revenue. A more detailed analysis of key influencers shows that total revenue is more likely to increase when the sentiment score is higher than 0.5 (neutral). I think that it is probably accurate.

Figure 3. Key Influencers Show that Customer Experience Influences Total Revenue

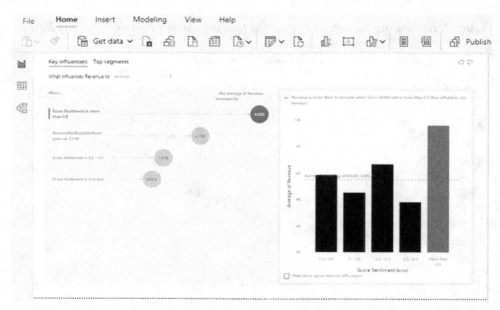

Of course, other ways to analyze data from the field of artificial intelligence are being added to business intelligence platforms all the time. As these become available, Socrates Digital™ can leverage them to enhance its ability to guide users in problem-solving on these platforms.

Another way that Socrates Digital™ could leverage these new analysis techniques is to identify new information, concepts, assumptions, conclusions, and implications. For example, Socrates Digital™ could have run the Key Influences analysis, shown in Figure 3, to discover the assumption that customer experience influences total revenue initially. Socrates Digital™ could also use such "discovery" methods to identify concepts, form conclusions, and predict implications.

CONSOLIDATION OF CONCEPTS, ASSUMPTIONS, CONCLUSIONS, AND IMPLICATIONS

A third way Socrates Digital™ can be enhanced builds on a subtle point you may have missed when Chapter 3 presented the investment example dialog. As the following excerpt shows, Socrates Digital™ asks the user persona if the answer provided is essentially the same as earlier. Although not described in Chapter 3, Socrates Digital™ uses natural language processing to match the user persona's answer for the implications of the conclusion to the other implications stored in the database. In this case, Socrates Digital™ matches it to an implication in the database and asks the user persona to verify that it is the same implication. When the user persona verifies that it is the same implication, Socrates Digital™, uses the implication from the database and does not add the new one to the database. This comparison to previous answers is an effort by Socrates Digital™ to consolidate similarly worded concepts, assumptions, conclusions, and implications. In this way, Socrates Digital™ attempts to make each concept, assumption, conclusion, and implication unique in its database. This consolidation reduces the storage and the amount of processing needed by the database. It also makes it easier for humans to consolidate similar concepts, assumptions, conclusions, and implications. Later versions of Socrates Digital™ will need more sophisticated natural language processing to infer and compare the intent behind the descriptions of worded concepts, assumptions, conclusions, and implications.

SP: Can you explain the implications of this conclusion? (Questions that Target the Parts of Thinking -- Questioning Implications and Consequences)

UP1: A viewpoint such as increasing marketing is needed to increase revenue per available room for motels in the Rosebud Motel chain.

SP: Is this the same as the implication that increased marketing is needed to raise the total revenue for motels in the Rosebud Motel chain? (Questions that Target the Quality of Reasoning -- Questioning Precision)

UP1: Yes.

IDENTIFYING AND MANAGING FAVORITE VIEWPOINTS

A fourth way that Socrates Digital™ can be enhanced is to provide a capability for the Problem-Solving Manager to rate "favorites" viewpoints for particular problems. This rating system is simply a more informal approach than the one presented in Chapter 10 for promoting some viewpoints as best practices for solving particular problems. Using our investment example dialog, when analysts use a viewpoint created by another analyst to solve a problem, they can "rate" the usefulness of that viewpoint for that problem. As a sort of "grassroots" movement, viewpoints become organizational favorites for solving particular problems by "bubbling to the top" of the rating scale. Over time, as problem-solvers tweak viewpoints to address variations of a problem, favorite solutions rise up for each variation of the problem. In this way, an organic process emerges to identify the best solutions for all the different problems an organization faces.

REMEMBER AND UNDERSTAND A SOLUTION

A fifth way to enhance Socrates Digital™ is to use natural language processing to select a previously created viewpoint for solving a problem from the database to solve a similar current problem. This selection process would involve using natural language processing to compare the problem description of the current problem with the problem descriptions of the viewpoints in the database. After selecting a previously created viewpoint, developing a viewpoint for the current problem proceeds like a regular Socrates Digital™ session. However, the user persona can use the selected viewpoint as a "blueprint' to complete the information analysis, concept application, assumption identification, conclusion development, and implication prediction steps to create a new viewpoint to solve the current problem.

Figure 4. Socrates Digital™ Remembering and Understanding a Previous Solution

Cognitive Dimension	Knowledge Dimension					
	Factual	Conceptual	Procedural	Metacognitive		
	Information	Concepts	Assumptions	Conclusions	Implications	Viewpoint
Experts — Create						
Evaluate						
Practitioners — Analyze						
Apply						
Novices — Understand	✓	✓	✓	✓	✓	✓
Remember	✓	✓	✓	✓	✓	✓

As Figure 4 shows, when Socrates retrieves a suitable solution to the problem at hand, it works at the human novice level of problem-solving. Socrates is "remembering" past solutions that have been created and "understand" them well enough to select one to create a new solution to the current problem.

ANALYZE AND APPLY A SOLUTION

A sixth way to enhance Socrates Digital™ is extending it for making suggestions for information analysis, concept application, assumption identification, conclusion development, and implication prediction. For example, suppose Socrates Digital™ matches the current question at hand with a question at hand in the database using natural language processing. Next, Socrates Digital™ looks at the information analysis for the viewpoint of the question at hand in the database. It runs the same analysis on the information for the current question at hand. (Note that this would require storing the information analysis in the database with the viewpoints during Socrates Digital™ sessions.) After the information analysis, Socrates Digital™ asks the user persona to evaluate the accuracy of the dataset -- just like in a "regular" Socrates Digital™ session. Suppose the user persona rates the accuracy of the dataset too low. In that case, Socrates Digital™ suggests that the user persona abandon the selected viewpoint as a possible viewpoint for solving the current problem.

If the dataset accuracy is high enough, Socrates Digital™ examines the concepts applied in the selected viewpoint and updates the concepts for the current viewpoint under consideration in the database. For each concept, Socrates Digital™ asks the user persona to evaluate the strength of the concept for data analysis. Socrates Digital™ then calculates the user persona input into a value representing the concept strength for each concept. If this value is too low, Socrates Digital™ recommends that the user persona abandon the current viewpoint.

Next, Socrates Digital™ identifies the assumptions in the selected viewpoint and runs the analysis on a larger dataset for the current viewpoint to see if the assumptions hold for that larger dataset. (Again, this would require storing the type of information analysis conducted on the larger dataset in the database with the viewpoints during Socrates Digital™ sessions.) After the analysis runs on the larger dataset, Socrates Digital™ asks the user persona to evaluate the confidence level for each assumption that underlies the analysis. Socrates Digital™ then calculates the user persona input into a value representing the assumption confidence. Socrates Digital™ reports it to the user persona; if this value is too low, the user persona considers abandonment.

Given a high enough confidence value for the assumptions, Socrates Digital™ next looks at the conclusions developed for the selected viewpoint. For each conclusion, Socrates Digital™ asks the user persona to evaluate the logic of the conclusion. Socrates turns this evaluation into a value for conclusion logic for each conclusion. Again, if this value is too low, Socrates Digital™ reports it to the user persona to consider abandoning the current viewpoint.

Socrates Digital™ next looks at the implications in the selected viewpoint. As with conclusions, Socrates Digital™ analyzes the implications predicted for the selected viewpoint. For each implication, Socrates Digital™ asks the user persona to evaluate the evidence for the implication. Socrates turns this evaluation into an implication evidence value for each implication. Furthermore, Socrates Digital™ reports it to the user persona to consider abandoning the current viewpoint if this value is too low.

Finally, Socrates Digital™ combines all these values into an overall confidence value for the viewpoint to solve the current problem. In this way, developers can enhance Socrates Digital™ to analyze and apply a viewpoint used to solve a previous problem for the current problem at hand. Note that, with this enhancement, Socrates Digital™ will only require a few answers to its questions to analyze and apply a viewpoint to the current problem.

Figure 5. Socrates Digital™ Analyzing and Applying a Previous Solution

Cognitive Dimension	Knowledge Dimension					
	Factual	Conceptual	Procedural	Metacognitive		
	Information	Concepts	Assumptions	Conclusions	Implications	Viewpoint
Experts — Create						
Evaluate						
Practitioners — Analyze	✓	✓	✓	✓	✓	✓
Apply	✓	✓	✓	✓	✓	✓
Novices — Understand	✓	✓	✓	✓	✓	✓
Remember	✓	✓	✓	✓	✓	✓

As noted in Figure 4, when Socrates retrieves a suitable solution to the problem at hand, it works at the human novice level of problem-solving.

Socrates Digital™ is "remembering" past solutions that have been created and "understand" them well enough to select one that could be a solution to the current problem to be solved. However, as Figure 5 shows, when Socrates Digital™ is "analyzing" and "applying" this selected solution for solving the current problem at hand, it is working at the practitioner level of problem-solving.

CREATE AND EVALUATE A SOLUTION

A sixth way to enhance Socrates Digital™ is to let it conduct the information analysis, concept application, assumption identification, conclusion development, implication prediction, and put them together into a viewpoint and calculate the confidence level. This solution creation, of course, is the most automated and ambitious enhancement for Socrates Digital™. It also seems to change the roles between the human user and Socrates Digital™. However, this is not entirely the case since the human user can examine the reasoning in each step – elect to change them – and judge each incremental value assigned in each step and the overall confidence value for the viewpoint as a solution to the current problem at hand. Alternatively, said another way, the human user is still in charge of the process of Socrates Digital™ and makes reasoned judgments about its calculations. The difference is that Socrates Digital™ will evaluate an information analysis, concept application, assumption identification, conclusion development, or implication prediction that it created – instead of the human problem-solvers who had the role for doing this in Chapter 3.

This automated process for Socrates Digital™ taking on some human problem-solving roles would look like the following. Socrates Digital™ would first engage the user persona in defining the problem. This defining of the problem would look the same as the investment example dialog in Chapter 3. Socrates Digital™ asks the user persona to define the problem. However, after the problem is defined, Socrates Digital™ assumes some of the human user roles and appears to come back with an immediate viewpoint for solving the problem.

In this enhanced version, Socrates Digital™ does a first-pass analysis of the problem-solving session's information. Most likely, this information would reside on a business intelligence platform. This first-pass analysis discovers what kind of information is available for more in-depth analysis. For example, Socrates Digital™ might find that the information is numerical.

This preliminary analysis could also reveal that the data is consistent and has few missing data values. Given these findings, Socrates Digital™ could assign a value to the dataset accuracy variable in the database based on the information used for the problem-solving session.

In this example, Socrates Digital™ next runs a correlation and other analyses to determine if any fields are related. Using our investment example dialog, Socrates Digital™ would find the following correlations between the data fields:

- Occupancy Rate is positively correlated with total revenue.
- Average Daily Rate is positively correlated with total revenue.
- Revenue per Available Room is positively correlated with total revenue.

These findings would be labeled "assumptions" and evaluated by Socrates Digital™ instead of a human user. For each of these assumptions, the stronger the correlation, the higher value Socrates Digital™ would assign to the assumption confidence variable before storing it in the database.

To identify the concepts used for information analysis, Socrates Digital™ would pull the information field names from all assumptions. Since "total revenue" appears in each assumption, it does not distinguish between assumptions, so Socrates Digital™ drops it. The remaining three fields, shown below, are listed as concepts and added to the database. Furthermore, like the dataset and assumptions, Socrates Digital™ would assign a value to the concept strength variable for each concept based on the strength of the correlation shown in the assumption.

- Occupancy Rate
- Average Daily Rate
- Revenue per Available Room

Next, Socrates Digital™ develops a conclusion from the information analysis, concept application, and assumption identification. It uses natural language processing to pull out "increase total revenue" from the main concept to make the investment decision. Then, using the three assumptions, Socrates Digital™ could knit together a conclusion. This conclusion would state, "Increase occupancy rate, average daily rate, and revenue per available room to increase total revenue." Socrates Digital™ then assigns a value to the conclusion logic variable based on the strength of the correlations of the assumptions. Socrates Digital™ then updates the database with this value.

At this point, this enhanced Socrates Digital™ would begin work on the implications of the conclusion. If this assumption were in the database, "Marketing is positively correlated with occupancy rate, average daily rate, and revenue per available room," Socrates Digital™ could use it to predict the implications of the above conclusion. The implication could then become, "Increase marketing to increase occupancy rate, average daily rate, and revenue per available room for increasing total revenue."

Suppose this assumption was not in the database. In that case, Socrates Digital™ could ask the user persona this question, "How can occupancy rate, average daily rate, and revenue per available room be increased?" Suppose the user persona responded, "Marketing increases occupancy rate, average daily rate, and revenue per available room." With this response, Socrates Digital™ could process this text with the conclusion to get the implication, "Increase marketing to increase occupancy rate, average daily rate, and revenue per available room for increasing total revenue." Socrates Digital™ then assigns a value to the implication prediction variable based on the strength of the correlations of the assumptions and updates the database with this value.

Socrates Digital™ has completed information analysis, concept application, assumption identification, conclusion development, and implication prediction. As with a human user session, Socrates Digital™ has to create a viewpoint for answering the question at hand. Using natural language processing, Socrates Digital™ knits together a statement that restates the implications in a viewpoint. In this case, Socrates Digital™ would take the implication "Increase marketing to increase occupancy rate, average daily rate, and revenue per available room for increasing total revenue" and join it with the string that describes how the main concept relates to the question at hand. Socrates Digital™ finds this main concept in the problem definition, "We need to know if the investment will increase the total revenue for the Rosebud Motel chain so that it can repay the investment at the projected rate of return." After adding some conversational text, Socrates Digital™ would generate the following to describe the viewpoint to the user persona, "This viewpoint is focused on increasing marketing to increase occupancy rate, average daily rate, and revenue per available room for increasing total revenue for the Rosebud Motel chain so that it can repay the investment at the projected rate of return."

As with working with a human user, the last step for Socrates Digital™ uses the Evaluate_Viewpoint subprocess to call the Evaluate_Viewpoint_Questioning_Depth subprocess, which will calculate the Viewpoint_Confidence from the datasets, concepts, assumptions, conclusions, and implications scores. This confidence score passes to the Evaluate_Viewpoint subprocess, and it updates the database with these values.

As with working with a human user, Socrates Digital™ would then see if more data could be analyzed to add to this viewpoint. If not, then Socrates Digital™ would output the viewpoint confidence score to the human user. From the user's perspective, this enhanced version of Socrates Digital™ was given the problem definition by the user persona, turned it around in a few seconds, and provided a viewpoint to solve the problem.

As Figure 4 shows, when Socrates retrieves a suitable solution to the problem at hand, it works at the human novice level of problem-solving. Socrates Digital™ is "remembering" past solutions that have been created and "understand" them well enough to select one that could be a solution to the current problem to be solved. As Figure 5 shows, when Socrates Digital™ is "analyzing" and "applying" this selected solution for solving the current problem at hand, it is working at the practitioner level of problem-solving. However, as Figure 6 also shows, when Socrates creates and evaluates a solution to the problem at hand, it works at the human expert level of problem-solving.

Figure 6. Socrates Digital™ Creating and Evaluating a Previous Solution

	Cognitive Dimension	Knowledge Dimension					
		Factual	Conceptual	Procedural	Metacognitive		
		Information	Concepts	Assumptions	Conclusions	Implications	Viewpoint
Experts	Create	✓	✓	✓	✓	✓	✓
	Evaluate	✓	✓	✓	✓	✓	✓
Practitioners	Analyze	✓	✓	✓	✓	✓	✓
	Apply	✓	✓	✓	✓	✓	✓
Novices	Understand	✓	✓	✓	✓	✓	✓
	Remember	✓	✓	✓	✓	✓	✓

As you probably noticed, this last enhancement to Socrates Digital™ poses technical challenges and issues as to how Socrates Digital™ should work with human-problem solvers. One technical challenge for this enhanced version of Socrates Digital™ is to develop reasonable estimates for the dataset accuracy, assumption confidence, concept strength, conclusion logic, implication prediction variables. As presented in this latest enhancement, Socrates Digital™ set these variables based on the strength of the correlations in the assumptions. This approach would undoubtedly be simplistic and problematic. A better way to look at this enhancement is to see it as a way for Socrates Digital™ to make "guesses" for possible viewpoints to solve the problem at hand for the human user to evaluate.

This enhancement brings up a not-so-subtle difference between single-loop and double-loop learning that is glaringly apparent for Socrates Digital™ (Argyris & Schön,1996). Taking a known solution and enhancing and adapting it to a similar problem is an example of single-loop learning. Socrates Digital™ can help human users do this with minor enhancement – as shown in the previous section, "Analyze and Apply a Solution." Socrates Digital™ can pull out the information, assumptions, concepts, conclusions, and implications from a previous solution and – working with human users – adapt it to address a similar problem. This adaption of a known viewpoint is creating a solution in the sense of single-loop learning.

As we saw in this section, starting from scratch to create a new and unique solution is hard for humans and Socrates Digital™. The reason is that it is double-loop learning. It requires a completely different viewpoint to solve a new problem that is significantly different from any other problem solved before. Therefore, this new solution has a different mix of information, assumptions, concepts, conclusions, and implications than any previous viewpoint created – some of which are entirely new.

This double-loop learning is difficult for Socrates Digital™ (and all computer programs) because it requires much knowledge about the world. In our investment example dialog, the analysts using Socrates Digital™ believed that marketing is one way to raise occupancy and total revenue for a motel chain. Socrates Digital™ did not know about the concept of marketing. It was not in its database. Therefore, without human user assistance, Socrates Digital™ could not use this concept. Researchers in artificial intelligence call this lack of knowledge "falling off the knowledge cliff" (Marcot, 1987; O'Keefe, Balci, & Smith, 1987; Yang, 1995). However, Socrates Digital™ could infer this concept and an associated assumption from access to data for solving problems in the problem area of marketing. This insight brings us to our last enhancement for Socrates Digital™.

INTEGRATION OF SOLUTIONS
ACROSS PROBLEM AREAS

The eighth way that Socrates Digital™ can be enhanced is by making more world knowledge accessible to it. Developers can accomplish this by integrating additional problem areas and their solutions for Socrates Digital™ during problem-solving sessions. Suppose that Socrates Digital™ had access to viewpoints created for solving marketing problems when it was creating implications for the conclusion, "Increase occupancy rate, average daily rate, and revenue per available room to increase total revenue." It could infer that marketing increases occupancy rate, average daily rate, and revenue per available room. This inference leads to the implication that "Increase marketing to increase occupancy rate, average daily rate, and revenue per available room for increasing total revenue." This example shows that the more problem areas accessible to Socrates Digital™, the more world knowledge it can bring to bear on solving the problem at hand.

Organizations can increase the world knowledge available to Socrates Digital™ by making all the viewpoints created in the business units available to each business unit. This principle of sharing is true for academic disciplines as well. When academic units share viewpoints for solving problems across disciplines, Socrates Digital™ can access viewpoints from other disciplines to solve a problem in one discipline. This cross-fertilization of viewpoints across multiple disciplines creates the opportunity for interdisciplinary solutions for complex problems.

SUMMARY

This chapter noted that before this book was published, most discussions around critical thinking and Socratic problem-solving described interactions between humans. However, computers can automate the Socratic problem-solving process and enhance its advantages for individuals, teams, and organizations in ways that only a computer can do.

This chapter looks at eight ways that Socrates Digital™ can be enhanced to create better solutions in less time which are listed below:

1.   Utilize a spoken interface between Socrates and the human users.

2. Integrate Socrates Digital™ with the data sources that the user persona is analyzing.
3. Develop a way for consolidating concepts, assumptions, conclusions, and implications so that each is a unique entry in the database.
4. Create a way for Socrates Digital™ to identify and manage "favorites" viewpoints for solving particular problems.
5. Develop a way to select viewpoints from the database and use them for solving the current problem.
6. Construct a means for Socrates Digital™ to make suggestions for information analysis, concept application, assumption identification, conclusion development, and implication prediction for solving a problem.
7. Develop the capability of Socrates Digital™ to conduct – on its own -- the information analysis, concept application, assumption identification, conclusion development, and implication prediction to solve a problem.
8. Provide a means for Socrates Digital™ to access problem descriptions and solutions from as many problem areas as possible to increase its world knowledge.

The discussion of 7) above – develop the capability for Socrates Digital™ to create a solution to a problem on its own – highlights the roles played by Socrates Digital™ and the humans that use it. We discussed that it is technically challenging to enhance Socrates Digital™ to do this task by itself. To be able to accomplish this satisfactorily is probably decades away. Nevertheless, the other question that we should ask ourselves is, "do we want Socrates Digital™ to solve our problems without our direction and input?" That answer will probably be "no" for the foreseeable future. If we were willing to turn decision-making over to machines, we would turn more and more of it over to machine learning algorithms – which we are reluctant to do since we do not really understand them. Turning over decision-making to machines is not where our future is going. We want to understand our problems and judge the tradeoffs between the different possible solutions for ourselves. Socratic problem-solving is the best way for us to do this. Socrates Digital™'s role is to help us reason in the best way that works for us. It just makes us better at what we do best.

REFERENCES

Argyris, C., & Schön, D. (1996). *Organizational learning II: Theory, method and practice*. Addison Wesley.

Marcot, B. (1987). Testing your knowledge base. *AI Expert*, 2(8), 42–47.

O'Keefe, R., Balci, O., & Smith, E. (1987). Validating expert system performance. *IEEE Expert*, 2(4), 81–90. doi:10.1109/MEX.1987.5006538

Yang, H. (1995). Information/knowledge acquisition methods for decision support systems and expert systems. *Information Processing & Management*, 31(1), 47–58. doi:10.1016/0306-4573(95)80005-E

Appendix A:
Flow Charts for Socrates Digital

Figure 1. Socrates Digital System Architecture

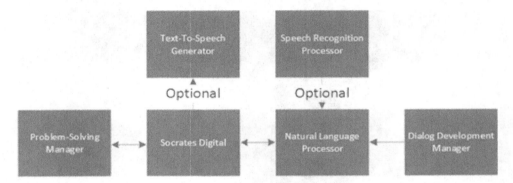

Figure 2. Define Problem Process of the Socrates Digital Module

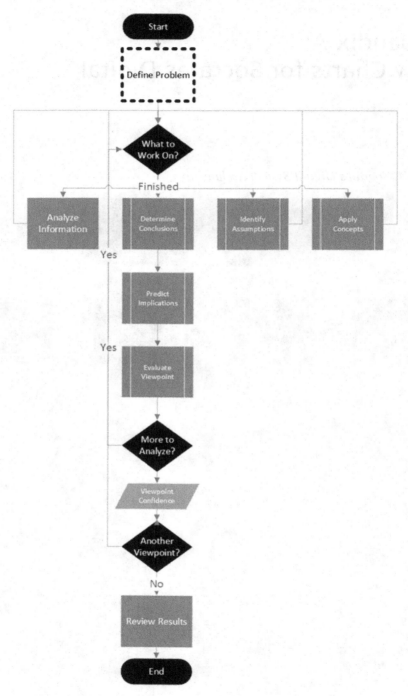

Figure 3. Apply Concepts Process of the Socrates Digital Module

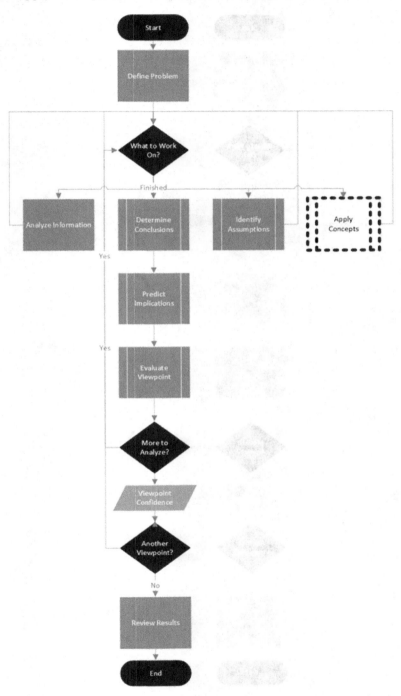

Figure 4. Analyze Information Process of the Socrates Digital Module

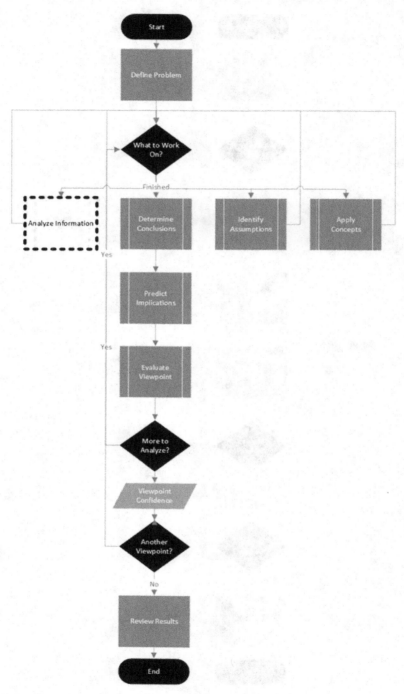

Figure 5. Determine Conclusions Subprocess of the Socrates Digital Module

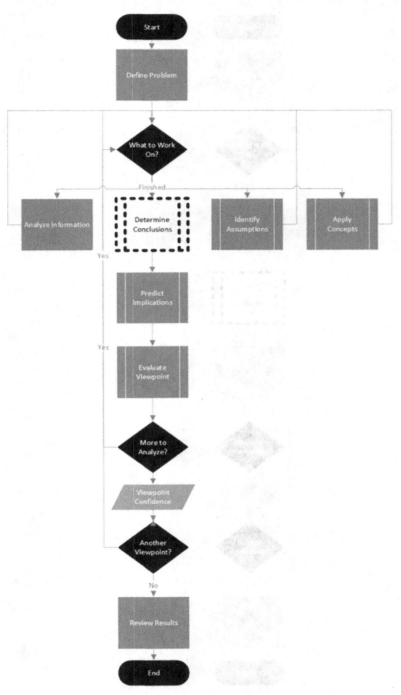

Figure 6. Predict Implications Subprocess of the Socrates Digital Module

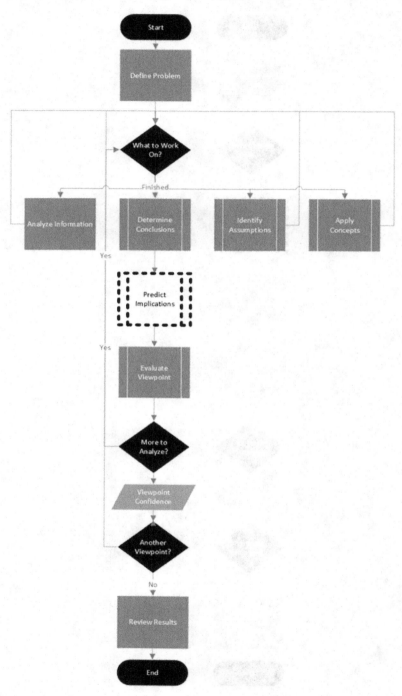

Figure 7. Review Results Process of the Socrates Digital Module

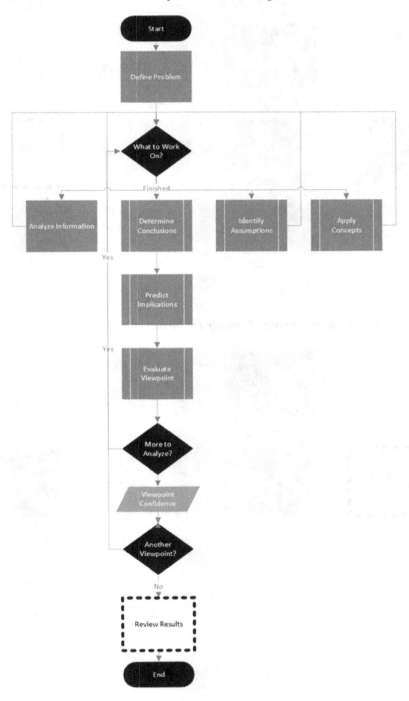

Figure 8. The Dialog Development Manager Process

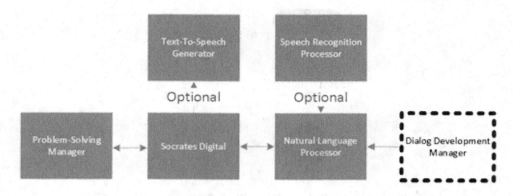

Figure 9. The Problem-Solving Manager Process

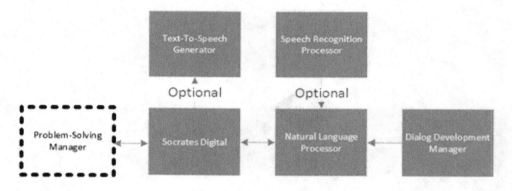

Figure 10. The Define Problem Process of the Socrates Digital Module

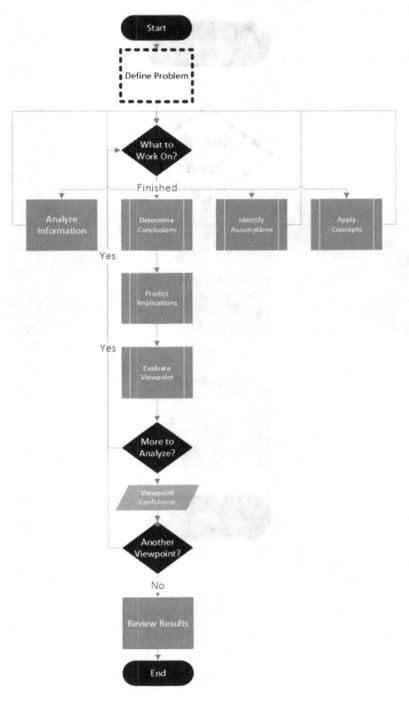

Figure 11. The Identify Area Process Starts the Define Problem Process

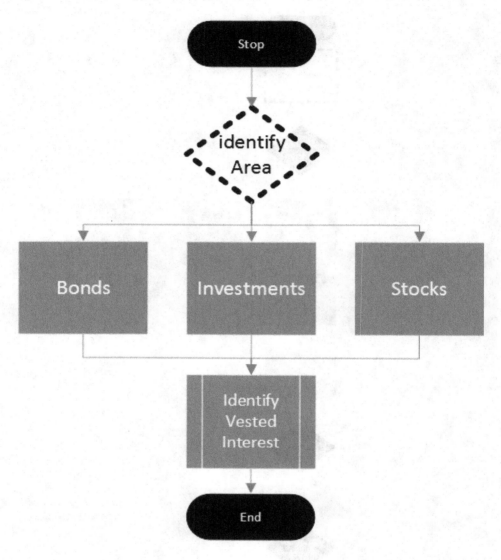

Figure 12. The Investments Process is a Second Step Option in the Define Problem Process

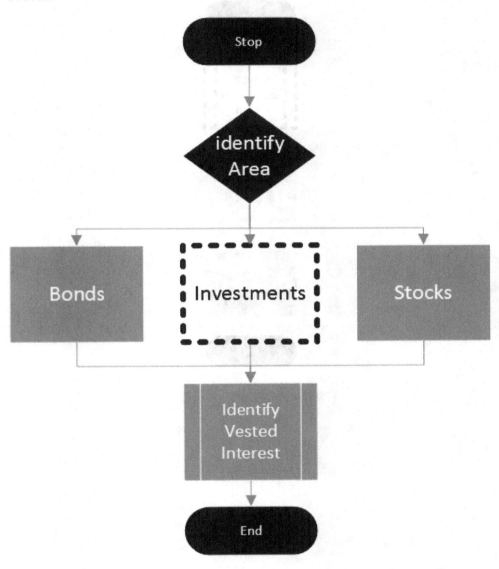

Figure 13. Identify Question at Hand is the First Subprocess in the Investment Process

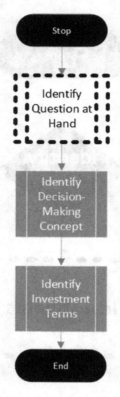

Figure 14. Identify Decision-Making Concept is the Second Subprocess in the Investment Process

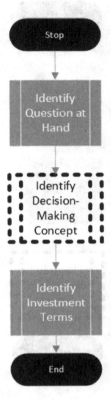

Figure 15. Identify Investment Terms is the Third Subprocess in the Investment Process

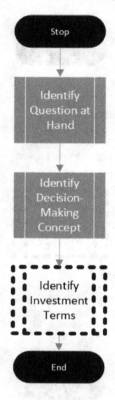

Figure 16. The Identify Vested Interest Subprocess of the Define Problem Process

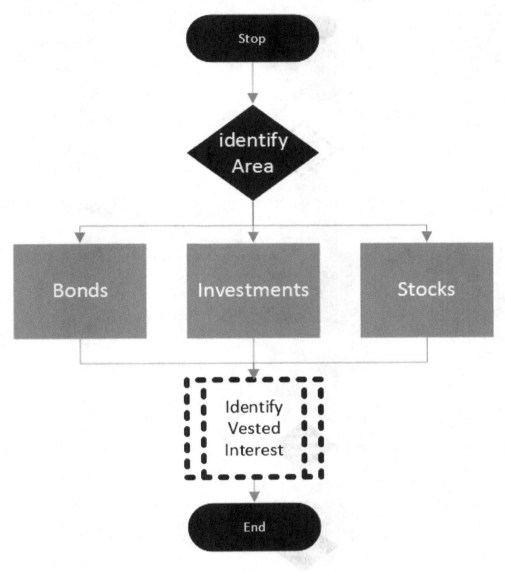

Figure 17. What to Work On? Decision Process in Socrates Digital

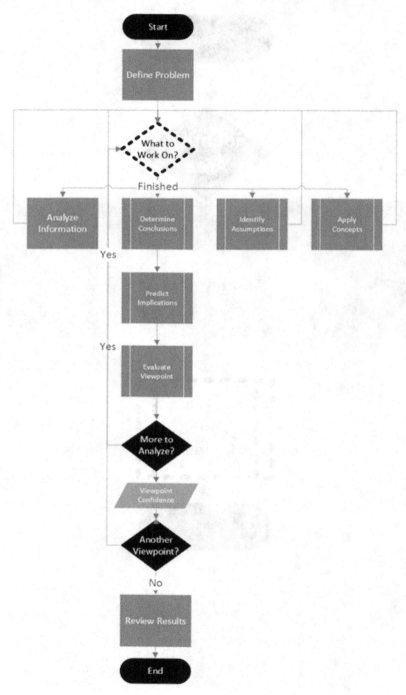

Figure 18. The Analyze Information Process of the Socrates Digital Module

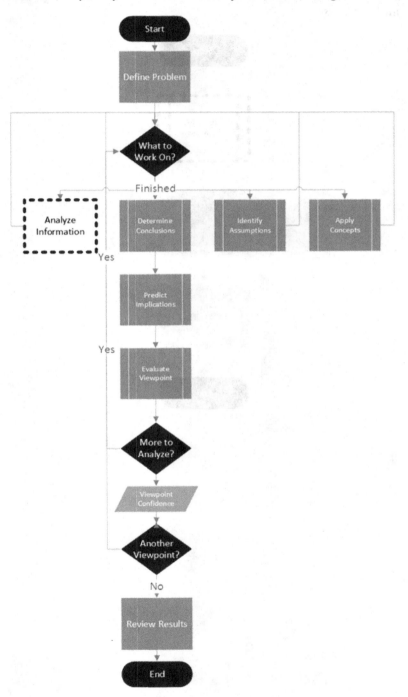

Figure 19. The Identify Assumptions Subprocess is the Second Step in the Analyze Information Process

Figure 20. The Identify Assumptions Subprocess of the Socrates Digital Module

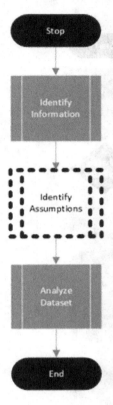

Figure 21. The Analyze Dataset Subprocess is the Third Step in the Analyze Information Process

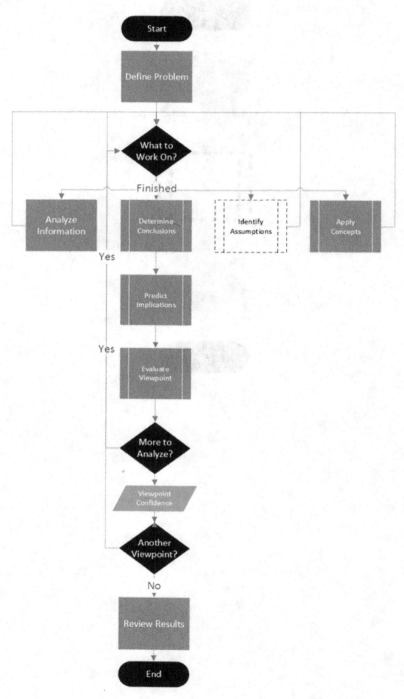

Figure 22. The Apply Concepts Subprocess of the Socrates Digital Process

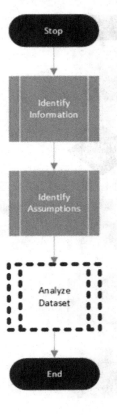

Figure 23. The Determine Conclusions Subprocess of the Socrates Digital Module

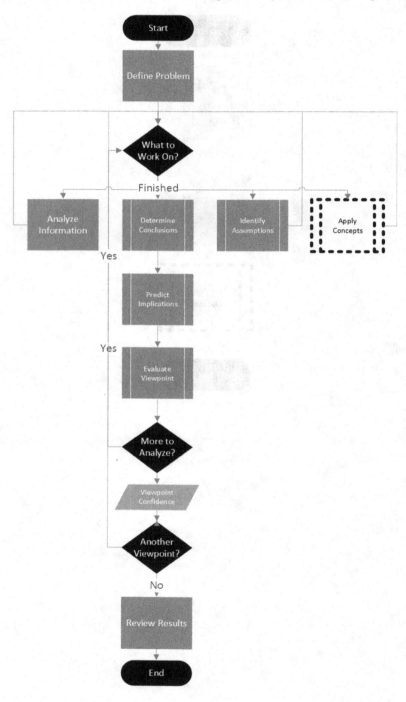

Figure 24. The Predict Implications Subprocess of the Socrates Digital Module

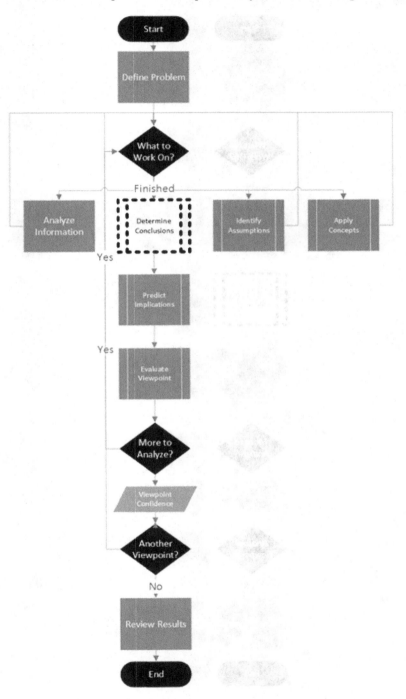

Figure 25. The Evaluate Viewpoint Subprocess of the Socrates Digital Process

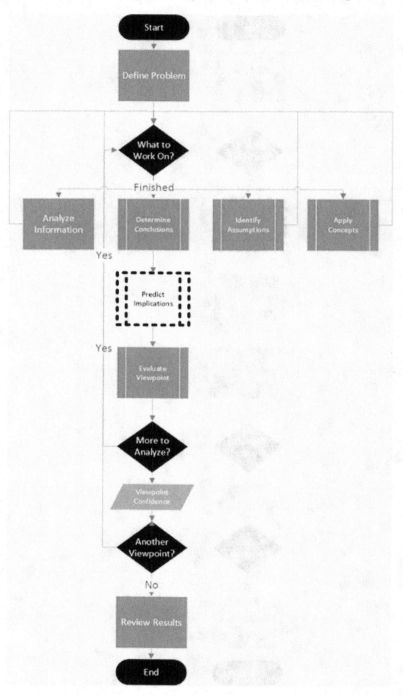

Figure 26. The More to Analyze? Subprocess of the Socrates Digital Module

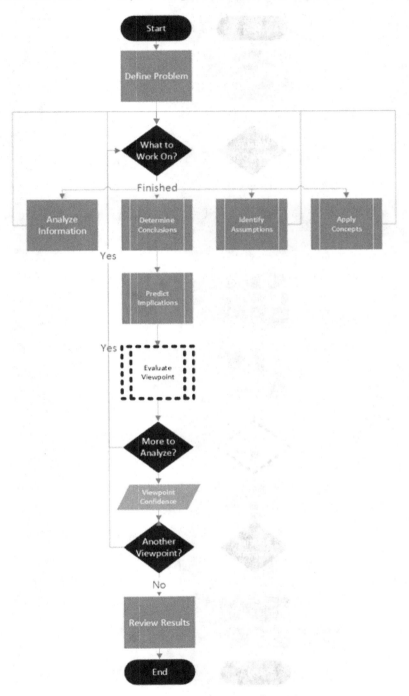

Figure 27. The Viewpoint Confidence Process in the Socrates Digital Module

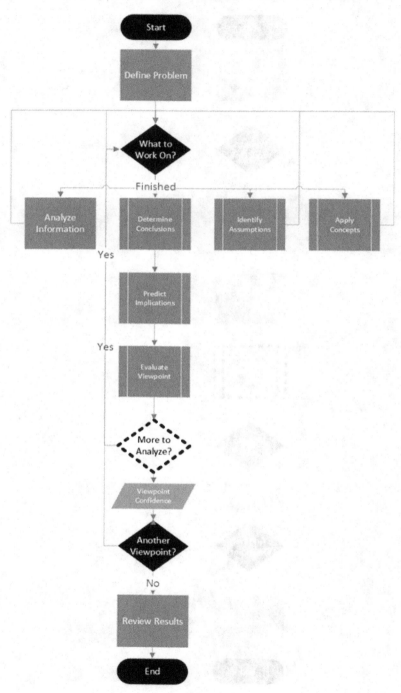

Figure 28. The Another Viewpoint? Subprocess of the Socrates Digital Module

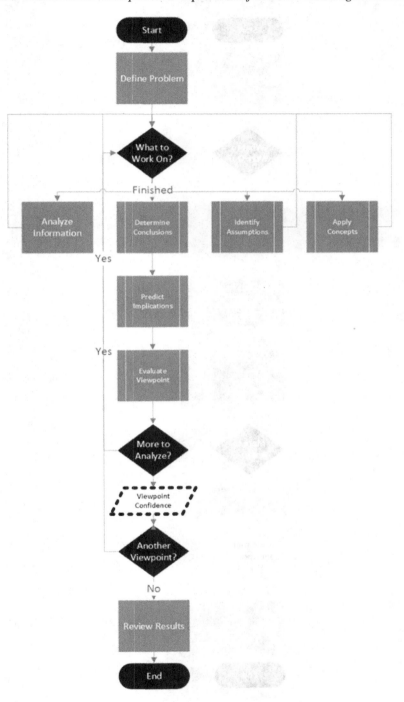

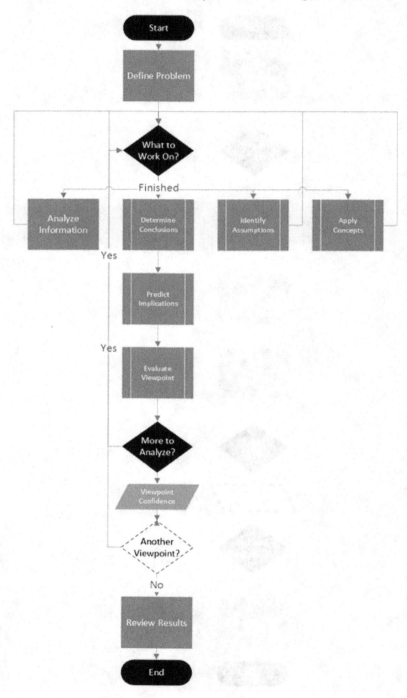

Figure 29. The Review Results Process of the Socrates Digital Module

Figure 30. The Report Results Subprocess of the Review Results Process

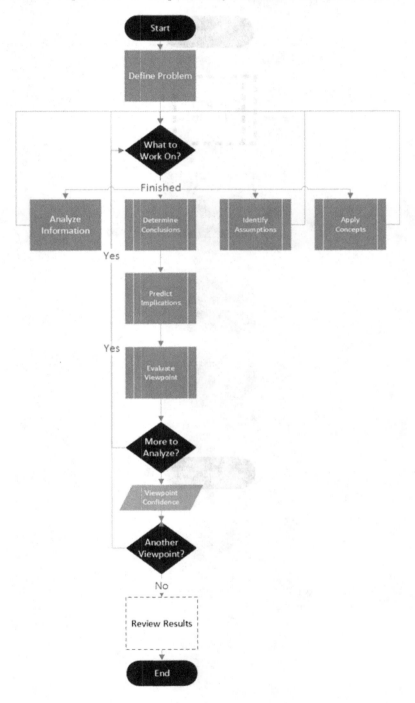

Figure 31. The Answer Question at Hand Subprocess of the Review Results Process

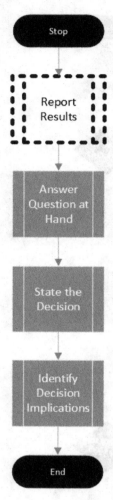

Figure 32. The State the Decision Subprocess of the Review Results Process

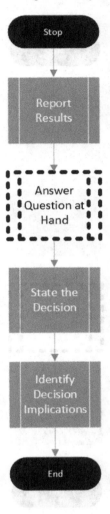

Figure 33. The Identify Decision Implications Subprocess of the Review Results Process

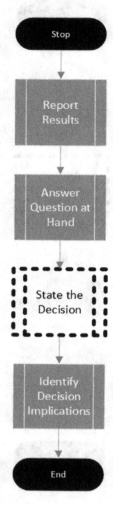

Figure 34. The Dialog Development Manager Process

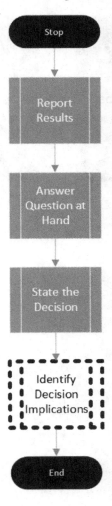

Figure 35. The Understand Subprocess in the Dialog Development Manager Process

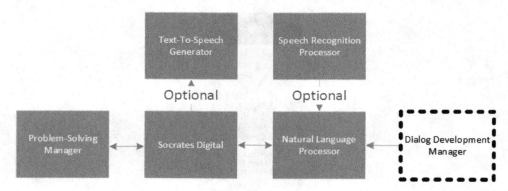

Figure 36. The Explore Subprocess in the Dialog Development Manager Process

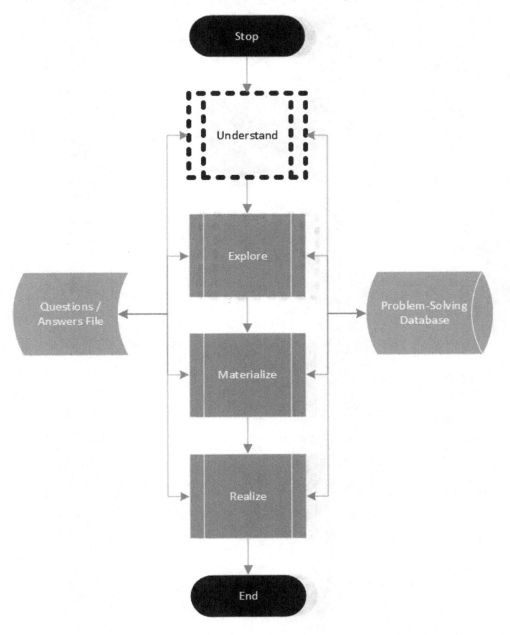

Figure 37. The Materialize Subprocess in the Dialog Development Manager Process

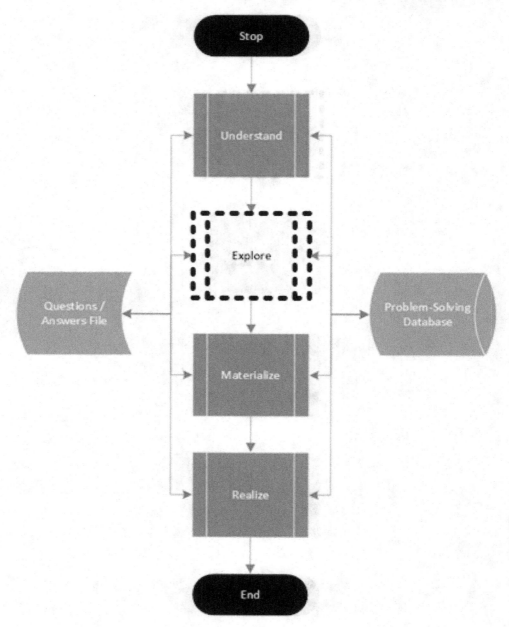

Figure 38. The Realize Subprocess in the Dialog Development Manager Process

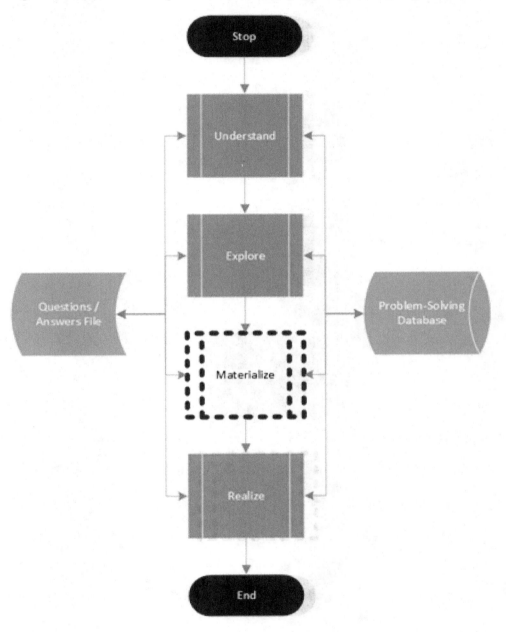

Figure 39. The Problem-Solving Manager Process

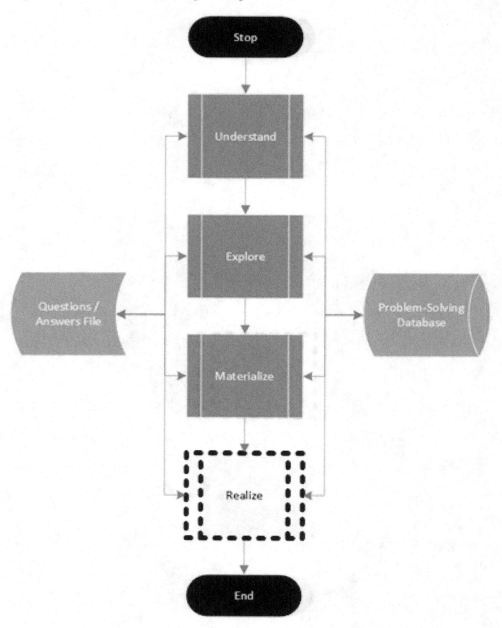

Figure 40. The Viewpoint_Approval Subprocess of the Problem-Solving Manager Process

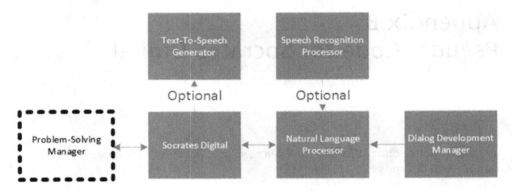

Appendix B:
Pseudo-Code for Socrates Digital

```
/* Questions that Target the Parts of Thinking -- Questioning
Goals and Purposes

/* Ask user persona to identify the area that help is needed
BEGIN Process Decision_Process_Identify_Area

/* Generate a Random Number Between 1 and 3 - the Possible
Forms of the Question
        RandomInteger:= GenerateRandomInteger[1,3]

/* Select a Form of the Question
        CASE RandomInteger OF
                1: Question:= "What can I help you with
today?"
                2: Question:= "What can I do for you?"
3: Question:= "Can I help you with something today?"
END_CASE

OUTPUT Question
INPUT Answer

Problem_Description:= Answer

User_Response:= Answer

/* Understood_Response should come back as "Bonds,"
"Investments," or "Stocks"
Natural_Language_Processor (User_Response, Understood_Response)

IF Understood_Response <>  "Bonds" OR "Investments" OR "Stocks"
THEN
        OUTPUT "Sorry I didn't understand you. Do you want
help with bonds, investments, or stocks?"
        INPUT Answer
User_Response:= Answer
END_IF
```

```
Problem_Area:= Understood_Response

/* Save Session_ID, Problem_Description, Problem_Area in
database
INSERT INTO Define_Problem_Table (Session_ID, Problem_
Description, Problem_Area) VALUES (Current_Session_ID, Problem_
Description, Problem_Area)

END Process Decision_Process_Identify_Area
```

PSEUDO CODE FOR THE DECISION_ PROCESS_IDENTIFY_AREA

```
/* Questions that Target the Parts of Thinking - Question at
Issue

/* Ask user persona to identify question at hand
BEGIN Subprocess Identify_Question_At_Hand

/* Generate a Random Number Between 1 and 3 - the Possible
Forms of the Question
        RandomInteger:= GenerateRandomInteger[1,3]

/* Select a Form of the Question
        CASE RandomInteger OF
        1: Question:= "So, the question at hand is " +
Problem_Description + "?"
        2: Question:= "Then, the question at hand is " +
Problem_Description + "?"
3: Question:= "OK, the question at hand is " + Problem_
Description + "?"

END_CASE

OUTPUT Question

INPUT Answer

User_Response:= Answer

Question:= Problem_Description

/* Understood_Response will come back as "Yes" or "No"
Natural_Language_Processor (User_Response, Understood_Response)
```

```
/* If no, then give user persona a chance to correct the
question at hand
IF Understood_Response <> "Yes" Then OUTPUT "Then what is the
question at hand?"
INPUT Answer
        Question:= Answer

END_IF

/* Save Question_At_Hand to database
UPDATE Define_Problem_Table
SET
Question_At_Hand:= Question
WHERE Problem_Area = "Investments"  AND Session_ID = Current_
Session_ID

END Subprocess Identify_Question_At_Hand
```

PSEUDO CODE FOR THE IDENTIFY_ QUESTION_AT_HAND SUBPROCESS

```
/* Questions that Target the Parts of Thinking -- Questioning
Concepts and Ideas
/* Ask user persona to identify concept that will be used to
make the decision
BEGIN Subprocess Identify_Decision_Making_Concept

/* Generate a Random Number Between 1 and 3 - the Possible
Forms of the Question
        RandomInteger:= GenerateRandomInteger[1,3]

/* Select a Form of the Question
        CASE RandomInteger OF
        1: Question:= "What is the main concept that you will
use to make your decision?"
        2: Question:= "To make your decision, what main
concept will you use?"
3: Question:= "What concept will you apply to make the
decision?"
END_CASE

OUTPUT Question
```

```
INPUT Answer

Description:= Answer

/* Call Subprocess Decision_Making_Concept_Questioning_
Relevance and Get Back an
/* Answer
Subprocess Decision_Making_Concept_Questioning_Relevance
(Answer)

Question_At_Hand:= Answer

/* Save Decision_Making_Concept_Description and
/* Decision_Making_Concept_Relates_Question_At_Hand to database
UPDATE Define_Problem_Table
SET
Decision_Making_Concept_Description:= Description
Decision_Making_Concept_Relates_Question_At_Hand:= Question_At_
Hand

WHERE Problem_Area = "Investments"  AND Session_ID = Current_
Session_ID

END Subprocess Identify_Decision_Making_Concept
```

PSEUDO CODE FOR THE IDENTIFY_DECISION_ MAKING_CONCEPT SUBPROCESS

```
/* Questions that Target the Quality of Reasoning --
Questioning Relevance

/* Generate Questioning Relevance question for user persona and
collect answer
BEGIN Subprocess Decision_Making_Concept_Questioning_Relevance
(Answer)

        /* Generate a Random Number Between 1 and 3 - the
Possible Forms of the
/* Question
        RandomInteger:= GenerateRandomInteger[1,3]

        /* Select a Form of the Question
        CASE RandomInteger OF
                1: Question:= "How does it relate to the
```

question at hand?"
                  2: Question:= "For the question at hand, how
does it relate?"
3: Question:= "Can you tell me how it relates to the question
at hand?"
END_CASE

OUTPUT Question

INPUT Answer

END Subprocess Decision_Making_Concept_Questioning_Relevance
*Pseudo Code for the Decision_Making_Concept_Questioning_*
Relevance Subprocess
/* Questions that Target the Parts of Thinking – Questioning
Questions
/* Ask user persona to identify investment terms
BEGIN Subprocess Identify_Investment_Terms

/* Generate a Random Number Between 1 and 3 – the Possible
Forms of the Question
        RandomInteger:= GenerateRandomInteger[1,3]

/* Select a Form of the Question
        CASE RandomInteger OF
        1: Question:= "OK – are you ready to answer some
questions about the terms
         of the investment?"
        2: Question:= "How about answering questions about the
terms of the
investment?"
3: Question:= "Would you answer some questions about the terms
of the
investment?"
END_CASE

OUTPUT Question

INPUT Answer

User_Response:= Answer

/* Understood_Response will come back as "Yes" or "No"
Natural_Language_Processor (User_Response, Understood_Response)

/* If no, then give user persona a chance to correct the
question at hand
IF Understood_Response = "Yes" THEN

316

```
Rate_Of_Return_Questioning_Precision (Rate)
Investment_Amount_Questioning_Precision (Amount)
Investment_Repayment_Period_Questioning_Precision (Repay)
Investment_Purpose_Questioning_Precision (Purpose)

/* Save terms of investment to database
UPDATE Define_Problem_Table
SET
Rate_Of_Return_Questioning_Precision:= Rate
Investment_Amount_Questioning_Precision:= Amount
Investment_Repayment_Period_Questioning_Precision:= Repay
Investment_Purpose_Questioning_Precision:= Purpose

WHERE Problem_Area = "Investments"  AND Session_ID = Current_
Session_ID

ELSE

OUTPUT "OK, we will skip this for now."

END_IF

END Subprocess Identify_Investment_Terms
```

PSEUDO CODE FOR IDENTIFY_ INVESTMENT_TERMS SUBPROCESS

```
/* Questions that Target the Quality of Reasoning --
Questioning Precision

/* Generate Questioning Precision question for user persona and
collect answer
BEGIN Subprocess Rate_Of_Return_Questioning_Precision (Answer)

Question:= "What is the projected rate of return?"

OUTPUT Question

INPUT Answer

END Subprocess Rate_Of_Return_Questioning_Precision


/* Questions that Target the Quality of Reasoning --
```

```
Questioning Precision

/* Generate Questioning Precision question for user persona and
collect answer
BEGIN Subprocess Investment_Amount_Questioning_Precision
(Answer)

Question:= "What is the investment amount?"

OUTPUT Question

INPUT Answer

END Subprocess Investment_Amount_Questioning_Precision


/* Questions that Target the Quality of Reasoning --
Questioning Precision

/* Generate Questioning Precision question for user persona and
collect answer
BEGIN Subprocess Investment_Repayment_Period_Questioning_
Precision (Answer)

Question:= "What is the repayment period?"

OUTPUT Question

INPUT Answer

END Subprocess Investment_Repayment_Period_Questioning_
Precision
```

PSEUDO CODE FOR RATE OF RETURN, INVESTMENT AMOUNT, AND REPAYMENT PERIOD SUBPROCESSES

```
/* Questions that Target the Quality of Reasoning --
Questioning Precision

/* Generate Questioning Precision question for user persona and
collect answer
BEGIN Subprocess Investment_Purpose_Questioning_Precision
(Answer)
```

```
Question:= "What will the investment be used for?"

OUTPUT Question
INPUT Answer

IF Answer < 100 Characters THEN
        Investment_Purpose_Questioning_Clarity (Clarified_
Answer)
Answer:= Clarified_Answer
END_IF

END Subprocess Investment_Purpose_Questioning_Precision


/* Questions that Target the Quality of Reasoning --
Questioning Clarity

/* Generate Questioning Precision question for user persona and
collect answer
BEGIN Subprocess Investment_Purpose_Questioning_Clarity
(Answer)

Question:= "Could you elaborate further about what the
investment will be used for?"

OUTPUT Question

INPUT Answer

END Subprocess Investment_Purpose_Questioning_Clarity
```

PSEUDO CODE FOR THE INVESTMENT PURPOSE QUESTIONING PRECISION SUBPROCESS

```
/* Questions that Target the Parts of Thinking - Questioning
Goals and Purposes
/* Ask user persona to identify any vested interests
BEGIN Subprocess Identify_Vested_Interest

Vested_Interest_Questioning_Fairness (Answer)

Vested_Interest_Questioning_Fairness:= Vested_Interest_
Questioning_Fairness
```

```
/* Save terms of investment to database
UPDATE Define_Problem_Table
SET
Vested_Interest_Questioning_Fairness:= Vested_Interest_
Questioning_Fairness

WHERE Problem_Area = "Investments"  AND Session_ID = Current_
Session_ID

END Subprocess Identify_Vested_Interest


/* Questions that Target the Quality of Reasoning --
Questioning Fairness

/* Ask Questioning Fairness question about vested interest of
user persona and collect answer
BEGIN Subprocess Vested_Interest_Questioning_Fairness (Answer)

Question:= "Before we get started, do you have vested interest
in the question at hand?  For example, you would have a vested
interest in this business opportunity if the Rosebud Motel were
owned by one of your relatives."

OUTPUT Question

INPUT Answer

END Subprocess Vested_Interest_Questioning_Fairness
```

PSEUDO CODE FOR IDENTIFY_VESTED_ INTEREST SUBPROCESS

```
/* Questions that Target the Parts of Thinking -- Questioning
Goals and Purposes

/* Ask user persona to what to work on - information,
assumptions, or concepts
BEGIN Subprocess What_To_Work_On

/* Generate a Random Number Between 1 and 3 - the Possible
Forms of the Question
        RandomInteger:= GenerateRandomInteger[1,3]
```

```
/* Select a Form of the Question
        CASE RandomInteger OF
        1: Question:= "OK, of the following, what would you
like to work on?"
        2: Question:= "What do you want to work on from this
list?"
3: Question:= "Given these options, what do you want to work
on?"
END_CASE

OUTPUT Question

/* If user persona has not worked on the identifying
information, then list it as an option
IF Information_Already_Visited = FALSE
        THEN OUTPUT "Information"
END_IF

/* If user persona has not worked on the identifying
assumptions, then list it as an option
IF Assumptions_Already_Visited = FALSE
        THEN OUTPUT "Assumptions"
END_IF

/* If user persona has not worked on the identifying concepts,
then list it as an option
IF Concepts_Already_Visited = FALSE
        THEN OUTPUT "Concepts"
END_IF

INPUT Answer

User_Response:= Answer

/* Understood_Response should come back as "Information,"
"Assumptions," or "Concepts"
Natural_Language_Processor (User_Response, Understood_Response)


/* Select a Form of the Question
        CASE Understood_Response OF
        "Information": Information_Already_Visited:= TRUE
        "Assumptions": Assumptions_Already_Visited:= TRUE
"Concepts": Concepts_Already_Visited:= TRUE
END_CASE


/* Given the value of Understood_Response, go to information,
assumptions, or concepts process
```

```
GOTO Understood_Response

END What_To_Work_On
```

PSEUDO CODE FOR THE WHAT_TO_ WORK_ON SUBPROCESS

```
/* Questions that Target the Parts of Thinking - Information,
Data, and Experience
/* Ask user persona to Identify Information for Analysis
BEGIN Subprocess Identify_Information

/* Generate a Random Number Between 1 and 3 - the Possible
Forms of the Question
        RandomInteger:= GenerateRandomInteger[1,3]

/* Select a Form of the Question
        CASE RandomInteger OF
        1: Question:= "What information, data, or experience
do you have that
          supports or informs this analysis?"
        2: Question:= "What information, data, or experience
do you have?"
3: Question:= "Do you have information, data, or experience
that illustrates
this?"
END_CASE

OUTPUT Question

INPUT Answer

Information_Description:= Answer

/* Call Subprocess Data_Point_Questioning_Clarity and Get Back
an Answer
Subprocess Data_Point_Questioning_Clarity (Answer)

Data_Point_Description:= Answer

/* Save Information_Description  and Data_Point_Description  in
database
INSERT INTO Datasets_Table (Session_ID, Information_
Description, Data_Point_Description) VALUES (Current_Session_
```

```
ID, Information_Description, Data_Point_Description)

END Subprocess Identify_Information


/* Questions that Target the Quality of Reasoning --
Questioning Clarity

/* Generate Questioning Clarity question for user persona and
collect answer
BEGIN Subprocess Data_Point_Questioning_Clarity (Answer)

        /* Generate a Random Number Between 1 and 3 - the
Possible Forms of the
         /* Question
        RandomInteger:= GenerateRandomInteger[1,3]

        /* Select a Form of the Question
        CASE RandomInteger OF
        1: Question:= "Can you give me an example data point
about this?"
        2: Question:= "Can you provide an example data point
that shows this?"
3: Question:= "Do you have an example data item that
illustrates this?"
END_CASE

OUTPUT Question

INPUT Answer

END Subprocess Data_Point_Questioning_Clarity
```

PSEUDO CODE FOR THE IDENTIFY INFORMATION PROCESS

```
/* Questions that Target the Parts of Thinking -- Questioning
Assumptions

/* Ask user persona to Identify assumption for analysis
BEGIN Subprocess Identify_Assumptions

/* Generate a Random Number Between 1 and 3 - the Possible
Forms of the Question
```

```
        RandomInteger:= GenerateRandomInteger[1,3]

    /* Select a Form of the Question
    CASE RandomInteger OF
    1: Question:= "Do any of the following assumptions
underlie this
      observation?"
    2: Question:= "Of the following assumptions, do any
underly this
observation?"
3: Question:= "Any of these assumptions underlie this
observation?"
END_CASE

OUTPUT Question

/* Display assumptions from the database for this session
SELECT Assumption_Description,
FROM Assumptions_Table
WHERE  Problem_Area = "Investments"

INPUT Answer

Assumption_Description:= Answer


/* Call Subprocess Apply_Assumptions_Questioning_Significance
and Get an Answer
Subprocess Apply_Assumptions_Questioning_Significance (Answer)

Assumption_Confidence:= Answer

/* Save Answer to Current Session Assumptions Description
INSERT INTO Assumptions_Table (Problem_Area, Session_ID,
Assumption_Description, Assumption_Confidence) VALUES
("Investment_Motel", Current_Session_ID, Assumption_
Description, Assumption_Confidence)

END Subprocess Identify_Assumptions
Psuedo Code for Subprocess Identify_Assumptions
/* Questions that Target the Quality of Reasoning --
Questioning Significance
/* Generate Questioning Significance question for user persona
and collect answer
BEGIN Subprocess Apply_Assumptions_Questioning_Significance
(Answer)

    /* Generate a Random Number Between 1 and 3 - the
Possible Forms of the Question
```

```
        RandomInteger:= GenerateRandomInteger[1,3]

        /* Select a Form of the Question
        CASE RandomInteger OF
        1: Question:= "Do you want to apply this assumption in
your reasoning?"
        2: Question:= "Is this the assumption you want to use
right now?"
3: Question:= "Do you want to apply this assumption for your
thinking on
this?"
END_CASE

OUTPUT Question

OUTPUT
"Definitely Apply It
  Probably Apply It
          Maybe Apply it
        Disregard It for Now
        Delete It"

INPUT User_Response

Natural_Language_Processor (User_Response, Understood_Response)

CASE Understood_Response OF

Definitely Apply It:  Answer: = 0.75
Probably Apply It:  Answer: = 0.5
        Maybe Apply it: Answer: = 0
        Disregard It for Now: Answer: =   -0.5
        Delete It: Answer: = -0.75

END_CASE

END Subprocess Apply_Assumptions_Questioning_Significance
```

PSEUDO CODE FOR APPLY_ASSUMPTIONS_ QUESTIONING_SIGNIFICANCE SUBPROCESS

```
/* Questions that Target the Parts of Thinking -- Questioning
Information, Data, and Experience
```

```
/* Ask user persona If Assumption Holds for Larger Dataset
BEGIN Subprocess Analyze_Dataset

/* Generate a Random Number Between 1 and 3 - the Possible
Forms of the Question
        RandomInteger:= GenerateRandomInteger[1,3]

        /* Select a Form of the Question
        CASE RandomInteger OF
        1: Question:= "Does this assumption hold for the
larger dataset?"
        2: Question:= "For the larger dataset, does this
assumption hold?"
3: Question:= "Is this assumption true for the larger dataset?"
END_CASE

OUTPUT Question

INPUT Answer

Dataset_Analysis_Description:= Answer

/* Call Subprocess Dataset_Analysis_Questioning_Accuracy and
Get an Answer
Subprocess Dataset_Analysis_Questioning_Accuracy (Answer)

Dataset_Accuracy:= Answer

/* Save Answer to Current Session Datasets Description
UPDATE Datasets_Table
SET
Dataset_Analysis_Description:= Dataset_Analysis_Description
Dataset_Accuracy:= Dataset_Accuracy
WHERE Problem_Area = "Investments"  AND Session_ID = Current_
Session_ID

END Subprocess Analyze_Dataset
```

PSEUDO CODE FOR THE ANALYZE_ DATASET SUBPROCESS

```
/* Questions that Target the Quality of Reasoning --
Questioning Accuracy
BEGIN Subprocess Dataset_Analysis_Questioning_Accuracy (Answer)
```

```
        /* Generate a Random Number Between 1 and 3 - the
Possible Forms of the
/* Question
        RandomInteger:= GenerateRandomInteger[1,3]

        /* Select a Form of the Question
        CASE RandomInteger OF
        1: Question:= "How would you rate the accuracy of this
information?"
        2: Question:= "How accurate is this information?"
3: Question:= "This information - how accurate is it?"
END_CASE

OUTPUT Question

OUTPUT
"Accurate
Probably Accurate
Unknown Accuracy
Probably Not Accurate
Inaccurate"
INPUT User_Response

Natural_Language_Processor (User_Response, Understood_Response)

CASE Understood_Response OF

Accurate:  Answer: = 0.75
Probably Accurate:  Answer: = 0.5
        Unknown Accuracy: Answer: = 0
        Probably Not Accurate: Answer: =    -0.5
        Inaccurate: = -0.75

END_CASE

END Subprocess Dataset_Analysis_Questioning_Accuracy
```

PSEUDO CODE FOR DATASET_ANALYSIS_ QUESTIONING_ACCURACY SUBPROCESS

```
/* Questions that Target the Parts of Thinking -- Questioning
Concepts
```

```
/* Ask user persona to apply concept for analysis
BEGIN Subprocess Apply_Concepts

/* Generate a Random Number Between 1 and 3 - the Possible
Forms of the Question
        RandomInteger:= GenerateRandomInteger[1,3]

        /* Select a Form of the Question
        CASE RandomInteger OF
        1: Question:= "Which concept do you want to use to
explain how to answer the
         question at hand? " + Question_At_Hand
        2: Question:= "Of the following, which do you want to
use to answer the
         question at hand? " + Question_At_Hand
3: Question:= "Which concept do you want to use for this
question at hand? "
+ Question_At_Hand
END_CASE

OUTPUT Question

/* Display concepts from the database for this session
SELECT Concept_Description,
FROM Concepts_Table
WHERE  Problem_Area = "Investments"

OUTPUT "Another Concept"

INPUT User_Response

Natural_Language_Processor (User_Response, Understood_Response)

Concept_Description:= Understood_Response

IF Concept_Description = "Another Concept" THEN
        OUTPUT "What do you call this concept?"
        INPUT User_Response
Natural_Language_Processor (User_Response, Understood_Response
Concept_Description:= Understood_Response
END_IF


/* Call Subprocess Apply_Concepts_Questioning_Significance and
Get an Answer
Subprocess Apply_Concepts_Questioning_Significance (Answer)

Concept_Strength:= Answer
```

```
/* Save Answer to Current Session Concepts Description
INSERT INTO Concepts_Table (Problem_Area, Session_ID, Concept_
Description, Concept_Strength) VALUES ("Investment_Motel",
Current_Session_ID, Concept_Description, Concept_Strength)

END Subprocess Apply_Concepts
```

PSEUDO CODE FOR SUBPROCESS APPLY_CONCEPTS

```
/* Questions that Target the Quality of Reasoning --
Questioning Significance
/* Generate Questioning Significance question for user persona
and collect answer
BEGIN Subprocess Apply_Concepts_Questioning_Significance
(Answer)

        /* Generate a Random Number Between 1 and 3 - the
Possible Forms of the
        /* Question
        RandomInteger:= GenerateRandomInteger[1,3]

        /* Select a Form of the Question
        CASE RandomInteger OF
        1: Question:= "How well does this concept explain how
to answer the question
         at hand?"
        2: Question:= "For the question at hand, how well does
this concept explain
         how to answer it?"
3: Question:= "How well does it explain how to answer the
question at hand?"
END_CASE

OUTPUT Question

OUTPUT
"Always Explains
  Mostly Explains
  Sometimes Explains
  Rarely Explains
  Never Explains"

INPUT User_Response
```

```
Natural_Language_Processor (User_Response, Understood_Response)

CASE Understood_Response OF

Always Explains:  Answer: = 0.75
Mostly Explains:  Answer: = 0.5
Sometimes Explains: Answer: = 0
          Rarely Explains: Answer: =   -0.5
          Never Explains: Answer = -0.75

END_CASE

END Subprocess Apply_Concepts_Questioning_Significance
```

PSEUDO CODE FOR THE APPLY_CONCEPTS_ QUESTIONING_SIGNIFICANCE SUBPROCESS

```
/* Questions that Target the Parts of Thinking - Questioning
/* Inferences and Conclusions

/* Ask user persona to Determine Conclusion of the analysis
BEGIN Subprocess Determine_Conclusions

/* Generate a Random Number Between 1 and 3 - the Possible
Forms of the /* Question
     RandomInteger:= GenerateRandomInteger[1,3]

     /* Select a Form of the Question
     CASE RandomInteger OF
     1: Question:= "Given these concepts, assumptions, and
      information, what is the most reasonable conclusion?"
     2: Question:= "What is the most reasonable conclusion
with these
     concepts, assumptions, and information?"
3: Question:= "With these concepts, assumptions, and
information, what is the best conclusion?"
END_CASE

OUTPUT Question

INPUT Answer

Conclusion_Description: = Answer
```

```
/* Call Subprocess Determine_Conclusion_Questioning_Inferences
and Get
/* an Answer
Subprocess Determine_Conclusion_Questioning_Inferences (Answer)

Conclusion_Logic: = Answer

/* Save Answer to Current Session Data Point Description
INSERT INTO Conclusions_Table (Session_ID, Conclusion_
Description, Conclusion_Logic) VALUES (Current_Session_ID,
Conclusion_Description, Conclusion_Logic)

END Subprocess Determine_Conclusions
```

PSEUDO CODE FOR SUBPROCESS DETERMINE_CONCLUSIONS

```
/* Questions that Target the Quality of Reasoning --
Questioning Logic

/* Ask user persona to rate how logical the conclusion is
BEGIN Subprocess Determine_Conclusion_Questioning_Inferences
(Answer)

        /* Generate a Random Number Between 1 and 3 - the
Possible Forms
        /* of the Question
        RandomInteger:= GenerateRandomInteger[1,3]

        /* Select a Form of the Question
        CASE RandomInteger OF
        1: Question:= "Given this is all the evidence that you
currently
        have, how would you rate the logic of this
conclusion?"
        2: Question:= "Given all this evidence, how would you
rate this
        logic ?"
3: Question:= "How would you rate this logic, given this
evidence?"
END_CASE

OUTPUT Question
```

```
OUTPUT
"Very Logical
  Probably Logical
  Unknown How Logical
  Probably Not Logical
  Illogical"
INPUT User_Response

Natural_Language_Processor (User_Response, Understood_Response)

CASE Understood_Response OF

Very Logical:  Answer: = 0.75
Probably Logical:  Answer: = 0.5
        Unknown How Logical: Answer: = 0
        Probably Not Logical: Answer: =   -0.5
        Illogical: = -0.75

END_CASE

END Subprocess Determine_Conclusion_Questioning_Inferences
```

PSEUDO CODE FOR THE DETERMINE_CONCLUSION_ QUESTIONING_INFERENCES SUBPROCESS

```
/* Questions that Target the Parts of Thinking -- Questioning
Implications and Consequences

/* Ask user persona to Predict Implications of a Conclusion
BEGIN Subprocess Predict_Implications

/* Generate a Random Number Between 1 and 3 - the Possible
Forms of the Question
        RandomInteger:= GenerateRandomInteger[1,3]

        /* Select a Form of the Question
        CASE RandomInteger OF
        1: Question:= "What are the implications of this
conclusion?"
        2: Question:= "For this conclusion, what do you think
are the
           implications?"
3: Question:= "Can you explain the implications of this
conclusion?"
```

```
END_CASE

OUTPUT Question

INPUT Answer

Implication_Description: = Answer

/* Call Subprocess Predict_Implications_Questioning_Breadth and
Get an Answer
Subprocess Predict_Implications_Questioning_Breadth (Answer)

Implication_Evidence: = Answer

/* Save Answer to Current Session Data Point Description
INSERT INTO Implications_Table (Session_ID, Implication_
Description, Implication_Evidence) VALUES (Current_Session_ID,
Implication_Description, Implication_Evidence)

END Subprocess Predict_Implications
```

PSEUDO CODE FOR SUBPROCESS PREDICT_IMPLICATIONS

```
/* Questions that Target the Quality of Reasoning --
Questioning Breadth

/* Ask user persona to rate the implications of this conclusion
BEGIN Subprocess Predict_Implications_Questioning_Breadth
(Answer)

        /* Generate a Random Number Between 1 and 3 - the
Possible Forms of the Question
        RandomInteger:= GenerateRandomInteger[1,3]

        /* Select a Form of the Question
        CASE RandomInteger OF
        1: Question:= "How would you rate your confidence in
the
        implications of this conclusion?"
        2: Question:= "For this implication of the conclusion,
how would
        you rate your confidence?"
3: Question:= "How confident are you in this implication of the
```

conclusion?"
END_CASE

OUTPUT Question

OUTPUT
"Highly Justified
  Probably Justified
  Insufficient Evidence to Judge
  Not Justified by the Evidence
  Refuted by the Evidence"
INPUT User_Response

Natural_Language_Processor (User_Response, Understood_Response)

CASE Understood_Response OF

Highly Justified: Answer: = 0.75
Probably Justified: Answer: = 0.5
          Insufficient Evidence to Judge: Answer: = 0
          Not Justified by the Evidence: Answer: =   -0.5
          Refuted by the Evidence: = -0.75

END_CASE

END Subprocess Predict_Implications_Questioning_Breadth

PSEUDO CODE FOR THE PREDICT_IMPLICATIONS_ QUESTIONING_CONSEQUENCES SUBPROCESS

```
/* Questions that Target the Parts of Thinking - Questioning
/* Viewpoints and Perspectives

/* Ask user persona to restate implications as a viewpoint and
/* evaluate it - then system will calculate a confidence level
for it
BEGIN Subprocess Evaluate_Viewpoint

/* Generate a Random Number Between 1 and 3 - the Possible
Forms
/* of the Question
      RandomInteger:= GenerateRandomInteger[1,3]

      /* Select a Form of the Question
```

```
        CASE RandomInteger OF
1: Question:= "Can you restate the implications of the current
conclusions, listed below, as a viewpoint for answering the
question at hand?"
2: Question:= "Can you state a viewpoint for answering the
question at hand by using the implications of the current
conclusions, listed below?"
3: Question:= "Can you rephase these current implications,
listed below, into a viewpoint?"
END_CASE

OUTPUT Question

/* Display implications from the database for this session
SELECT Implication_Description, Implication_Confidence
FROM Implication_Table
WHERE Problem_Area = "Investments"  AND Session_ID = Current_
Session_ID

        INPUT Answer

Viewpoint_Description:= Answer

/* Calculate Viewpoint_Confidence from the Dataset, Concept,
Assumption, Conclusion, and Implications scores
Subprocess Evaluate_Viewpoint_Questioning_Depth (Answer)

Viewpoint_Confidence:= Answer

/* Save Viewpoint_Description and Viewpoint_Confidence to
Viewpoints_Table table in the database
INSERT INTO Viewpoints_Table (Session_ID, Viewpoint_
Description, Viewpoint_Confidence) VALUES (Current_Session_ID,
Viewpoint_Description, Viewpoint_Confidence)

END Subprocess Evaluate_Viewpoint
```

PSEUDO CODE FOR SUBPROCESS EVALUATE_VIEWPOINT

```
/* Questions that Target the Quality of Reasoning --
Questioning Depth

/* Calculate the Viewpoint_Confidence in this viewpoint (values
```

```
range
/* between 0 and 1).  A value of 0 is no confidence; 1 is high
/* confidence

/* The complete pseudo code listing for the subprocess
/* Evaluate_Viewpoint_Questioning_Depth

BEGIN Subprocess Evaluate_Viewpoint_Questioning_Depth (Answer)


/* Count the number of datasets in the current session
Number_Of_Datasets:= SELECT COUNT (Dataset_Accuracy)
 FROM Dataset_Table
 WHERE  Session_ID = Current_Session_ID

/* Calculate the average confidence score across the datasets
/* used in the current session
Dataset_Average:= SELECT AVG (Dataset_Accuracy)
       FROM Dataset_Table
       WHERE  Session_ID = Current_Session_ID

/* Increase the average confidence score for each additional
/* dataset to add more confidence
Dataset_Accuracy_Adjusted_Ave:= Dataset_Average + ((Dataset_
Average * (Number_Of_Datasets * Additional_Dataset_
Multiplier)))

/* If dataset average confidence score is over 1, then set to 1
IF Dataset_Accuracy_Adjusted_Ave > 1.0 THEN Dataset_Accuracy_
Adjusted_Ave:= 1.0


/***************


/* Count the number of datasets in the current session
Number_Of_Concepts:= SELECT COUNT (Concept_Strength)
 FROM Concept_Table
 WHERE  Session_ID = Current_Session_ID

/* Calculate the average confidence score across the concepts
/* used in the current session
Concept_Average:= SELECT AVG (Concept_Strength)
       FROM Concept_Table
       WHERE  Session_ID = Current_Session_ID

/* Increase the average confidence score for each additional
/* concept to add more confidence
Concept_Strength_Adjusted_Ave:= Concept_Average + ((Concept_
```

```
Average * (Number_Of_Concepts * Additional_Concept_
Multiplier)))

/* If concept average confidence score is over 1, then set to 1
IF Concept_Strength_Adjusted_Ave > 1.0 THEN Concept_Strength_
Adjusted_Ave:= 1.0


/***************


/* Count the number of assumptions in the current session
Number_Of_Assumptions:= SELECT COUNT (Assumption_Confidence)
 FROM Assumption_Table
 WHERE  Session_ID = Current_Session_ID

/* Calculate the average confidence score across the
assumptions
/* used in the current session
Assumption_Average:= SELECT AVG (Assumption_Confidence)
       FROM Assumption_Table
       WHERE  Session_ID = Current_Session_ID

/* Increase the average confidence score for each additional
/* assumption to add more confidence
Assumption_Confidence_Adjusted_Ave:= Assumption_Average +
((Assumption_Average * (Number_Of_Assumptions * Additional_
Assumption_Multiplier)))

/* If assumption average confidence score is over 1, then set
to 1
IF Assumption_Confidence_Adjusted_Ave > 1.0 THEN Assumption_
Confidence_Adjusted_Ave:= 1.0


/***************


/* Count the number of conclusions in the current session
Number_Of_Conclusions:= SELECT COUNT (Conclusion_Logic)
 FROM Conclusion_Table
 WHERE  Session_ID = Current_Session_ID

/* Calculate the average confidence score across the
conclusions
/* used in the current session
Conclusion_Average:= SELECT AVG (Conclusion_Logic)
       FROM Conclusion_Table
       WHERE  Session_ID = Current_Session_ID
```

```
/* Increase the average confidence score for each additional
/* conclusion to add more confidence
Conclusion_Logic_Adjusted_Ave:= Conclusion_Average +
((Conclusion_Average * (Number_Of_Conclusions * Additional_
Conclusion_Multiplier)))

/* If conclusion average confidence score is over 1, then set
to 1
IF Conclusion_Logic_Adjusted_Ave > 1.0 THEN Conclusion_Logic_
Adjusted_Ave:= 1.0


/***************

/* Count the number of implications in the current session
Number_Of_Implications:= SELECT COUNT (Implication_Evidence)
 FROM Implication_Table
 WHERE   Session_ID = Current_Session_ID

/* Calculate the average confidence score across the
implications
/* used in the current session
Implication_Average:= SELECT AVG (Implication_Evidence)
     FROM Implication_Table
     WHERE   Session_ID = Current_Session_ID

/* Increase the average confidence score for each additional
/* implication to add more confidence
Implication_Evidence_Adjusted_Ave:= Implication_Average +
((Implication_Average * (Number_Of_Implications * Additional_
Implication_Multiplier)))

/* If implication average confidence score is over 1, then set
to 1
IF Implication_Evidence_Adjusted_Ave > 1.0 THEN Implication_
Evidence_Adjusted_Ave:= 1.0


/***************

/* Calculate Viewpoint_Confidence from the adjusted average
/* values for datasets, concepts, assumptions, conclusions, and
/* implications

Viewpoint_Confidence:=                       (Dataset_Accuracy_
Adjusted_Ave * Dataset_Weight)+
(Concept_Strength_Adjusted_Ave * Concept_Weight)+
(Assumption_Confidence_Adjusted_Ave * Assumption_Weight)+
(Conclusion_Logic_Adjusted_Ave * Conclusion_Weight)+
```

```
(Implication_Evidence_Adjusted_Ave * Implication_Weight)


/* Return Viewpoint_Confidence as the decimal value between 0
and
/* 1 that reflects the total confidence in the viewpoint
Answer:= Viewpoint_Confidence

END Subprocess Evaluate_Viewpoint_Questioning_Depth
```

PSEUDO CODE FOR THE EVALUATE_VIEWPOINT_QUESTIONING_DEPTH SUBPROCESS

```
/* Questions that Target the Parts of Thinking -- Questioning
Goals and Purposes

/* Ask user persona if more confirming evidence is available
BEGIN Subprocess More_To_Analyze

/* Generate a Random Number Between 1 and 3 - the Possible
Forms
/* of the Question
        RandomInteger:= GenerateRandomInteger[1,3]

/* Select a Form of the Question
        CASE RandomInteger OF
        1: Question:= "Can we get more confirming evidence
about
        this?"
        2: Question:= "Is there more information that supports
        this?"
3: Question:= "Can you provide more data that backs this
up?"
END_CASE

OUTPUT Question
INPUT Answer

Problem_Description:= Answer

User_Response:= Answer

/* Understood_Response should come back as "Yes " or "No"
Natural_Language_Processor (User_Response, Understood_Response)
```

```
IF Understood_Response <>  "Yes" OR "No" THEN
      OUTPUT "Sorry I didn't understand you. Is it yes or no
that
         you have more confirming evidence?"
      INPUT Answer
User_Response:= Answer
END_IF

IF Understood_Response  = "Yes"  THEN
GOTO WHAT_TO_WORK_ON
END_IF

END Subprocess More_To_Analyze
```

THE PSEUDO CODE FOR THE MORE TO ANALYZE? SUBPROCESS

```
/* Questions that Target the Quality of Reasoning --
Questioning Depth

/* Tell user persona the confidence (between 0 and 1) in the
viewpoint and the description of the viewpoint
BEGIN Subprocess Viewpoint_Confidence

OUTPUT User_Persona_Identity " has expressed an overall
confidence of " + Viewpoint_Confidence + " for the following
viewpoint " + Viewpoint_Description
END Subprocess Viewpoint_Confidence
```

PSEUDO CODE FOR THE VIEWPOINT CONFIDENCE SUBPROCESS

```
/* Questions that Target the Parts of Thinking -- Questioning
Goals and
/* Purposes

/* Ask user persona if another viewpoint that should be
considered
```

```
BEGIN Subprocess Another_Viewpoint

/* Generate a Random Number Between 1 and 3 - the Possible
Forms
/* of the Question
RandomInteger:= GenerateRandomInteger[1,3]

/* Select a Form of the Question
CASE RandomInteger OF
1: Question:= "Is there another viewpoint that should be
considered?"
2: Question:= "Should we consider another viewpoint?"
3: Question:= "At this time, is there another viewpoint we
should look at?"
END_CASE

OUTPUT Question

INPUT Answer

Problem_Description:= Answer

User_Response:= Answer

/* Understood_Response should come back as "Yes " or "No"
Natural_Language_Processor (User_Response, Understood_Response)

IF Understood_Response <>  "Yes" OR "No" THEN
        OUTPUT "Sorry I didn't understand you. Is it yes or no
that
         another viewpoint that should be considered?"
        INPUT Answer
User_Response:= Answer
END_IF

IF Understood_Response   = "Yes"   THEN
GOTO WHAT_TO_WORK_ON
END_IF

END Subprocess Another_Viewpoint
```

THE PSEUDO CODE FOR THE ANOTHER VIEWPOINT? SUBPROCESS

```
/* Questions that Target the Parts of Thinking - Questioning
/* Viewpoints and Perspectives

/* Ask user person if he or she wants to see all the viewpoints
and
/* their confidence levels for answering the question at hand
BEGIN Subprocess Report_Results (Answer)

        /* Generate a Random Number Between 1 and 3 - the
Possible Forms
         of the Question
        RandomInteger:= GenerateRandomInteger[1,3]

        /* Select a Form of the Question
        CASE RandomInteger OF
        1: Question:= "Would you like to see all the
viewpoints and
          their confidence levels for answering the question at
hand?"
        2: Question:= "Display all the viewpoints and their
confidence
          levels for answering the question at hand?"
3: Question:= "Show all the viewpoints and confidence levels
for
answering the question at hand?"
END_CASE

OUTPUT Question

INPUT Answer

User_Response:= Answer


Natural_Language_Processor (User_Response, Understood_Response)

IF Understood_Response = "Yes" THEN

/* Display viewpoints from the database for this question /* at
hand
SELECT User_Persona_Identity, Viewpoint_Description, Viewpoint_
Confidence
FROM Viewpoint_Table
WHERE Problem_Area = "Investments"  AND Session_ID =
```

```
Current_Session_ID

END_IF

/* Save the user persona's Viewed_Viewpoints answer to database
UPDATE Define_Problem_Table
SET
User_Persona_Identity:= User_Persona_Identity
Viewed_Viewpoints:= Understood_Response
WHERE Problem_Area = "Investments"  AND Session_ID =
Current_Session_ID

END Subprocess Report_Results
```

PSEUDO CODE FOR THE REPORT_ RESULTS SUBPROCESS

```
/* Ask user persona to identify question at hand
BEGIN Subprocess Answer_Question_At_Hand

/* Generate a Random Number Between 1 and 3 - the Possible
Forms
/* of the Question
RandomInteger:= GenerateRandomInteger[1,3]

/* Select a Form of the Question
        CASE RandomInteger OF
        1: Question:= "Does this help answer the question at
hand about
        " + Question_At_Hand + "?"
        2: Question:= "Is the question at hand answered -- " +
        Question_At_Hand + "?"
3: Question:= "Does this answer the question at hand -- " +
Question_At_Hand + "?"

END_CASE

OUTPUT Question

INPUT Answer

User_Response:= Answer

/* Understood_Response will come back as "Yes" or "No"
```

```
Natural_Language_Processor (User_Response, Understood_Response)

/* If no, then give user persona a chance to correct the
question
/* at hand
IF Understood_Response = "No" THEN OUTPUT "Then, it looks
unresolved for now"

END_IF

/* Save Answer_Question_At_Hand to database
UPDATE Define_Problem_Table
SET
Answer_Question_At_Hand:= Understood_Response
WHERE Problem_Area = "Investments"  AND Session_ID =
Current_Session_ID


END Subprocess Answer_Question_At_Hand
```

PSEUDO CODE FOR THE ANSWER_ QUESTION_AT_HAND SUBPROCESS

```
/* Questions that Target the Parts of Thinking -- Questioning
Goals and Purposes

/* Ask user persona to state the decision
BEGIN Subprocess State_The_Decision

/* Generate a Random Number Between 1 and 3 - the Possible
Forms
/* of the Question
        RandomInteger:= GenerateRandomInteger[1,3]

/* Select a Form of the Question
        CASE RandomInteger OF
        1: Question:= "What is your decision?"
        2: Question:= "What have you decided?"
3: Question:= "So, what is the decision?"

END_CASE

OUTPUT Question
```

```
INPUT Answer

What_Is_The_Decision:= Answer

/* Save What_Is_The_Decision to database
UPDATE Define_Problem_Table
SET
What_Is_The_Decision:= What_Is_The_Decision
WHERE Problem_Area = "Investments" AND Session_ID =
Current_Session_ID

END Subprocess State_The_Decision
```

PSEUDO CODE FOR THE STATE_THE_DECISION SUBPROCESS

```
/* Ask User Persona to identify the implications of the
decision
BEGIN Subprocess Identify_Decision_Implications

/* Generate a Random Number Between 1 and 3 - the Possible
Forms
/* of the Question
        RandomInteger:= GenerateRandomInteger[1,3]

/* Select a Form of the Question
        CASE RandomInteger OF
        1: Question:= "What are the implications of this
decision?"
        2: Question:= "For this decision, what are the
implications?"
3: Question:= "So, what do you think are the implications of
this decision?"
END_CASE

OUTPUT Question

INPUT Answer

Decision_Implications:= Answer


/* Save Decision_Implications to database
UPDATE Define_Problem_Table
```

```
SET
Decision_Implications:= Decision_Implications

WHERE Problem_Area = "Investments"  AND Session_ID =
Current_Session_ID

OUTPUT "OK, that completes this session."

END Subprocess Identify_Decision_Implications
```

PSEUDO CODE FOR THE STATE THE IDENTIFY_ DECISION_IMPLICATIONS SUBPROCESS

```
/* Questions that Target the Parts of Thinking - Questioning
Questions
/* Ask the analyst to create a user persona profile, define
system
/* persona behavior, and identify user journey mapping
BEGIN Subprocess Understand

Question:= "Are you ready to answer some questions about the
user persona profile, Socrates Digital behavior, and user
journey mapping?"

OUTPUT Question

INPUT Answer

User_Response:= Answer

/* Understood_Response will come back as "Yes" or "No"
Natural_Language_Processor (User_Response, Understood_Response)

/* If no, then give the analyst an opportunity to skip this.
IF Understood_Response = "Yes" THEN

Subprocess Create_Profile_Questioning_Precision (ProfileFile)
Subprocess Define_Behavior_Questioning_Precision (BehaviorFile)
Subprocess Identify_Journey_Questioning_Precision (MappingFile)

/* Save Understand phase answers to database
UPDATE Understand_Table
SET
Create_Profile:= ProfileFile
```

```
Define_Behavior:= BehaviorFile
Identify_Journey:= MappingFile

WHERE Problem_Area = "Investments"

ELSE

OUTPUT "OK, we will skip this for now."

END_IF

END Subprocess Understand
```

PSEUDO CODE FOR THE UNDERSTAND SUBPROCESS

```
/* Questions that Target the Quality of Reasoning --
Questioning Precision

/* Generate Questioning Precision question for user persona and
/* collect answer
BEGIN Subprocess Create_Profile_Questioning_Precision (Answer)

Question:= "How would you describe the profile of your user
persona?  You should include what the problem area is and the
level of experience of the user persona.  For example, you
could describe the user persona as a member of an investment
firm who is considering investing in a commercial real estate
opportunity. After you have completed your user persona
profile, upload the file so it can be found with the click of a
mouse."

OUTPUT Question

UPLOAD_FILE Answer

Subprocess Provide_Initial_Background

END Subprocess Create_Profile_Questioning_Precision
```

PSEUDO CODE FOR CREATE_PROFILE_ QUESTIONING_PRECISION SUBPROCESS

```
/* Questions that Target the Parts of Thinking - Questioning
Questions
/* Ask user persona to provide some initial information,
concepts, and
/* assumptions to start the learning and problem-solving
process for the
/* user persona
BEGIN Subprocess Provide_Initial_Background


Question:= "It's important to provide some initial information,
concepts, and assumptions to start the learning and problem-
solving process for the user persona of the system.

Do you want to provide some initial information, concepts, and
assumptions to start the learning and problem-solving process
for the user persona."

OUTPUT Question

INPUT Answer

User_Response:= Answer

/* Understood_Response will come back as "Yes" or "No"
Natural_Language_Processor (User_Response, Understood_Response)

/* If no, then give the analyst an opportunity to skip this.
IF Understood_Response = "Yes" THEN

Subprocess Provide_Initial_Information
Subprocess Provide_Initial_Concepts
Subprocess Provide_Initial_Assumptions

ELSE

OUTPUT "OK, we will skip this for now."

END_IF

END Subprocess Provide_Initial_Background
```

PSEUDO CODE FOR PROVIDE_INITIAL_
BACKGROUND SUBPROCESS

```
/* Questions that Target the Quality of Reasoning --
Questioning Precision

/* Generate Questioning Precision question for user persona to
provide
/* initial information and update database

BEGIN Subprocess Provide_Initial_Information


Question:= "Let's start with information. Do you want to add a
source of information for the user persona?"

OUTPUT Question

INPUT User_Response
/* Send off to natural language processor to determine yes/no
answer
Natural_Language_Processor (User_Response, Understood_Response)

If Understood_Response = "Yes"

WHILE Understood_Response = "Yes"
OUTPUT "How would describe the information?"
        INPUT Information_Description
        OUTPUT "What is the URL for the information?"
        INPUT Information_URL
        /* Save Information Description and URL Information
Table
/* in Database
INSERT INTO Information_Table (Problem_Area, Information_
Description, Information_URL, VALUES("Investment_Motel",
Information_Description, Information_URL)
OUTPUT "Do you want to add another source of information for
the user persona?"
INPUT User_Response
/* Send off to natural language processor to determine
/* yes/no answer
Natural_Language_Processor (User_Response, Understood_Response)

END WHILE

END Subprocess Provide_Initial_Information
```

PSEUDO CODE FOR PROVIDE_INITIAL_ INFORMATION SUBPROCESS

```
Precision

/* Generate Questioning Precision question for user persona to
provide
/* initial concepts and update database

BEGIN Subprocess Provide_Initial_Concepts


Question:= "Let's start with concepts. Do you want to add a
concept for the user persona?"

OUTPUT Question

INPUT User_Response
/* Send off to natural language processor to determine yes/no
answer
Natural_Language_Processor (User_Response, Understood_Response)

If Understood_Response = "Yes"

WHILE Understood_Response = "Yes"
OUTPUT "What is the name for the concept?"
        INPUT Concept_Name
        OUTPUT "How would describe the concept?"
        INPUT Concept_Description
/* Save concept name and description in Concepts Table in
database
INSERT INTO Concepts_Table (Problem_Area, Concept_Name,
Concept_Description, VALUES("Investment_Motel", Concept_Name,
Concept_Description)
OUTPUT "Do you want to add another concept for the user
persona?"
INPUT User_Response
/* Send off to natural language processor to determine yes/no
answer
Natural_Language_Processor (User_Response, Understood_Response)

END WHILE

END Subprocess Provide_Initial_Concepts
```

PSEUDO CODE FOR PROVIDE_INITIAL_ CONCEPTS SUBPROCESS

```
/* Questions that Target the Quality of Reasoning --
Questioning Precision

/* Generate Questioning Precision question for user persona to
provide
/* initial assumptions and update database

BEGIN Subprocess Provide_Initial_Assumptions


Question:= "Let's turn to assumptions. Do you want to add an
assumption for the user persona?"

OUTPUT Question

INPUT User_Response
/* Send off to natural language processor to determine yes/no
answer
Natural_Language_Processor (User_Response, Understood_Response)

If Understood_Response = "Yes"

WHILE Understood_Response = "Yes"
OUTPUT "What is the name for the assumption?"
        INPUT Assumption_Name
        OUTPUT "How would describe the assumption?"
        INPUT Assumption_Description
/* Save assumption name and description in Assumptions Table in
database
INSERT INTO Assumptions_Table (Problem_Area, Assumption_Name,
Assumption_Description, VALUES("Investment_Motel", Assumption_
Name, Assumption_Description)
OUTPUT "Do you want to add another assumption for the user
persona?"
INPUT User_Response
/* Send off to natural language processor to determine yes/no
answer
Natural_Language_Processor (User_Response, Understood_Response)

END WHILE

END Subprocess Provide_Initial_Assumptions
```

PSEUDO CODE FOR PROVIDE_INITIAL_ ASSUMPTIONS SUBPROCESS

```
/* Questions that Target the Quality of Reasoning --
Questioning Precision

/* Generate Questioning Precision question for user persona and
collect
/* answer
BEGIN Subprocess Define_Behavior_Questioning_Precision(Answer)

Question:= "What is the behavior of Socrates Digital? In other
words, how does it help the user persona solve a problem?  The
overall behavior should guide the user persona in conversation
to analyze the information, concepts, and assumptions of the
problem, then to the discover the conclusions, identify the
implications of those conclusions, and how all of this forms
a viewpoint about how to solve the problem. The behavior of
Socrates Digital should describe how it does this within the
problem area. Afterwards, upload the file so it can be found
with the click of a mouse."

OUTPUT Question

UPLOAD_FILE Answer

END Subprocess Define_Behavior_Questioning_Precision
```

PSEUDO CODE FOR DEFINE_BEHAVIOR_ QUESTIONING_PRECISION SUBPROCESS

```
/* Questions that Target the Quality of Reasoning --
Questioning Precision

/* Generate Questioning Precision question for user persona and
collect answer
BEGIN Subprocess Identify_Journey_Questioning_Precision
(Answer)

Question:= "User journey mapping begins by deciding what are
the most important parts of the conversation that Socrates
Digital and user persona will have.  These important parts are
```

then scripted for Socrates Digital and user persona to ensure
that Socrates Digital provides the user persona what it needs
to decide about the problem at hand. The next step is to
document this journey mapping in a file. Afterwards, upload the
file so it can be found with the click of a mouse."

OUTPUT Question

UPLOAD_FILE Answer

END Subprocess Identify_Journey_Questioning_Precision

PSEUDO CODE FOR IDENTIFY_JOURNEY_ QUESTIONING_PRECISION SUBPROCESS

```
/* Questions that Target the Parts of Thinking - Questioning
Questions
/* Ask the analyst to create a sample dialog, perform a table
reading
/* and conduct Wizard of Oz testing.
BEGIN Subprocess Explore

Question:= "Are you ready to answer some questions about
creating a sample dialog, performing a table reading, and
conducting Wizard of Oz testing?"

OUTPUT Question

INPUT Answer

User_Response:= Answer

/* Understood_Response will come back as "Yes" or "No"
Natural_Language_Processor (User_Response, Understood_Response)

/* If no, then give the analyst an opportunity to skip this.
IF Understood_Response = "Yes" THEN

Subprocess Create_Sample_Questioning_Precision (SampleFile)
Subprocess Perform_Reading_Questioning_Precision (ReadingFile)
Subprocess Conduct_Wizard_Test_Questioning_Precision
(WizardFile)

/* Save Explore phase answers to database
```

```
UPDATE Explore_Table
SET
Create_Sample:= SampleFile
Perform_Reading:= ReadingFile
Conduct_Wizard_Test:= WizardFile

WHERE Problem_Area = "Investments"

ELSE

OUTPUT "OK, we will skip this for now."

END_IF

END Subprocess Explore
```

PSEUDO CODE FOR THE EXPLORE SUBPROCESS

```
/* Questions that Target the Quality of Reasoning --
Questioning Precision

/* Generate Questioning Precision question for user persona and
collect
/* answer
BEGIN Subprocess Create_Sample_Questioning_Precision (Answer)
```

Question:= "For the sample dialog, take those conversations
identified from the journey mapping step in the Understand
subprocess and flesh them out into conversations. These
conversations use the 'happy path' approach that assumes
there are not any misunderstandings in the conversations
between Socrates Digital and the user persona. This keeps the
conversations simple and allows the designers to focus on the
information that will be exchanged in the conversation.

For all Socrates Digital systems, this sample dialog should
guide the user persona through the steps to identify the
information the user persona will examine, what concepts it
will use to make sense of the information, and what assumptions
underlie the analysis of the data.

The sample dialog should conclude with guiding the user
persona to make a conclusion and identify the implications of
that conclusion. Finally, the sample dialog should guide the

user into taking all the information, concepts, assumptions, conclusions, and implications into account to create a viewpoint to solving the problem at hand.

The next step is to document this sample dialog in a file. Afterwards, upload this file so it can be found with the click."

OUTPUT Question

UPLOAD_FILE Answer

END Subprocess Create_Sample_Questioning_Precision

PSEUDO CODE FOR CREATE_SAMPLE_ QUESTIONING_PRECISION SUBPROCESS

```
/* Questions that Target the Quality of Reasoning --
Questioning Precision

/* Generate Questioning Precision question for user persona and
collect
/* answer
BEGIN Subprocess Perform_Reading_Questioning_Precision (Answer)
```

Question:= "In this next step of the Explore Phase, volunteers are used as actors to see if the sample dialog created in the previous step captures the important things for the user persona to solve his or her problem. Have one volunteer read Socrates Digital part and another volunteer read the user persona part.

Afterwards, conduct a debrief where you ask both volunteers for their impressions of Socrates Digital. Specifically, ask them if Socrates Digital asked the right questions – and in the right way. Ask them if some questions were missing. The most important aspect of the debrief is to have your volunteer actors look at the line of reasoning to see if it makes sense.

The last thing to do in this step is to take this feedback and use it to update the sample dialog so that it represents a clear and logical progression from reasoning about information to constructing a viewpoint for solving the problem at hand.

Afterwards, document this sample dialog in a file and upload it."

OUTPUT Question

UPLOAD_FILE Answer

END Subprocess Perform_Reading_Questioning_Precision

PSEUDO CODE FOR PERFORM_READING_ QUESTIONING_PRECISION SUBPROCESS

/* Questions that Target the Quality of Reasoning -- Questioning Precision

/* Generate Questioning Precision question for user persona and collect answer
BEGIN Subprocess Conduct_Wizard_Test_Questioning_Precision (Answer)

Question:= "After the updates to the sample dialog during the Table Reading step, this is next step called Wizard of Oz Testing. The idea with this step is to have an actor play the role of the user persona and have that person communicate with the unseen Socrates Digital who is in another room. This provides a way to further test the sample dialog in a setting that more closely represents the way communication is planned between Socrates Digital and user persona.

The first thing to do in this step is have your volunteers go through the sample dialog. As before, you will be looking to see if the sample dialog represents a clear and logical progression from reasoning about information to constructing a viewpoint for solving the problem at hand. As before, look for weak spots where the reasoning makes too big of leap such as a conclusion that is made on shaky concepts or assumptions. Make revisions as needed.

Afterwards, provide the revisions of the sample dialog in a new file and upload it."

OUTPUT Question

UPLOAD_FILE Answer

```
END Subprocess Conduct_Wizard_Test_Questioning_Precision
```

PSEUDO CODE FOR CONDUCT_WIZARD_TEST_ QUESTIONING_PRECISION SUBPROCESS

```
/* Questions that Target the Parts of Thinking – Questioning
Questions
/* Ask the analyst to create user flow charts, voice scripts,
and define
/* multimodal interactions.
BEGIN Subprocess Materialize

Question:= "Are you ready to answer some questions about
creating user flow charts, voice scripts, and defining
multimodal interactions?"

OUTPUT Question

INPUT Answer

User_Response:= Answer

/* Understood_Response will come back as "Yes" or "No"
Natural_Language_Processor (User_Response, Understood_Response)

/* If no, then give the analyst an opportunity to skip this.
IF Understood_Response = "Yes" THEN

Subprocess Create_FlowCharts_Questioning_Precision (ChartsFile)
Subprocess Develop_Scripts_Questioning_Precision (ScriptsFile)
Subprocess Define_Multimodal_Questioning_Precision
(MultimodalFile)

/* Save Materialize phase answers to database
UPDATE Materialize_Table
SET
Create_FlowCharts:= ChartsFile
Develop_Scripts:= ScriptsFile
Define_Multimodal:= MultimodalFile

WHERE Problem_Area = "Investments"

ELSE
```

```
OUTPUT "OK, we will skip this for now."

END_IF

END Subprocess Materialize
```

PSEUDO CODE FOR THE MATERIALIZE SUBPROCESS

```
/* Questions that Target the Quality of Reasoning --
Questioning Precision

/* Generate Questioning Precision question for user persona and
collect answer
BEGIN Subprocess Create_FlowCharts_Questioning_Precision
(Answer)

Question:= "This first step of the Materialize phase is to
create the user flow charts for the subprocesses that capture
answers with questions that make up the parts of thinking. The
subprocesses that capture answers with questions that make up
the parts of the quality of reasoning are not seen in the flow
charts.  That is because they are called from the subprocesses
that focus on the parts of thinking.

As shown in the previous chapters of this book, using the
sample dialog that resulted from the Wizard of Oz testing and
revision, the details of the flow of control are defined so
that all the possible user persona's responses are addressed.

After the flow charts have been created, the last step is to
place the flowcharts in a file and upload the file so it can be
found with the other design documentation."

OUTPUT Question

UPLOAD_FILE Answer

END Subprocess Create_FlowCharts_Questioning_Precision
```

PSEUDO CODE FOR CREATE_FLOWCHARTS_ QUESTIONING_PRECISION SUBPROCESS

```
/* Questions that Target the Quality of Reasoning --
Questioning Precision

/* Generate Questioning Precision question for user persona and
collect answer
BEGIN Subprocess Develop_Scripts_Questioning_Precision (Answer)

Question:= "In this step of the Materialize Phase, all
questions and possible responses are documented in a word
processing document or spreadsheet application.  Since most
natural language processing services can process single
question / answer pairs, there is a temptation to skip this
step.  It turns out that there are two good reasons to document
the question / answer pairs and upload them as a file to a
natural language processing service.

The first reason is that with a documented "knowledge base" of
question / answer pairs, designers can easily see what needs
to be changed, make those changes, and upload the question /
answer pairs as a batch to make those systematic changes.

The second reason to put the question / answer pairs in a
file is to have a way to divide up the work.  The upfront
design work described in these first three phases of design
and development can be done by a designer.  Then, the file
containing the knowledge base of questions and answer pairs can
be handed off to a programmer for the Realize Phase.

The last thing to do in this step is to take this file
and upload it."

OUTPUT Question

UPLOAD_FILE Answer

END Subprocess Develop_Scripts_Questioning_Precision
```

PSEUDO CODE FOR DEVELOP_SCRIPTS_ QUESTIONING_PRECISION SUBPROCESS

```
/* Questions that Target the Quality of Reasoning --
Questioning Precision

/* Generate Questioning Precision question for user persona and
collect answer
BEGIN Subprocess Define_Multimodal_Questioning_Precision
(Answer)

Question:= "In this third step of the Materialize Phase, the
possible multimodal interactions between the system and user
personas are examined. In the investment dialog example, the
user persona interacts with data sources such as spreadsheets,
databases, and business intelligence platforms at the same time
the user persona is interacting with Socrates Digital. However,
Socrates Digital is not integrated with the data sources.
Socrates Digital relies on the user persona to provide the
requested values from the data sources to it.

If Socrates Digital is expected to interact directly with
the data sources during its conversation with the user
persona, that would be addressed here.  For example, when
Socrates Digital asks the user persona if a correlation found
in an individual data item holds for the larger dataset,
Socrates Digital could interact with the data source, run the
correlation, and present the results to the user to evaluate.
This level of interaction between the Socrates Digital, user
persona, and the data sources would require additional design,
development, and system user testing to ensure the system works
as envisioned.


After these multimodal aspects of design have been addressed
and stored in a file, then upload the file."

OUTPUT Question

UPLOAD_FILE Answer

END Subprocess Define_Multimodal_Questioning_Precision
```

PSEUDO CODE FOR DEFINE_MULTIMODAL_ QUESTIONING_PRECISION SUBPROCESS

```
/* Questions that Target the Parts of Thinking - Questioning
Questions
/* Ask the analyst to create vocabulary, develop implementation
logic, and set calculation weights.
BEGIN Subprocess Realize

Question:= "Are you ready to answer some questions about
creating vocabulary, developing implementation logic, and
setting calculation weights?"

OUTPUT Question

INPUT Answer

User_Response:= Answer

/* Understood_Response will come back as "Yes" or "No"
Natural_Language_Processor (User_Response, Understood_Response)

/* If no, then give the analyst an opportunity to skip this.
IF Understood_Response = "Yes" THEN

Subprocess Create_Vocabulary_Questioning_Precision (VocabFile)
Subprocess Develop_Logic_Questioning_Precision (LogicFile)
Subprocess Set_Weights_Questioning_Precision (WeightsFile)

/* Save Realize phase answers to database
UPDATE Realize_Table
SET
Create_Vocabulary:= VocabFile
Develop_Logic:= LogicFile
Set_Weights:= WeightsFile

WHERE Problem_Area = "Investments"

ELSE

OUTPUT "OK, we will skip this for now."

END_IF

END Subprocess Realize
```

PSEUDO CODE FOR THE REALIZE SUBPROCESS

/* Questions that Target the Quality of Reasoning --
Questioning Precision

/* Generate Questioning Precision question for user persona to
create vocabulary file
BEGIN Subprocess Create_Vocabulary_Questioning_Precision
(Answer)

Question:= "In this first step of the Realize phase, the
vocabulary is built for the natural language processing
service. This is typically a simple, straight-forward, and
well documented process. This process to create the vocabulary
for the natural language processing service is similar across
artificial intelligence service providers such as Apple,
Microsoft, Google, and Amazon.

Creating a vocabulary for a natural language processing service
typically has the following steps:

1)Create an account with the artificial intelligence service
provider.
2)Create an entity that will process the string of words that
you send it. These are usually called something like a "bot,"
"agent," or similar name.
3)Upload the knowledge base of question / answer pairs.
4)Train the bot on the knowledge base.
5)Test the bot to see if it answers the questions in the way
you expect.
6)Revise the question / answer pairs.
7)Publish the bot.
8)Access the bot from the Socrates Digital system. This is
usually done by using the published endpoint of the bot.

After the vocabulary for a natural language processing service
has been created and saved in a file, the last step is to
upload the file to the natural language processor for it
to use in recognizing answers by the user persona during a
session with Socrates Digital. In addition, upload the file to
Socrates Digital for safe keeping in the Dialog Manager."

OUTPUT Question

UPLOAD_FILE Answer

END Subprocess Create_Vocabulary_Questioning_Precision

PSEUDO CODE FOR CREATE_VOCABULARY_ QUESTIONING_PRECISION SUBPROCESS

```
/* Questions that Target the Quality of Reasoning --
Questioning Precision

/* Generate Questioning Precision question for user persona to
develop implementation logic
BEGIN Subprocess Develop_Logic_Questioning_Precision (Answer)

Question:= "In this second step of the Realize phase, the
implementation logic is developed for the Socrates Digital
system.  This can be done in more than one way and your choice
will depend on several factors.  One factor is concerns which
artificial intelligence service provider is selected.  Some
have no code application programming interfaces (APIs) while
others have APIs that can only be accessed by a general
programming language such as Java, C, or Python.

This book presents the pseudo code for developing most of the
logic in a general programming language. Developers can then
use this pseudo code to implement the parts they choose in a
general programming language.

By the time this book is published, there will be many options
to develop implementation logic across all of the artificial
intelligence service providers including Apple, Microsoft,
Google, and Amazon.
The last thing to do in this step is to put this implementation
logic to use for your Socrates Digital system.  In addition,
take this file
and upload it to Socrates Digital to be managed by the Dialog
Development Manager."

OUTPUT Question

UPLOAD_FILE Answer

END Subprocess Develop_Logic_Questioning_Precision
```

PSEUDO CODE FOR DEVELOP_LOGIC_ QUESTIONING_PRECISION SUBPROCESS

```
/* Questions that Target the Quality of Reasoning --
Questioning Precision

/* Generate Questioning Precision question for user persona to
set calculation weights
BEGIN Subprocess Set_Weights_Questioning_Precision (Answer)

Question:= "The last step in the Realize Phase is setting the
numerical weights for the calculations in the implementation
logic.

As presented in Chapter 8, they are used to empirically adjust
the Viewpoint Confidence according to the problem area.

/* Set Multiplier for each factor - investment example dialog
/* shown

Additional_Dataset_Multiplier:= 0.1
Additional_ Concept_Multiplier:= 0.1
Additional_ Assumption_Multiplier:= 0.1
Additional_ Conclusion_Multiplier:= 0.1
Additional_ Implication_Multiplier:= 0.1

/* Set Weight for each factor - investment example dialog shown
Dataset_Weight:= 0.3
Concept_Weight:= 0.1
Assumption_Weight:= 0.1
Conclusion_Weight:= 0.2
Implication_Weight:= 0.3

First, set these multipliers and weights for all the factors
in the implementation logic of your Socrates Digital system.
Second, upload a copy of the settings in a file to Socrates
Digital for safe keeping in the Dialog Development Manager."

OUTPUT Question

UPLOAD_FILE Answer

END Subprocess Set_Weights_Questioning_Precision
```

PSEUDO CODE FOR SET_WEIGHTS_ QUESTIONING_PRECISION SUBPROCESS

```
/* Questions that Target the Parts of Thinking - Questioning
Questions
/* Ask the analyst if he or she has a viewpoint to submit for
approval
/* as a best practice for the organization
BEGIN Subprocess Viewpoint_Approval

Question:= "Do you want to submit a viewpoint used in a
problem-solving session to be considered as a "best practice"
for the organization?"

OUTPUT Question

INPUT Answer

User_Response:= Answer

/* Understood_Response will come back as "Yes" or "No"
Natural_Language_Processor (User_Response, Understood_Response)

/* If no, then give the analyst an opportunity to skip this.
IF Understood_Response = "Yes" THEN

Question:= "What is the ID number of this viewpoint?"

OUTPUT Question

INPUT Answer

User_Response:= Answer

/* Understood_Response will come back as a number
Natural_Language_Processor (User_Response, Understood_Response)

        ID:= Understood_Response

Subprocess Submitted_Questioning_Precision (Submittal_
Rationale)
Subprocess Reviewed_Questioning_Precision (ID, Reviewed,
Opinion)
Subprocess Approved_Questioning_Precision (ID, Approved,
Reason)

/* Save Understand phase answers to database
```

```
UPDATE Approved_Viewpoints_Table
SET
Submitted_Viewpoint:= Submittal_Rationale

Reviewed_Viewpoint:= Reviewed
Reviewed_Opinion:= Opinion

Approved_Viewpoint:= Approved
Approved_Reason:= Reason

WHERE Viewpoint_ID = Viewpoint_ID_Number

ELSE

OUTPUT "OK, we will skip this."

END_IF

END Subprocess Viewpoint_Approval
```

PSEUDO CODE FOR THE VIEWPOINT_ APPROVAL SUBPROCESS

```
/* Questions that Target the Quality of Reasoning --
Questioning Precision

/* Generate Questioning Precision question for user persona and
/* collect answer
BEGIN Subprocess Submitted_Questioning_Precision (Answer)

Question:= "Why are you submitting this viewpoint for
consideration as a 'best practice' for our organization?"

OUTPUT Question

INPUT Answer


END Subprocess Submitted_Questioning_Precision
```

PSEUDO CODE FOR SUBMITTED_ QUESTIONING_PRECISION SUBPROCESS

```
/* Questions that Target the Quality of Reasoning --
Questioning Precision

/* Generate Questioning Precision question for user persona and
collect
/* answer
BEGIN Subprocess Reviewed_Questioning_Precision (ID, Answer,
Opinion)

        SELECT Viewpoint_Description, Viewpoint_Confidence
FROM Viewpoints_Table
WHERE Viewpoint_ID = ID


Question:= "Please review this viewpoint.  In your opinion,
should it become a best practice for our organization"

OUTPUT Question

INPUT Opinion

Answer:= "yes"

END Subprocess Reviewed_Questioning_Precision
```

PSEUDO CODE FOR REVIEWED_ QUESTIONING_PRECISION SUBPROCESS

```
/* Questions that Target the Quality of Reasoning --
Questioning Precision

/* Generate Questioning Precision question for user persona and
collect answer
BEGIN Subprocess Approved_Questioning_Precision  (ID, Answer,
Reason)

SELECT Viewpoint_Description, Viewpoint_Confidence
FROM Viewpoints_Table
WHERE Viewpoint_ID = ID
```

Question:= "Do you want to approve this viewpoint as a best practice?"

OUTPUT Question

INPUT Answer

User_Response:= Answer

/* Understood_Response will come back as "yes" or "no"
Natural_Language_Processor (User_Response, Understood_Response)

Answer:= Understood_Response

Question:= "What is the reason behind your answer for approval?"

OUTPUT Question

INPUT Reason

END Subprocess Approved_Questioning_Precision

Appendix C:
Demo of Microsoft's Power Virtual Agent

STARTING THE SOCRATES DIGITALTMDEMO IN TEAMS

This appendix documents a demonstration of a Socrates DigitalTM application created in Microsoft Power Virtual Agent and deployed in Microsoft Teams. The narration and screenshots were copied and formatted for this book from the webpage, https://www.socrates.digital/virtual-agent-demo, (Salisbury, 2021). These materials are used with permission. This Socrates DigitalTMapplication is called a "no-code" implementation of Socrates Digital. Some logic requires configuration, but the implementation requires no code in a general-purpose programming language like Java, C, or VBA. If you have Microsoft Office 365, this application is essentially free since a version of Microsoft Power Virtual Agent comes with Microsoft Teams.

Figure 1.

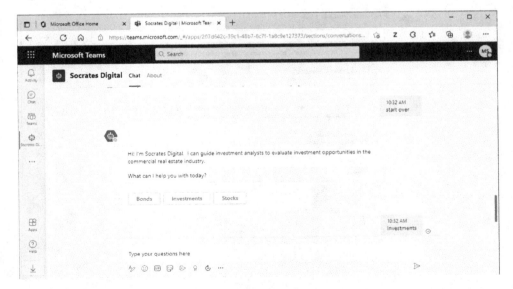

The screen capture in Figure 1 shows that this demo begins with Socrates DigitalTM asking the user what it can help with today. The knowledge base for this demo is about evaluating investments in the commercial real estate industry. The user responds with a request for help with investments.

DECIDING WHAT A GOOD SOLUTION LOOKS LIKE

In the next screen capture, shown in Figure 2, Socrates DigitalTM asks how the user will decide to invest. The response is that the user will decide by determining if the investment will boost total revenue enough to pay back the investors. Socrates DigitalTM then asks precisely how this statement relates to the question at hand. In other words, it asks the user to state all the decision criteria. The user responds by saying it must boost revenue enough to pay back the investors, but it must be enough to meet the projected rate of return for the investors.

Figure 2.

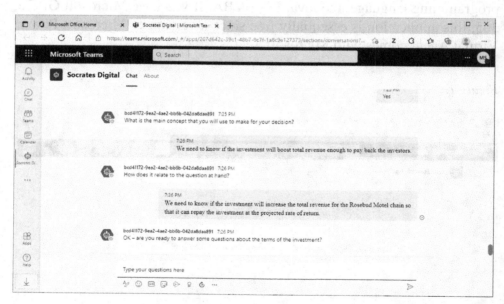

PICKING THE SOCRATIC QUESTIONS TO ANSWER

The user tells Socrates DigitalTM that the investment under consideration is the Rosebud Motel chain in this screen capture, shown in Figure 3. Socrates DigitalTM responds by asking what the user would like to work on next. The options for the user relate to the information available for the Rosebud Motel chain[1], the known assumptions, the applied concepts, the developed conclusions, the predicted implications of those conclusions, and the viewpoint created by answering the questions.

[1]Any similarity to the Rosebud Motel in the situation comedy "Schitt's Creek" (TV Series 2015–2020) is merely coincidental.

Figure 3.

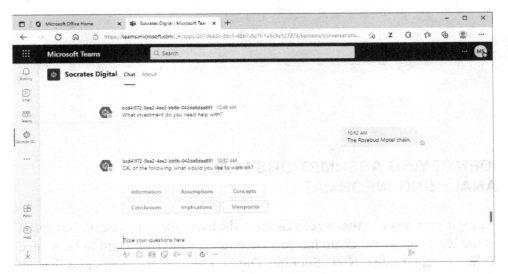

FINDING FACTS THAT SUPPORT CONCEPTS

The following screen capture, displayed in Figure 4, shows that the user selected to answer questions in the information category. Socrates DigitalTMfollows up by asking what information the user has. The user responds by saying that information about occupancy rates and revenue is available in a Rosebud Motel chain spreadsheet. Socrates DigitalTMthen asks for specific data from the spreadsheet to provide insight into occupancy rates and revenue for the Rosebud Motel chain.

Figure 4.

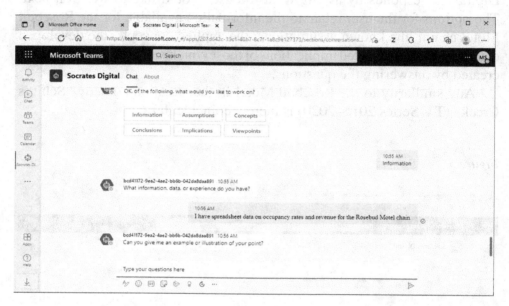

IDENTIFYING ASSUMPTIONS FOR ANALYZING INFORMATION

As Figure 5 shows, in this screen capture, the user notes that one of the motels in the Rosebud Motel chain has low occupancy rates that seem to be related to low revenue rates. Now, Socrates DigitalTM switches gears and lists all the assumptions it knows about evaluating investments in the commercial real estate industry. For this demo, the analysts supplied the listed assumptions that created the knowledge base in this area for Socrates Digital. Next, the application asks the user if any of these supplied assumptions make sense of the data point, suggesting that low occupancy rates are related to low revenue rates. The user responds that the assumption "Occupancy rate is positively correlated with total revenue" explains the data.

Figure 5.

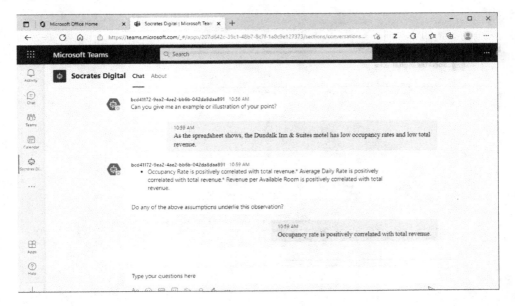

Checking if Assumption Holds for Larger Dataset

Socrates DigitalTM, shown in Figure 6, asks the user a question about applying this assumption. Socrates DigitalTM uses this answer by the user to later calculate the level of confidence the user has in this assumption for evaluating if the Rosebud Motel chain is a good investment. Socrates DigitalTM now asks the user if this assumption holds for a larger dataset in a follow-up question. The user responds that the occupancy rate is positively correlated with total revenue for a larger dataset.

Developing a Conclusion and Evaluating the Logic

The screen capture in Figure 7 shows that Socrates DigitalTM now moves toward getting the user to state a conclusion based on the analysis of the information, assumptions, and concepts (skipped in this demo) gathered so far. Socrates DigitalTM will continue to work with the user to analyze additional information, assumptions, and concepts until the user has no more additional ones to add.

After the user states a conclusion, Socrates DigitalTM asks the user to evaluate the logic of the conclusion. Socrates DigitalTM will also use this

Figure 6.

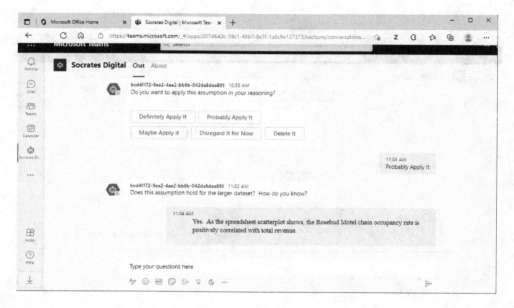

Figure 7.

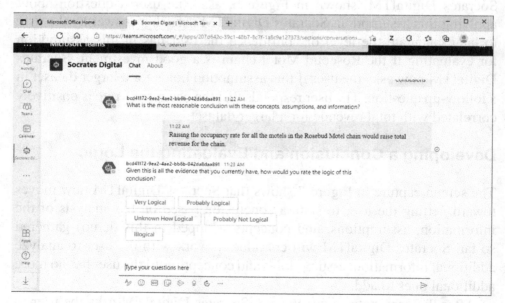

answer later to calculate the level of confidence the user has in this conclusion for evaluating if the Rosebud Motel chain is a good investment. (This demo also skips the questions put to the user about the implications drawn from the conclusions.)

Restate Implications to Create a Viewpoint

After ensuring that there are no more information, assumptions, concepts, conclusions, and implications to consider, Socrates DigitalTM asks the user to restate the implications of the developed conclusions into an overarching viewpoint that summarizes the results from all the questions Socrates DigitalTM asked the user. Figure 8 shows that Socrates DigitalTM now goes to work to calculate a value for each Socratic questioning category -- information, assumptions, concepts, conclusions, and implications.

Figure 8.

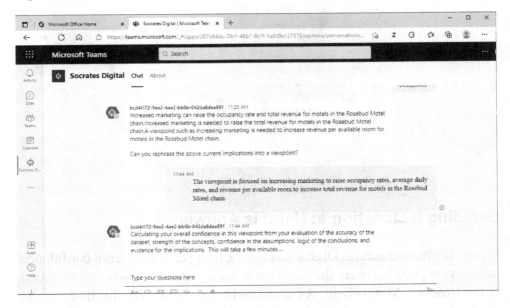

Calculating Overall Confidence in Viewpoint

In this next screen capture, shown in Figure 9, Socrates DigitalTM calculates a value for each Socratic questioning category -- information, assumptions, concepts, conclusions, and implications – and a final overall level of confidence that the user has in the viewpoint for deciding to invest in the Rosebud Motel chain. In this demo, the overall confidence level is .84 – a high level of confidence that this viewpoint is a good solution. In the more extended demo of this example, the user examines the average daily rates and the revenue by available room. Additionally, other users have built on this viewpoint with more information, assumptions, concepts, conclusions, and implications in the more extended demo.

Figure 9.

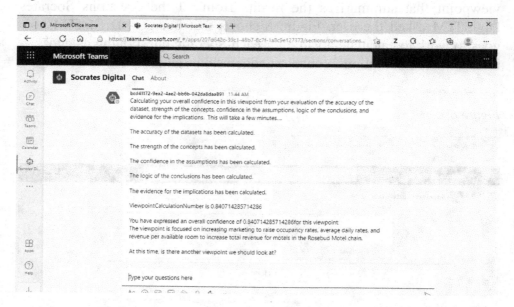

Deciding if Question at Hand is Answered

Figure 10 shows Socrates DigitalTM asking the user if the overall confidence in this viewpoint answers the question at hand – deciding whether to invest in the Rosebud Motel chain. As noted earlier, not shown in this demo is the discussion about the implications of this decision. At this point, Socrates DigitalTM has brought the users to a solution for their problem and has stored the results of the problem-solving process in SharePoint and the calculations in Excel. The results can now be accessed for review and reuse – providing the basis for organizational learning.

Figure 10.

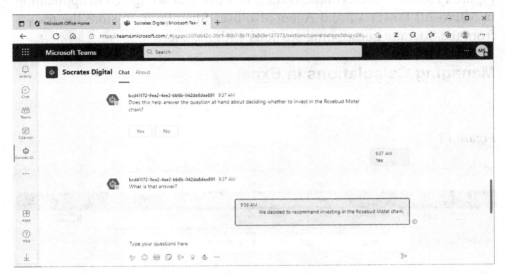

Storing Session Results in SharePoint

Figure 11.

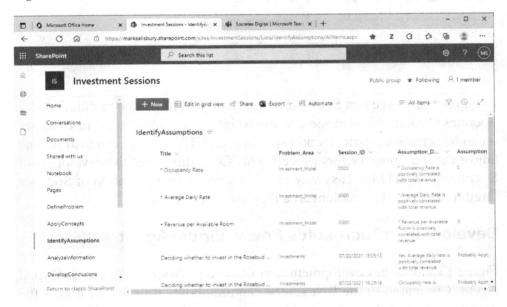

Figure 11 shows that this implementation of a Socrates DigitalTM application in Microsoft Power Virtual Agent also uses SharePoint to store the results from the Socratic questioning sessions with the user.

Managing Calculations in Excel

Figure 12.

In Figure 12, we see that Microsoft Excel Excel performs the calculations for Socrates Digital. We also see that the weights for each factor – or category – can be set and empirically adjusted in Excel. Developers can also set and adjust the multiplier factors as well. This flexibility gives the developers of Socrates DigitalTMan easy way to "fine-tune" their application of Socrates DigitalTM to fit the problem area they are working. in

Developing in Microsoft's Power Virtual Agent

Figure 13 shows the development environment for Microsoft's Power Virtual Agent. Compared to the first screen capture above, we see that it asks the user what it can help with today. Next, the logic shows that it offers the user the options of bonds, investments, and stocks. These options are branches of a tree created through a "click and drag" environment called the Canvas in Power Virtual Agent. With this environment, the developer can create a visual representation of the logic that presents user questions, captures user responses, and presents follow-on questions based on those user responses.

Figure 13.

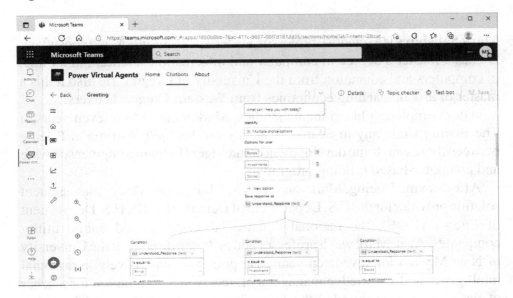

REFERENCES

Salisbury, M. (2021). *Microsoft Power Virtual Agent Demo*. Vitel, Inc. Retrieved September 9, 2021, from https://www.socrates.digital/virtual-agent-demo

About the Author

Mark Salisbury is a scientist, professor, leader, speaker, author, and consultant. He has a master's degree in computer and information science and a Ph.D. in computers and education from the University of Oregon. He also holds a master of arts in teaching economics from Western Oregon University.

After completing his graduate studies, Mark worked for eleven years at The Boeing Company in Seattle, Washington. He spilt his time at Boeing between the research and development of intelligent human/computer software and computer-based training programs.

After leaving Boeing, Mark founded *Vitel*, Inc., a knowledge management solution provider for the U.S. Department of Defense (DOD), U.S. Department of Energy (DOE), the national defense laboratories, and public utility companies. Also, Mark was a professor and program director at the University of New Mexico for seventeen years. He published extensively in artificial intelligence and knowledge management, received a nomination for teacher of the year, and co-founded the Organization, Information, and Learning Sciences program.

Currently, he is a professor of Computer Science and Organizational Development and Change at the University of St. Thomas.

Index

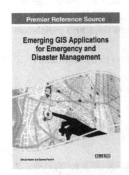

IGI Global Author Services

Providing a high-quality, affordable, and expeditious service, IGI Global's Author Services enable authors to streamline their publishing process, increase chance of acceptance, and adhere to IGI Global's publication standards.

Benefits of Author Services:

- **Professional Service:** All our editors, designers, and translators are experts in their field with years of experience and professional certifications.
- **Quality Guarantee & Certificate:** Each order is returned with a quality guarantee and certificate of professional completion.
- **Timeliness:** All editorial orders have a guaranteed return timeframe of 3-5 business days and translation orders are guaranteed in 7-10 business days.
- **Affordable Pricing:** IGI Global Author Services are competitively priced compared to other industry service providers.
- **APC Reimbursement:** IGI Global authors publishing Open Access (OA) will be able to deduct the cost of editing and other IGI Global author services from their OA APC publishing fee.

Author Services Offered:

English Language Copy Editing
Professional, native English language copy editors improve your manuscript's grammar, spelling, punctuation, terminology, semantics, consistency, flow, formatting, and more.

Scientific & Scholarly Editing
A Ph.D. level review for qualities such as originality and significance, interest to researchers, level of methodology and analysis, coverage of literature, organization, quality of writing, and strengths and weaknesses.

Figure, Table, Chart & Equation Conversions
Work with IGI Global's graphic designers before submission to enhance and design all figures and charts to IGI Global's specific standards for clarity.

Translation
Providing 70 language options, including Simplified and Traditional Chinese, Spanish, Arabic, German, French, and more.

Hear What the Experts Are Saying About IGI Global's Author Services

Learn More or Get Started Here:

For Questions, Contact IGI Global's Customer Service Team at cust@igi-global.com or 717-533-8845

IGI Global
PUBLISHER of TIMELY KNOWLEDGE
www.igi-global.com

Printed in the United States
by Baker & Taylor Publisher Services